VIEWS

OF

LOUISIA

TOGETHER WITH A JOURN
UP THE MISSOURI R

---

b

ENRY MARIE

AMER

A

First edition published 1814, Pittsburgh
This edition published 1962 by
Quadrangle Books, Inc./Chicago

Library of Congress Catalog Card Number: 62-12187

MANUFACTURED IN THE UNITED STATES OF AMERICA
BY BOOK CRAFTSMEN ASSOCIATES, INC., NEW YORK

CONTENTS.

BOOK I.

To the reader 3
CHAP. I.
Discovery and first Settlement of Louisiana , . . . 9
CHAP. II.
Boundaries of Louisiana 23
CHAP. III.
Face of the Country—Change which a part has probably under-
gone—Climate—Extent and Importance 27
CHAP. IV.
Lakes and Rivers 36
A Table of navigable rivers in Louisiana—Extent of navigation . 51
CHAP. V.
Natural or Indigenous productions—Animal, Vegetable and Mi-
neral 54
CHAP. VI.
A view of the Indian nations of Louisiana—Of the Indian trade
for furs, &c —Of the Missouri and Mississippi . . . 69
A Table of the Indian nations of Louisiana—Their trade, &c. , 85
CHAP. VII.
View of the country on the Columbia 95

BOOK II.

CHAP. I.
Territory of the Missouri—Boundaries—Extent—Rivers—Gene-
ral view 99
CHAP. II.
Soil—Face of the conntry, &c from New Madrid to the Missouri
—Forks of the Missouri 103
CHAP. III.
Climate—Diseases 111
CHAP. IV.
Political divisions—Inhabitants—Settlements—Population . . 112
CHAP. V.
Towns and villages 119

CONTENTS.

CHAP. VI.
Historical Character of the ancient inhabitants—change of Government 132

CHAP. VII.
Lead Mines in the District of St. Genevieve—Mode of mining—Produce, &c. 146

CHAP. VIII.
Resources—Agriculture—Manufactures—Trade . . . 156

CHAP. IX.
State of Louisiana—Boundaries—General Surface, &c. . 157

LEVEES. 175

CHAP. X.
Antiquities in the Valley of the Mississippi . . . 181

JOURNAL.

CHAP. I. 199

CHAP. II. 207

CHAP. III. 219

CHAP. IV. 227

CHAP. V. 239

CHAP. VI. 247

CHAP. VII. 259

A TABLE of distances, &c. . . 265

APPENDIX.

(No. 1.) Extracts from Humboldt's New Spain 269

(No. 2.) The mound near Sultzertown, M. T. 278

(No. 3.) A communication from the Rev. Mr. Miller on the same 280

(No. 4.) Account of Madisonville, and a part of the Mississippi Territory 281

(No. 5.) A description of the Trappists 287

(No. 6.) Articles of treaty respecting the boundaries of Louisiana 291

(No. 7.) Extract from an account of Mr. Sibly's journey, &c. . 293

(No. 8.) American Enterprise 297

TO THE READER.

IN the spring of 1810, I landed at New Madrid in Upper Louisiana, and proceeded from thence by land to St. Genevieve, with the intention of settling myself in some part of the territory as a lawyer. But finding after a short residence, that prospects of success in that part of the world, were not such as I could have wished, I resolved to employ the time I should remain there, in making observations and remarks on such things as appeared most worthy of attention. I was in a short time, pleased with the employment, which drew me into a more extensive research than I had at first contemplated, and gave rise to a degree of earnestness in a pursuit, to which I had before been almost a stranger; my studies having been chiefly directed to abstract subjects, to history, belles lettres, and to those in some way connected with my profession.

In the winter of 1811, I published at St. Louis, the capital of Upper Louisiana, a series of essays descriptive of the country, many of which were reprinted in periodical papers in the states, and spoken of in terms of approbation. It were needless to declare how gratifying this was to my feelings, or, as the reader will choose to think, to my vanity. In the heyday of youth, when the mind is filled with romantic conceits, there is nothing so pleasant as this taste of fame. It is however, sometimes productive of dangerous effects, for where this first manifestation of applause, does not intoxicate the brain and paralize the energies, causing the infatuated being to believe, that he has already arrived at the highest degree of earthly honors, it is apt to confirm one in that pursuit, where accident may have crowned him with success.—Hence, I have been in no small danger of becoming an author, perhaps an indifferent one: a professed author in our country, alas! is pitiable indeed. A mere abstract man, without any degree of importance, or consequence, attached to him; he is not ranked as having any employment in the state, ecclesiastical, civil, or military, and necessarily takes up his abode next door to starvation. It has been supposed by some of my friends who read my essays in the public prints, that I had in reality relinquished my profession, and that I was wandering about the western country, writing geography, philosophy, history, and the Lord knows what; but, I thank heaven, I have had sufficient firmness to resist this temptation to prove a recreant to the delightful pages of my Lord Coke, to the erudite commentator, Blackstone, or to neglect my new friends, the code of Justinian, and commentators thereon, the Portidas, the ordonnances of Bilbao, and Domat.

During the winter before mentioned, I became acquainted with Mr. Bradbury, Fellow of the Linnean Society; a gentleman as distinguished for his agreeable manners, sound understanding, and general science, as for his attainments in the department of natural history. My acquaintance with him naturally nourished the fondness I had begun to feel for the subjects treated of in this volume. In the spring following, this gentleman set off to ascend the Missouri in the party of Mr. Wilson P. Hunt, for the purpose of pursuing his researches in those unfrequented regions. Shortly after his departure, Mr. Manuel Lisa, one of the members of the Missouri Fur Company, ascended with a small party, for the purpose of retrieving the affairs of the company, which had become considerably deranged : being solicited by this gentleman to accompany him, my wish to visit those countries was so strong, that I did not hesitate, notwithstanding that there was much to be feared from the hostilities of the Indians, who of late had been unfriendly to the whites ; in so much, that it was generally supposed, that even the considerable party of Mr. Hunt would not be able to make its way through the Sioux bands. The pleasure of being in company with Mr. Bradbury, whom we expected to overtake, was not a light consideration. I accordingly ascended, and after an absence of four or five months, returned to St. Louis, with two boats loaded with furs and peltry of the company, placed under my command. Remaining at St. Louis until the month of November, I embarked for New Orleans, where I arrived in December 1811. Here I met with one of the publishers of this work, Mr. Cramer, and proposed to him the publication of the essays before mentioned, with the journal of my voyage up the Missouri ; to which he assented, on condition that I would extend it, and add something relative to the state of Louisiana.

Such is the history of the volume now offered to the public, respecting which, I have observed with regret, that expectations have been excited, much beyond its real importance. I say regret, because those expectations, will most probably be disappointed, if, instead of the cursory observations of an ordinary traveller, the reader shall look for a complete and scientific account of Louisiana, emulating the famed productions of Depons, Molini, or Humboldt.

The extensive country which constitutes the subject of these essays, although, one of the most interesting portions of the new world, appears to have been amongst the last in becoming known. The Spaniards, who possessed it from 1769, until after 1800, cannot be said to have done any thing towards its further discovery. The French, who were first settlers, had made considerable progress in exploring it, but those exploring parties originating principally with private individuals, unsupported by the government, or any wealthy society, were consequently neither sufficiently extensive nor accurate. It is a singular fact, that so great a portion of it, should to this day remain an entire blank on the map, and that there should be no correct standard work, to refer to, for knowledge of a country inhabited by Europeans for more than one hundred years. A few writers, such as Charlevoix, Du Pratz, Dumont, de la Harpe, &c. collected the materials furnished by a variety of individuals, who passed over different parts of it, and formed their books by joining to them the observations made by themselves; but they were unfortunately too ready to receive all the falsehoods with which they were fraught. In fact, but little was accurately known of this country, until it fell into the possession of the United States. Besides the observations of a number of individuals, there have been some exploring expeditions sanctioned and equipped by the government; these are too well known to require enumeration. The sources of the Mississippi, Missouri, Arkansas, Red river, Washita, and of White river, are known to the world for the first time. In the course of the last eight or ten years, such a number of authentic accounts have appeared, that the time may be regarded as not distant, when the geographer will be able to speak of Louisiana with as much certainty, as of any other part of the United States. The materials for its history have also been augmented: a variety of facts, scattered through the pages of writers almost obsolete, or of transactions known but to tradition, have been carefully collected and preserved. I have no higher aim in these " Views," than to be considered one of those who furnish materials for abler hands. Mr. William Darby, to whom I am indebted for the statistical view and table, has been engaged for a number of years in preparing an elaborate work on Louisiana. Possessing strong original genius, with considerable acquirements, and indefatigable industry, the public may expect something substantially useful in his labors. He has already almost completed, from actual survey, a map of the new state of Louisiana; a work of vast difficulty and labor, from the strange configuration of the country, being cut up, and infinitely diversified, by bayoux, swamps, lakes, lagoons, and a thousand other objects calculated to impose difficulties on the undertaking.

It has always appeared to me, that the observations of travellers, if made with any tolerable degree of accuracy, should rank amongst the most useful productions, and should, moreover, be entitled to great indulgence. What can be more pleasing and instructive than the testimony of eye witnesses, relative to objects of the most interesting nature, which we are precluded from visiting ourselves, or than the remarks of intelligent persons on what chances to come under their notice during their peregrinations through distant countries? In the early ages of society, travelling from one nation to another, was almost the only means of acquiring superior knowledge,

> Multorumque hominum urbes, et mores cognovit,

a wise man and a great traveller were regarded as synonymous, and treated with equal respect. When in the form of narrative, this species of composition has all the attractions of romance, combined with the usefulness of truth. I have always perused the book of travels with peculiar delight, no matter how aukward its style, or humble the adventurer. In this kind of writing, the fidelity of truth is far to be preferred to the mere artifice or elegance of diction.* It may be said to be a species of composition free alike to the illiterate and the learned, requiring no peculiar and appropriate style ; demanding neither the dignified march of history, the brilliancy of works of the imagination, nor the precision and regularity of those which are purely scientific, yet, admitting with propriety something of them all. Men of the most common acquirements are not excluded, or thought presumptuous in attempting it, for it may be the fortune of such only, to have witnessed facts of the highest interest, or to have passed through countries not likely to be visited by the learned. Hence the various modes adopted by travellers, from the regular and systematic essay, down to the simple diary or journal.

Before the reader decides upon this work, he must recollect, that travels through countries little known, must necessarily be of a different cast from those in countries highly cultivated, and already described by innumerable writers. Instead of amusing incident, descriptions of manners and customs, characters of distinguished persons, political and moral reflections, historical reminiscence, and a multitude of other topics, the traveller has only to describe the face of nature in its primitive state, the character of a few wandering savages, or the situation of settlements yet in their infancy. He that would aspire to the highest order of travellers for having traversed such a country, ought to be

---

* The travels of a Frenchman are bedizened with conceits of the fancy, those of an Englishman loaded with sluggish prejudice. I must declare (perhaps the result of partiality) that such American travels as I have perused, have always struck me as more impartial, and containing a more perfect stamp of authenticity than either.

a proficient in natural history; to this I must confess, I have but slender pretensions. Devoted to a profession, which my lord Coke, observeth, " is a jealous mistress, and will not abide a rival," I have not been able to spare the time requisite for such attainment. It is with regret I reflect, that I have devoted so much time to this employment, which was necessarily withdrawn from my profession, or studies connected with it. To become a botanist, mineralogist, or geologist, requires long and undivided attention. I have therefore been compelled to content myself with admiring merely the face of nature, without attempting to analize, or seek out her hidden character. I have dwelt as little in political and statistical detail, as on the phenomena of nature, the countries through which I passed affording but little of interest on these topics. The reader will find here little else, than geographical outlines, descriptions of the surface of the country, the navigation of rivers, the nature or quality of soils, the appearance of towns or villages, and whatever else would be likely to meet the eye of a transient passenger.

The greater part of what is here offered is original, though it will be seen that I have read what has been written by others, and occasionally adopted their ideas. In forming a table of the Indian nations, much of my materials are derived from Gen. Clark, Dr. Sibly, and Pike. In my observations on the Mississippi, &c. the writings of Mr. Ellicot, the late Sir William Dunbar, and Dr. Mease, furnished me with hints.

I now lay this volume before the public, with all the reverence and awe, with which that tribunal is usually approached, feeling conscious of the temerity of my attempt. It is a tribunal whose attention, in the republic of letters, we are all entitled to demand, but if we abuse it, by exhibiting what proves unworthy of that attention, we are soon consigned to merited contempt.

VIEWS

OF

LOUISIANA.

IN TWO BOOKS.

———

CHAPTER I.

DISCOVERY, AND FIRST SETTLEMENT OF LOUISIANA.

THE early history of nearly all the colonies planted by European nations, on this continent, presents us with a series of hardships and misfortunes, encountered by the first settlers, and of injudicious management by those entrusted with their superintendence. From these Louisiana in its first settlement was by no means exempt, on the contrary they were all experienced here, in the severest manner. It was not until after repeated failures, and the lapse of a century, from the first attempt, that a colony could take root, and not for half a century more that it could flourish. It is intended in this imperfect sketch, to pass those events in review, and as far as in the writer's power, to develope their causes.

The Spaniards from their establishments in Cuba, and in Mexico, at an early period became acquainted with the continent lying opposite the island before mentioned, and had given it the name of Florida. Under this name, they comprehended and claimed, east of the province of Penuco, indefinitely, north, east, and south ; and declared that all the French and English possessions in America, belonged to Florida, and were unjust usurpations on the dominions appertaining to the crown of Spain.* They

* Kerr of Kerrslands Memoirs, 1727—History of European Settlements an. 1775, and Postlethwayte on Commerce, published in 1745,— Don Andres Gonzales de Boreca.

B

were, however, by no means the first to take possession, or to explore it. The liberal gift of Pope Alexander the sixth, of all the *new world*, might be supposed to supersede the necessity of such formalities.

It is true, that some adventurers in the hopes of discovering in this unexplored region, kingdoms of civilized Indians, and fired by the success of Cortez, penetrated into the country now called Louisiana, but were deplorably unsuccessful. These adventurers the better to obtain followers, had artfully circulated a story, suited to the superstition of the age, that in this country, there existed a miraculous fountain, possessing the desirable qualities of restoring youth, or rendering it perpetual to him who should be so fortunate as to bathe himself in its enchanted waters. The Spanish expeditions had not for their object the taking possession of a wilderness, thinly peopled, by wandering Indians, of populating and improving it, but to plunder the natives of the gold and silver they were supposed to possess : nor did the world, or even they, become better acquainted with the country in consequence of their expeditions. Pontio de Leon, was the first adventurer. In 1512, he penetrated Florida, at the head of a considerable party, ostensibly in pursuit of the before mentioned fountain ; but his stay was short, he did not even build a fort, the natives considering him as an invader, and opposing him with great ferocity. Thus Pontio, and such of his men as survived returned home, worn out with the hardships sustained in the expedition.* In 1520, Vasques de Ayllon, landed and explored the neighbourhood of a river which he called the Jourdan, in that part of Florida which is now South Carolina ; but his stay was not long and his success no better than that of Pontio de Leon. A few years after this, Pamphile de Narvaès, obtained from the emperor Charles the fifth, the government of Florida. Narvaès coasted along the northern shore of the gulph of Mexico, landed several times, had frequent rencounters with the Indians, who killed many of his people, and at length perished miserably himself without having even built a fort.

* History of European Settlements.

Hernandes de Soto, being afterwards made captain-general
of Florida, in the year 1539 at the head of eight or nine hundred
men landed in this country and penetrated a considerable distance into the interior. He continued for several years wandering
in search of gold, of civilized Indians, and of miraculous fountains; in the mean time he was much harassed by the natives,
his party was divided and dispersed in small bands, the greater
part of which, were never afterwards heard of, and finally de
Soto himself died on the banks of the Mississippi.* The unhappy issue of these successive expeditions, entirely dissuaded adventurers from any further attempt, until establishments were
formed by the French.

In the year 1523, Verazzani, an Italian mariner, in the service of France, had discovered Florida, but had not attempted
any settlement. This discovery was not followed up by the French,
owing to the almost total inattention to America, during the
troubled reigns of Francis II, and of Charles IX. The celebrated
Coligny, desirous of obtaining freedom of religious worship, for
the persecuted sect to which he belonged, conceived the idea of
going in search of the country discovered by Verazzani, and of
planting a colony of protestants: a scheme rather encouraged by
the king who was desirous of chasing off the Hugonots. He cast
his eye upon that part of Florida, which Verazzani, had described
as most suitable for the establishment of a colony; for besides
the mildness of the climate, and the fertility of the soil, he fancied the French would find no one to dispute their right or even
to trouble them. Jean de Ribaut being chosen by the admiral
to undertake the expedition, set off the 18th of February 1562.
He first touched at a place which he called *Cape Francois*, about
the 30°, of N. lat. and turning to the right he perceived a short
time after, a river which he named *la riviere des Dauphins*, but

---

* In the account of this expedition by Herrera, it is mentioned that de
Soto in 1541 reached Mavilla, an Indian town enclosed with wooden walls.
He had an engagement there in which 2000 natives were killed and 83
Spaniards, who also lost 45 horses. An Indian village named Chicaca
was burnt. See Amer. ann. 1. vol. 91.—A tradition prevailed amongst the
Kaskaskia Indians of their having slain the first white men they had
ever seen--this might have been one of de Soto's parties.

did not enter. Pursuing this course, at the distance of fifteen leagues he discovered another river and entered it on the first of May, from which circumstance he gave it the name of *la riviere de Mai.* Here he found a great number of savages, by whom, from that conciliatory policy, which the French have so successfully pursued towards these people, he was well received: reciprocal presents were made, to the great satisfaction of the Indians. But having in view the river Jourdan, he hastened his departure from this place, but not without having first erected a pillar on which were engraven the arms of France, and taking possession of the country in the name of the king and of the admiral: a vain and idle ceremony. He afterwards gave to the rivers which he successively discovered for sixty leagues, the names of French rivers, and at length cast anchor in what he supposed the Jourdan, but which was called afterwards by the Spaniards, St. Cruz, and by the natives Shawano,* at present Savana. Ribaut at this place built a fort which he called Fort Charles; the Indians manifested the greatest friendship. Leaving here the persons who had accompanied him for the purpose of establishing a colony, he took his departure. Unfortunately the direction and government of it, were resigned to a person no ways capable. He soon manifested great imprudence, and the most ferocious severity. The colony in a short time, suffered severely from famine, and a complication of miseries: and were at length compelled to leave the country and endeavor to regain their native land, in a vessel built by them under the most discouraging circumstances.

It is indeed strange, how men can be induced voluntarily to tear themselves from the bosom of a refined and civilized society, retire to a wilderness and become the neighbours of savages. But the sweet and cheering hope of regaining their native soil, after having acquired a competency, has been found never to abandon the emigrants from France. Even the powerful incentive of religious freedom, was not sufficient alone. The belief that eve-

---

* The Shawanese Indians were originally from Georgia; they exchanged their country with the Cherokees for that on the Cumberland river, from whence they were afterwards driven by the same people across the Ohio.

ry part of America was equally rich in mines of precious metals, will account both for the readiness with which adventurers, embarked in colonizing enterprises, and the ill success of the first attempts; for instead of cultivating the earth, the greater part of their time was spent in running about in search of gold and silver.

The admiral, not discouraged by the failure of this attempt, soon succeeded in preparing another armament, consisting of three vessels provided with every thing which might be required by a young colony, and gave the command to René de Laudamère. Fifty thousand crowns were advanced to this expedition by the king. Several gentlemen of fortune, and young persons of family were desirous of making this voyage at their own expense; and there were joined to it some detachments of soldiers chosen from among the veteran corps. On the 26th of June 1564, he entered the Dauphin river, but did not land, to the great regret of the Indians who appeared disposed to receive them in the most friendly manner. He continued his course to the May river where he landed, ascended some distance, and, being well received by the natives, commenced an establishment. Notwithstanding all these advantages, and flattering auspices, the same fate attended this colony as the first. The colonists were soon carried away by the delusion of searching after gold. This became almost a mania, and was taken advantage of by a neighbouring PARAOUSTI, who succeeded in drawing them into a war with his enemies, a powerful tribe. This chief perceiving the thirst after gold and silver which prevailed, exhibited some pieces of silver, and informed that he had procured them from his enemies, who had the same metal in abundance. The colony now began to feel the usual calamities, from dissention, famine from neglect of tillage, and at the same time an Indian war which they had unjustly provoked. In this state they at length came to the resolution of re-embarking, when of a sudden, to the general surprise, seven brigantines, appeared in the river. It proved to be Ribaut who had brought succors to the colony.

About this time the attempt of France to colonize Florida, became known in Spain, who claimed the country in virtue of the Pope's bull, and the particular discoveries of Pontio de Leon and

the other adventurers. Pedro de Menendez, was immediately
despatched by that monarchy to establish a colony and to drive
away the French. The armament, might be considered for that
period, and for the occasion, a formidable one, consisting of ten
vessels and upwards of two thousand men. Before he could reach
the place of his destination, a storm arose, which dispersed and
scattered his ships, so that he only arrived with five. These were
attacked by some English vessels then at the mouth of the river,
and compelled to fall down to the Dauphin river, which they
entered, giving it the name of St. Augustin ; here they commenced an establishment. In the mean while Ribaut, contrary to the
advice of his officers, embarked nearly all his force, in order to
attack and destroy the Spanish fleet, and left but sixty or seventy
men in his fort.*   Ribaut could only come in sight of the Spaniards when a dreadful tempest drove him off the coast.   The
Spanish commander, rightly conjecturing that the greater part
of the garrison had been embarked on this occasion, resolved to
march over by land and storm the fort. This he did in five days
after his discovering the English squadron, and succeeded completely, meeting in fact with but little or no resistance : Mons.
Laudamère and a few soldiers only escaped. This achievment
honorable in its commencement, was however wound up by one
of those acts of barbarity, which causes humanity to shudder even
when related of the most ferocious savages, and which stamps
infamy and shame on civilized men ; the prisoners who surrendered, and the miserable fugitives, who were afterwards caught,
were hung upon a tree, on which was suspended this sentence,
worthy of that bigotry, " whose forces are congregated from the
abysses of hell :" NOT AS FRENCHMEN, BUT AS HERETICS AND
ENEMIES OF GOD.

Menendez, giving the name of St. Matteo, to the fort he had
taken, left a garrison in it, and returned to St. Augustin. Ribaut at
the same time paid dearly for his imprudence, being ship-wreck-
ed on the Bahama banks, he attempted with the remainder of his
forces to regain the fort by land. Having approached it after incredible hardships, he learned that it was in the possession of
the Spaniards. One of his officers was sent with proposals, and

---

* It had been called Fort Charles.

it was solemnly agreed on both sides, that the commander of the fort, should supply them with a vessel to return to France; but he no sooner got these unfortunate people in his power, than regardless of humanity and justice, he caused them to be barbarously butchered.

Such is the tragic fate of these early colonies; the story is related by Charlevoix, with minute detail, in his loose and rambling way. This writer expresses the strongest indignation at the abominable and atrocious conduct of the Spaniards, and denies in the strongest terms that Spain ever had any just right to this country.

France and Spain were at this moment in profound peace, nor does this outrage, seem in the least to have excited the indignation of the former, owing to the circumstance of the unfortunate victims having been protestants and heretics. But it was left to a private gentleman, to avenge the indignity offered to his country, and to chastise the barbarous usurpers of Florida. This was the Chevalier de Gourgues a man who in those times had distinguished himself in various countries for that romantic valour, which was then so highly esteemed; the indignation which he felt for the insult offered his country was heightened by a sense of personal wrongs, having been for many years confined in Spanish prisons. Under pretence of forming an expedition to Africa, he raised at his own expense and with the assistance of his friends, a considerable armament and steered for Florida. On his arrival he was joined by the Indians who had become greatly dissatisfied with the Spaniards, stormed St. Matteo, and carried it with little difficulty. The greater part of the garrison was killed in the assault, the remainder were taken to the same tree on which the French had been hanged, and in the execution of a severe but not unjust retaliation, served in the same manner, the former inscription being replaced by one to this effect—NOT AS SPANIARDS, BUT AS MURDERERS AND CUT-THROATS. Having destroyed the fort, and completed the object of his expedition, he soon after embarked; St. Augustin was considered as too formidable for his party.

The attention of France seems to have been altogether withdrawn from this quarter of the continent, during an interval of many years : being at this time chiefly occupied with her settle-ments in Canada, which had begun to flourish. St. Augustin and all Florida were about the same time abandoned by the Spa-niards.

About the year 1671, it was known in Canada, from the in-formation of Indians, that there was a great river to the west of New France, which neither flowed to the east nor to the north.* It was thought, it must either discharge itself into the gulph of Mexico or into the south sea; and it therefore became a matter of importance that this should be ascertained.

Frontenac the governor of Canada, accordingly sent the priest Marquette, with a trader named Joliet, accompanied by three or four men to explore this river. These persons ascend-ed the river of the Foxes, crossed to the Ouisconsing, which they descended to the Mississippi. They sailed down this river discovering some considerable tributary streams, the chief of which, the celebrated Missouri, was named by the Indians *Pe-kitanoni*. A few leagues below it, they found three large Indian villages of Illinois.†

Little was done towards the further discovery of this region, until it was undertaken by the enterprising La Salle. This gen-tleman having descended the Mississippi in company with the Chevalier Tonti, discovered the mouth of the river, returned with a fixed resolution of attempting further discoveries, and of establishing a colony. He succeeded in obtaining a considerable force from the king of France and about the year 1684, set sail from la Rochelle. But according to Charlevoix, from an unfortu-nate severity of temper which often produced acts very ill-timed, and from an over-weening confidence in his own abilities and resources, which led him to treat the opinions of others with

* Charlevoix.

† The decrease of these people is astonishingly great. The Illinois in the recollection of the whites could bring eight or ten thousand warriors into the field. Shortly after the discovery of the Mississippi, a missiona-ry who went to establish himself amongst the Miamies, found three thousand warriors preparing for a war party. The Onlogamies were reckoned at a thousand families.

contempt, he soon became the object of dislike to all. This was the cause of his ultimate failure. He passed by the mouth of the river which he sought, though it was seen by every person on board the ships; and persisted with such obstinacy that he would not even listen to proposals, of going with a boat to examine. It seems that from theoretic notions he had placed it further south. He arrived at the bay of St. Bernard, and now discovered his error, but too late, for the naval commander, became as obstinate as himself, positively refused to return, and set him on shore with all his men and equipments. La Salle, built a fort at this place, and in a short time afterwards set out for the Mississippi, but was assassinated by his own people, before he could reach it. His whole company, with the exception of three or four persons who reached Canada, finally perished, being either destroyed by the Indians or taken prisoners by the Spaniards and condemned to the mines.

The colonization of the Mississippi was not abandoned. In the year 1698, Mons. D'Iberville, a gentleman of considerable note in his day, as a naval commander and intrepid adventurer, was sent with two ships in company with M. Chateaumorand to explore and settle the mouth of that mighty river. In 1699, he arrived at the bay of Pensacola, where three hundred Spaniards had lately landed, having been sent from Vera Cruz, for the purpose of forming a colony. D'Iberville sent to them to request permission to water, but was refused.

Continuing his route, he entered the Mobile, which at that time afforded a fine harbor, but which was afterwards choked up by sand during a tempest. The first place at which he landed was an island, *L'isle de Massacre* (so named from the mangled bodies of Indians which first struck his sight, apparently butchered in a wanton manner,) but which was afterwards called the Isle of Dauphin. D'Iberville from this island proceeded to the main land, and afterwards, accompanied by a number of his men, to the Mississippi; which being discovered, he returned to his vessels, entered and ascended the river a considerable distance, and erected a fort. He afterwards ascended as far as the Natchez, with which place he was so much pleased, that he conceived the idea of building a city there, to be named Rosali.

c

The Mississippi was at this time called St. Louis, the name given to it by La Salle, but the country on both sides of it was still known by the name of Florida; D'Iberville was the first to change it, to that of LOUISIANA.

About this period two English vessels arrived in search of the Mississippi, induced by the glowing descriptions of Father Hennepin, who had ascended, or pretended to have ascended, this river to its source. One of these vessels entered the river but did not attempt to land, or form any settlement. It appeared that this country was also claimed by Britain, from the discoveries of Sebastian Cabot, who sailed along the coast, without landing any where, and also by another title even more absurd than the Pope's bull, to wit, *in virtue of her own Charters.** Thus had our infant French colony to contend with two great powers, one jealous of supposed encroachments, and the other envious of any new scheme of colonization on this continent.

M. D'Iberville left Louisiana in 1700; the colony was very inconsiderable and far from advancing rapidly. The principal settlement was at the Isle of Dauphin, noway suited to the purpose. It, however, still continued to live until the year 1712, receiving occasional supplies from France and maintaining a good understanding with the Spanish colony of Pensacola; they seem to have forgotten former animosities and frequently rendered each other mutual assistance. The Indians were also conciliated and lived in friendship with the colonists. In this year the commerce and government of Louisiana, was granted to Crosat who had two objects in view, the discovery of mines in the Illinois, and the trade with Mexico. In both these he completely failed. About this time the Natchez first began to display that enmity to the French, (occasioned perhaps by the injudicious conduct of the officers who commanded the different posts within the country) which afterwards proved so fatal to themselves. The gold and silver mines of the Illinois could not be discovered; and St. Denys, an active and enterprising indivi-

---

* See Marshall's Life of Washington and Bozman's History of Maryland.

dual who had been sent by land to obtain permission of trading from the viceroy, returned without success. St. Denys was afterwards despatched to build a fort at the Natchitoches, in order to prevent the Spaniards from encroaching in that quarter. About the same time they made a settlement at the Assinais.*

Crosat not obtaining those profits, from his grant of the exclusive trade of Louisiana which were expected, gave up his privilege to the king in 1717, before the term of its duration had expired. The famous company of Law, had been formed, which by degrees engrossed the whole commerce within and without the kingdom of France; this company under the name of " the Company of the Indies," took possession of Louisiana, and appointed Mons. Bienville governor of the colony. This gentleman was welcomed at the Isle of Dauphin by the deputies of twenty-five Indian nations; he commenced an establishment but had been here but a short time when a hurricane completely closed up the port. M. Bienville, then chose the position, where the city of New Orleans now stands, and nearly all the settlers of the Isle of Dauphin removed to Beloxi.†

In 1719, war broke out between France and Spain; and put an end to the friendly intercourse which had existed between the two colonies. Pensacola was taken; the company having seized the opportunity of the breach between the two nations, of making itself master of the only port, on all the northern coast of Florida, from the Bahama banks to the Mississippi. The Spaniards, after this event, mortified and chagrined at the loss, made great preparations for retaking the place, and for the total destruction of the French colony. They succeeded in retaking Pensacola but in their attack on the Isle of Dauphin were repulsed; shortly after which, a squadron under the command of M. Champlain, made its appearance, and the siege of Pensacola was once more undertaken. Bienville was ordered to come in a sloop, with the soldiers and volunteers of the Company, to the river Perdido, in order to meet and unite with their Indian allies, who

---

* According to La Harpe even this settlement was made by St. Denys, who brought the Spaniards from the interior for the purpose.

† Charlevoix—Du Pratz—Postlethwayte.

were there ready to join them. The fort was invested by sea and land, and in a short time compelled to surrender at discretion.

In the year 1721, peace was concluded between the two powers; one of the articles of the treaty was the restoration of Pensacola: about the same time the council general ordered the establishments of the Beloxi to be removed to New Orleans. At this period violent dissentions prevailed in the colony; a great proportion of the colonists were persons of the most worthless and despicable class; these dissentions were in some measure fomented by the English of Carolina, who were at the same time in the habit of exciting the Indian nations. Fortunately for the French the Choctaws then the most powerful nation were generally faithful to them; these people more than once saved the infant colony of Louisiana from total destruction. This was particularly shewn in the wars with the Natchez. In the year 1729 in consequence of a plot formed with great art and finesse, for the general massacre of the whites, the colony narrowly escaped destruction; the settlements at Natchez and at the Yazoo were entirely destroyed.* The discovery was made by the mother of the principal Sun, or chief, who delayed and in a great measure frustrated its execution. The mode agreed on by the nations in the plot, and who were at a distance from each other, in different parts of the colony, in order to secure concert in striking the blow on the same day, was a bundle of rods of the same number, deposited with each. A rod was to be taken from the bundle each day, and when there should remain but one, on that day the massacre was to take place. The woman just mentioned, drew out several rods, and in this manner hastened the attack by the Natchez; a few who escaped gave the intelligence and saved the rest of the colony. The Indians rose, but it was too late, the colonists were on their guard, and the Choctaws, came forward with alacrity in their defence. The settlements on the Mobile owed their preservation entirely to these people.

M. Perier, who succeeded Bienville as governor, prepared to take vengeance; he marched to the Natchez, with seven hundred Choctaws, joined to his own forces. He defeated one of their

* See a minute account of this affair in Du Pratz.

parties before his arrival at their town. The Natchez were shut up in two forts, constructed after their own manner, and defended themselves with great obstinacy, holding out for upwards of a month, notwithstanding that seven pieces of cannon were brought against them. The principal cause of this delay, however, was the number of prisoners in the possession of the besieged ; it was justly feared that should they be driven to extremity, these might be butchered. The forts at length surrendered, but on favorable terms ; delivering up their prisoners and giving hostages for their future good conduct.

Several writers have taken it for granted that the Indians were never in the habit of fortifying ; but the detail of the foregoing siege, minutely given by Charlevoix and others, sufficiently refute the idea. The approaches were made in the usual forms, and in the course of the siege there were frequent sorties. The remains of Indian fortifications seen throughout the western country, have given rise to strange conjectures, and have been supposed to appertain to a period extremely remote ; but it is a fact well known, that in some of them the remains of palisadoes were found by the first settlers.

The Natchez were neither reconciled nor induced to relinquish their hostile designs. In 1731, it was found necessary to raise another army of whites and Indian auxiliaries, with the intention of putting an end for the future to all apprehensions from this troublesome nation. Under the command of M. Perier, this army ascended Red river, and afterwards Black river its tributary stream, to the place where the Natchez had fortified themselves in the greatest force. The siege was commenced on the 30th of January ; the trench was opened and all the different works of the besiegers begun, and advanced apace during the rest of the day, and the whole of the night. The day following, the mortars and all things necessary for the attack, were brought on shore. Some bombs were thrown, which fell in the fort. The besieged made a sortie, killed a Frenchman and a negro but were repulsed. On the 22d, bombs were thrown during the whole day but produced no great effect, and the besieged wounded two soldiers. On the 24th, they hoisted a white flag ; M. Perier at the same time caused one to be hoisted at the head of a mast ; a short time after, an Indian was seen advancing with a calumet in each hand. He brought proposals of peace, and offered on the part of his chief to return the prisoners and negroes in their possession. Terms of any kind would not be attended to unless the chief came in person; this the Indian declared could not take place, but observed to M. Perier, if he would advance to the corner of his entrenchment, the great chief would come to the end of his Fort. The Indian was dismissed with the message to his chief, that if the prisoners and negroes were delivered up, the general would then declare his further determination. These being brought and delivered to M. Perier, he declared that unless the great chief came to him in person he would continue the siege, and deny all quarter. The chiefs finally agreed to surrender, and with them the greater part of the people; the remainder who refused to give themselves up found means during some very heavy rains to escape and join the rest of the nation. About two hundred were fortified some distance up the Red river, but were attacked and destroyed by St. Denys. Those that fell into the hands of the French were disposed of as slaves; a thing very unusual in their conduct towards the Indians, which has been marked with a greater degree of kindness than perhaps that of any of the European nations, but which on this occasion, may be ascribed to the known treachery and unconquerable enmity of these people. From that day the Natchez no longer existed as a nation.

I have been more minute in detailing the circumstances of this affair, than perhaps might be deemed necessary; but it has excited much interest, and is generally viewed by writers as of importance in history.

In the same year Louisiana was retroceded to the king of France, and Monsieur Perier appointed governor. I have taken a rapid view of the first settlement of Louisiana; it is not my intention to enter upon a history of the province, this would not accord with the plan of these cursory Views. I shall only observe that even as late as the year 1736, the colony was inconsiderable, confined to some trifling settlements at the Beloxi, on the Mobile, and on the Mississippi, at New Orleans and Natchez. The greatest draw back on the prosperity of the colony was the injudicious practice of monopolies. The inhabitants could only dispose of their produce to the Company, and at such prices as it chose to establish.

Charlevoix complains that although the Spaniards did not act as openly as the English, against a colony at which they had taken great umbrage: yet that they had taken their measures more effectually to arrest its progress, and to prevent the formation of any new establishment. He says, " They have in fact succeeded even till now,[*] in retaining us by the pursuit of a contemptible trade, between the stream which was neglected to be settled,[†] and Pensacola, on a sandy coast,[‡] on an island[||] not better, and upon a river,[§] which, although well enough to occupy, is yet not fitted for any great plan of colonization. It must be confessed, that on this occasion M. D'Iberville was not judicious, or that he had no time to carry his designs into execution."

CHAPTER II.

BOUNDARIES OF LOUISIANA.

HAVING taken a cursory view of the discovery and first settlement of Louisiana, I now enter upon a subject of no small difficulty and perplexity ; the discussion of the boundaries of this province. Difficulties have already occurred, and it is feared that others will yet arise, before the matter be finally adjusted.

From the foregoing chapter, it will appear to the reader, that although in point of settlement and first discovery, the French might fairly be considered as having the best claim to Florida, yet the subsequent dereliction, for so great a number of years, gave the Spaniards a just right to occupy it, as a country owned only by the natives. We have seen, that Pensacola, during the war which preceded the treaty of 1721, was taken by the French, but afterwards surrendered in consequence of that treaty.—

---

[*] 1736. [†] Mississippi. [‡] Beloxi. [||] Isle Dauphin. [§] Mobile.

France, was therefore confined to the limits tacitly stipulated or agreed on, before the war, or at least to the part, of which she actually enjoyed possession : it does not appear that this was ever altered until the country was transferred by France to Spain. What those limits were, between what retained the name of Florida, and the French possessions to the east of the Mississippi, is tolerably well defined by several writers ; the French were undoubtedly in possession on the Mobile, and La Harpe expressly declares the *Rio Perdido* to be the boundary.

But the boundaries of this province like those of many other of the American colonies, were very vague, and given by writers who were influenced by national vanity, or guided by the political views of government. It is certain that Louisiana in the hands of France, did extend a very considerable distance east of the Mississippi ; this is acknowledged by early writers most disposed to dispute her title. Dr. Postlethwayte in his Dictionary of Commerce, after speaking of the difficulties of ascertaining the boundaries of Louisiana, observes, " that certain it is, that Louisiana contains the greater part of those new discovered lands east and west of the Mississippi, which at first had the name of Florida."

I. A question has arisen whether Louisiana by virtue of the cession to us, is held in the same extent as it was holden by France previous to the 3d of November 1762 ; that is, to the Perdido on the east side of the Mississippi ; for it can scarcely be doubted that previous to the period just mentioned, it did extend to that river. To render the subject more clear it will be necessary to ascend to first causes, and to take a view of those which induced the different transfers. As soon as the settlements on the Mississippi and in the Illinois, had taken a firm footing, the design was formed of uniting them with Canada, under the name of New France ; a young scion that in time would have rivalled and perhaps surpassed New-England. M. D'Anville under the patronage of the Duke of Orleans, executed a map of New France which included the whole extent of country west of the Allegany mountains. To the whole of the valley of the Mississippi, France had probably the most just claim, as the discoverer of the American Nile, and as the first to form establishments on all its great rivers. But this, interfered with the British charters which extended indefinitely to the west; another map was published (probably under the direction of the ministry) restricting France to much narrower limits. The dispute was settled by a war in which France lost all her possessions in this quarter of the world. Canada falling into the hands of Britain, and France fearing that the like fate might attend Louisiana, by a secret treaty of the 3d Nov. 1762, ceded to Spain *so much* of this province as lies beyond the Mississippi, together with the isle of Orleans; and by the treaty of peace which followed in 1763, the whole territory of *France and Spain,* eastward of the river Mississippi to the river Iberville, thence through the middle of that river and the lakes Pontchartrain to the sea, was ceded to Great Britain.

It will be recollected that during the American revolution, Spain taking part with the United States, conquered the Floridas from Great Britain, and they were confirmed to her by the treaty of 1783; she thus re-attached to Louisiana, the part, which, by her *joint act with France*, had been separated from it, at the same period that Florida was ceded by Spain to Britain. That part of Louisiana once more came under the government of the province. A separate one was formed of Florida of which Pensacola became the capital.

By the treaty of St. Ildefonso, Spain ceded back to the French republic, " the colony or province of Louisiana, with the same extent that it *actually had in the hands of Spain*, and *that it had when France possessed it*, and such as it ought to be after the treaties subsequently entered into between Spain and other States." This treaty was confirmed by that of Madrid 1801. To the United States, it was ceded by France on the 30th April 1803, with a reference to the foregoing clause as descriptive of its limits.

This brief exposition might be deemed sufficient, and the able view of the subject by Mr. Gallatin places it beyond doubt. It is a fact well known in this country, that the commandants at Baton Rouge and at Mobile had prepared to deliver up their posts to the United States, and that it was owing to some oversight in the commissioners that possession was not actually taken.

It is not a new claim set up on the spur of the occasion ; the first
acts of congress relative to Louisiana, expressly provided for the
government of this, as well as of other parts of the province. A
recapitulation of the facts will place the subject in a clearer light.
1. France, previous to the year 1762, possessed as far as the Perdido. 2. By the treaty of that date, she ceded to Spain not the
whole of Louisiana, but only *so much* of it, as lay west of the Mississippi, &c. 3. France jointly with Spain, ceded to Britain east
of the same river, &c. 4. Spain re-attached to Louisiana, that part
which she had jointly with France ceded in the manner before
mentioned. Spain ceded the province to France in the same extent as was then held by her, and as it had been held by France
when she possessed it, and was again ceded by the latter to the
United States in the same extent. Some have been deceived by
the term *West Florida*, and have supposed a separate government to have existed under this name, but the fact is that it was
first distinguished in this manner after it fell into the hands of
Britain.

II. The boundaries of Louisiana to the S. W. and the N. E.
still remain in doubt and obscurity. In fact, from the variety of
claimants, and the ignorance of the geography of the country in
the first instance, it was scarcely to be expected that the limits
could be clearly and satisfactorily defined. Father Hennepin and
Mons. La Salle, bounded Louisiana on the east by the Alleghe-
ny mountains, on the south by the gulph of Mexico, and on the
S. W. by the Spanish settlements ; on the N. and W. they deny
any boundary. De Lisle and Mons. D'Anville assign as the
boundary in the quarter of Mexico, the Rio Bravo. Others
contend that it was contained within the 25° and 40 of N. latitude. France certainly claimed to the Rio Bravo ; and this has
been expressed in an official act, the Grant to Crosat. It is not
clear that our executive is not bound to maintain this claim until expressly waved by the competent authority ; the sovereign
which our government suceeds, had declared the right, and actually exercised jurisdiction. These are political acts, and it is difficult to say how just or reasonable the causes which induced
them. There is no question but that France had undisturbed
possession as far as the Rio Hondo, (west of Natchitoches) and

that a fort was built by La Salle, on the bay of St. Bernard; it is said that its remains are still visible. The United States have declared the Sabine to be the boundary of the State of Louisiana, but there is no declaration how much further our claim may be considered as extending. Should Mexico achieve her independence, the amicable disposition which will probably be felt will render this more easy of arrangement. It would not be difficult to fix this boundary by taking either the Trinity, Brassos de Dios, or Guadaloupe, of the bay of St. Bernard, following the course of one of these rivers to its source, from thence pursuing a N. W. direction to the Cordilleras, and following these so as to include all the waters of the Mississippi and of the Missouri. Nacogdoches, St. Antonio, Labourdi, and a few other inconsiderable settlements, would be the only ones included. Other arrangements might perhaps be made still more to the satisfaction of the parties.

It is not more easy to assign the boundary to the N. W. and N. Perhaps the 50° of N. latitude would be the most certain and just.

CHAPTER III.

FACE OF THE COUNTRY—CHANGE WHICH A PART HAS PROBA
BLY UNDERGONE—CLIMATE—EXTENT AND IMPORTANCE.

This extensive portion of North America, has usually been described from a small part which is occupied by the settlements; as though it were limited to the borders of the Mississippi, as Egypt is confined to the vicinity of the Nile. Some represent it, in general description, as a low flat country, abounding in swamps and subject to inundation. Others speak of it as one vast wilderness;

"Missouri marches through his world of woods."

But if Louisiana were to be described like other countries not from a particular spot, but from its general appearance, we should say that it is an extensive region of open plains and meadows, interspersed with bare untillable hills, and having some resemblance to the Stepps of Tartary, or the Saara's of Africa, but without the morasses and dull uniformity of the one, or the dreary sterility of the other. The tracts lying on the great rivers constitute the most important parts of Louisiana, but are very inconsiderable in geographical extent, when compared with the remainder. These tracts are principally on the Mississippi, Missouri, Arkansas and Red river. They are vallies, seldom exceeding ten or twelve miles in width, of a soil exceedingly rich and productive, but much interspersed with lakes and refluent currents or bayous. To give a more perfect and satisfactory view of this extensive country, it will be found convenient to divide it into three parts.

1. The regions beyond the settlements.
2. The territory of the Missouri.
3. The state of Louisiana.

Volney has properly called the country drained by the Mississippi and its waters, a valley; but it is to be observed that the western side is nearly three times as large as the other, and traversed by much more considerable rivers. The mountains which bound it on the west and S. W. are of a much greater magnitude than the Alleganies.

To pursue some plan in these Views, I propose to take up the first book, with some general description of Louisiana, its rivers, soil and productions, and to give in the next book, a more detailed account of the territory of the Missouri, and of the state of Louisiana—

The Rocky Mountains are without doubt a continuation of the Andes. Their course is nearly north and south; in extent and magnitude they fall little short of the mountains of South America. There are in some places peaks of an immense height, and covered with perennial snows. The highest point is in lat. 41°, and may be considered the table land of North America. It is from this place that many of the greatest rivers take their rise, and flow in opposite directions;* the Colorado of California, Rio del Norte, the Arkansas, the Platte, and the Roche Jaune (yellow stone.) It will be to the geologist an interesting work,

* See Pike's Journal,

..o trace the various ridges, connections, spurs and dependencies of these mountains. There is a long chain of hills which generally separate the waters of the Missouri from those of the Arkansas and Mississippi, these are commonly called the Black mountains. The hills in the White river country, and those west of the Mississippi, towards the head of the St. Francis and the Maramek, so abundant in minerals, may be dependencies of the Black mountains. There are high rugged hills, approaching to mountains, between the upper part of the Washita river and the Arkansas, of which some account may be found in Hunter and Dunbar's voyage up the Washita.

Taking the distance from the Mississippi to the mountains, to be about nine hundred miles, of the first two hundred miles, the larger proportion is fit for settlements. There is a great deal of well timbered land and the soil is generally good : this quality, however, diminishes as we ascend north, where the soil becomes unproductive and almost barren, and as we advance westward the land becomes more bare of woods. For the next three hundred miles the country can scarcely be said to admit of settlements; the wooded parts form but trifling exceptions to its general appearance, and are seldom found except in the neighbourhood of streams; we may safely lay it down as a general remark, that after the first hundred miles, no timber is found on the upland except it be pine or cedar. The rest of the country is made up of open plains of immense extent, chequered with waving ridges which enable the traveller to see his journey of several days before him. Yet a great proportion of the soil would bear cultivation, the river bottoms, being generally fine, and many spots truly beautiful: there are other places, however, barren in the extreme, producing nothing but hyssop and prickly pears. The same description will suit the rest of the country to the Rocky mountains; except that it is more mountainous, badly watered, and a greater proportion entirely barren.*
In the two last divisions the bodies of land fit for settlements,

* There are extensive tracts of moving sands similar to those of the African deserts. Mr Makey informed me that he was several days in passing over one of these between the Platte and the Missouri, and near the mountains; there was no sign of vegetation.

are so distant from each other, that there is scarcely any proba
bility of any being formed for centuries, if ever.

A great proportion of the country watered by the Missouri
and its tributary streams, appears to have undergone some wonderful change, from causes not easy to ascertain; the influence
of fire, is however evident. I have seen in many places banks of
clay burnt almost to the consistence of brick; of this kind, there
is above the Poncas village, what is called the tower, a steep
hill one hundred and fifty feet in height, and four or five hundred in circumference: it is so hard, as not to be affected by the
washing of the rains. Large masses of pumice are seen near
these places, and frequently in the high bluffs of the river banks.
These appearances were formerly attributed to the existence
of volcanoes on the Missouri, but they are now generally supposed to be the effects of coal-banks continuing a long time on
fire. I am well satisfied that this fossil abounds in every part of
the great valley of the Mississippi. Many of the river hills present the appearance of heaps of clay, great quantities of which,
on the melting of the snows, and in heavy rains, are precipitated
and carried to the principal river. This clay, is of a grey color
extremely tenacious, being mixed with a large proportion of calcarious earth: the incumbent soil having been first carried away;
the rock on which it reposed being laid bare to the frost and
sun, and perhaps affected by the burning of coal-banks near it,
gradually crumbled and united with the clay. In taking up a
handful, one may pick out pieces of gypsum, (sulphat of lime)
some of half an ounce weight. Near these spots are usually
found glaubers salt, (sulphat of soda) and common salt, oozing
with water out of the ground, and crystallized on the surface.
The most remarkable fact, is the appearance on these heaps of
clay, of the remains of trees, in a state of petrifaction and some
of enormous size. Fragments may be every where picked up,
but stumps of four or five feet in height, perfectly turned to
stone, and the trunks of tall trees, may be seen and traced. This
is extraordinary in a country, where even in the richest alluvions,
the timber attains but a stinted growth.

From these facts an ingenious theorist might conjecture, that
the Missouri has not always brought down in its channel, that

astonishing quantity of earth which it does at the present day.—
It is probable, that other causes, as in Tartary, might have ope-
rated in preventing the growth of woods, in a great proportion
of this western region; but something of a different kind, must
have effected a change in this country, which apparently was
once covered with trees. What immense quantities of the earth
must have been carried off to form the great alluvions of the
Mississippi, by means of the Arkansas, Red river, and chiefly
from the Missouri! not to mention the vast quantities lost in
the gulph of Mexico. The result of a calculation would be curious. The marks of this loss, are very evident in the neighbourhood of nearly all the rivers which discharge themselves into the Missouri above the Platte. Some of the appearances,
may rank amongst the greatest natural curiosities in the world.
The traveller on entering a plain, is deceived at the first glance
by what appears to be the ruins of some great city; rows of
houses for several miles, in length, and regular streets. At the
first view, there appears to be all the precision of design, with
the usual deviations in single buildings, representing palaces,
temples, &c.; which appearances, are caused by the washing
away of the hills as before described. These remains, being composed of more durable substance continue undecayed while the
rest is carried off. The strata, have the appearance of different
stories: the isolated, and detached hills, constitute the remainder. I had this description from hunters, and from persons of
intelligence who have met with them, and I have myself, seen
places near the Missouri, very similar.

There is but a small portion of this extensive region, which
is not calcarious; in this respect, resembling the section of the
valley which lies east of the Mississippi. A fact which is singular enough, on the summits of many of the river hills, about one
thousand miles up, large blocks of granite are found, of several
tons weight; .these continue to be seen until we reach the first
range of primitive mountains. It is possible, there may have
been a lower range, which from the change produced by the
wearing away of the earth has gradually disappeared.

Some of the peculiarities of climate may be noted in this
place. The height of this western region, and the open plains

which compose it, cause it to possess a pure elastic air. The sky has a more delightful blue, than I ever saw any where else; the atmosphere in a serene, calm evening is so clear, that a slight smoke can be discerned at a distance of many miles; and is of great importance to the Indians in detecting their enemies, and in giving warning; but it also exercises their caution in the highest degree. In point of health, it is unnecessary to say any thing; such a country must necessarily be salubrious. The heat of the sun is greatest in the month of July, and at that time is not less intense than in other parts of the continent, but it is rendered more supportable by the breezes which continually fan the air. Spring opens about the last of April, and vegetation is in considerable forwardness by the middle of May. Such fruits as the country affords, principally, berries, sand cherries, currants, do not ripen until the latter end of July. I found strawberries ripe about the fourth of that month, near the Mandan villages. Plumbs ripen in the latter end of August. The winter sets in the beginning of October, but there is frost very frequently in August and September. The cold is excessive during the winter season; there are frequent storms which continue for several days, and render it dangerous for any but Indians to stir out, without running the risk of being frozen. These observations, apply to the greater portion of this region, but with respect to the part which lies south of the Arkansas, must be taken with considerable allowance.

To the north of the river just mentioned, rains are not frequent, but when they set in, pour down in torrents. To the south, there is seldom any rain, its place being supplied by heavy dews. In the dry season, at a distance from the great rivers, water is every where exceedingly scarce. The Indians in their journeys, usually pass by places where they know there are ponds, but generally, they are under the necessity of carrying water in bladders. In this season, a person in traversing the country will be frequently surprised at crossing the beds, or channels of large rivers, without finding a drop of water. After rains, or the melting of snows, torrents roll down these channels. It is not surprising that a country so distant from the sea, drained by a river which has a course of three thousand miles, before it reaches the great reservoir, should not be so well watered. This deficiency, is another amongst the impediments to the settlement of that vast waste.

According to the boundaries before laid down, Louisiana is at least, one third larger than the rest of the United States, and contains little short of one million and an half square miles. But we should be greatly deceived if in estimating its importance we take into view only its geographical extent. Constituting the central or interior part of North America, the greater portion of it, is at too remote a distance from the ocean to have an easy and advantageous communication with the rest of the world.— When compared to other parts of America it may be considered as badly watered, and devoid of that facility of intercourse from navigable rivers which they possess. I am to be understood, as speaking of Louisiana generally; there are exceptions to these general observations: the territory of the Missouri, and the state of Louisiana, are amply sufficient to make amends for the unpromising character of the remainder, they may be justly reckoned amongst the most interesting portions of the American empire.

From what has been already said, it will be seen that the prevailing idea of those western regions, being like the rest of the United States, susceptible of cultivation, and affording endless out-lets to settlements, is erroneous. These out-lets when compared to the extent of country are extremely limited; they are much less considerable than on the eastern side of the Mississippi. The natives will probably remain in quiet and undisturbed possession, for at least a century, for until our country becomes in some degree surcharged with population, there is scarcely any probability of settlers venturing far into those regions. A different mode of life, habits altogether new and suited to the situation, would have to be adopted. Settlements would have to be strung along water courses at such distances from each other, that they could not protect themselves from the wandering tribes. The distance from market, and the difficulties of reaching it, would render the agricultural produce of little or no value. Yet, I am convinced, that did not the Indians possess it, there would in a very short time, be many small groups of set-

E

tlements scattered through it. This country, it is certain, can never become agricultural, but it is in many respects highly favourable to the multiplication of flocks and herds Those delightful spots where the beauty and variety of landscape, might challenge the fancy of the poet, invite to the pastoral life. How admirably suited to that interesting animal, the sheep, are those clean smooth meadows, of a surface infinitely varied by hill and dale, covered with a short sweet grass intermixed with thousands of the most beautiful flowers, undeformed by a single weed!

This contraction of the settlements will have its advantages. The territory we possessed before the acquisition of Louisiana, would not have been filled up for a great length of time : it will require ages, and even centuries before our lands can be cultivated as in Europe, or before the population presses on the means of subsistence. A thin and scattered population is a disadvantage as it weakens a nation, and retards the progress of improvements. There is also a consideration which will strike at the first view ; the vast open plains which separate us from the Mexican provinces will for a long time prevent any serious difficulties as to boundary where there exists so little data for determining it.

To dilate upon the political advantages of the acquisition of Louisiana would fill a volume. It may be regarded as one of the most fortunate occurrences in our history. Had this country continued in the hands of any other power, it is highly probable that we should have been involved in expensive wars, or perhaps a separation of the western states might have taken place. To these states the free navigation of the Mississippi is absolutely necessary, and while Louisiana remained in the possession of any European nation it would always have been subject to interruption. This consideration alone would have been worth the price paid for the province. The connection between the existence of a republic and the extent of its territory, is still a *vexata questio* amongst politicians, and can only be decided by the experiment of ours. I will only venture to suggest one idea. In a small extent of country there is danger from the momentary bias of popular opinion ; the *permanent interests*, may not be sufficiently diversified, and should the confederacy divide on this subject, into two great parties, nothing can long retain them in union. In an extensive region like ours, even with the aid of our *thousand newspapers*, popular feeling cannot be suddenly aroused to such a pitch of passion and phrenzy, as to break down the barriers of reason; and the northern and southern interests, (of which we hear) are neutralized by the weight of several important states whose interests are connected with that of both. The western states, like the southern, are devoted to agriculture, but at the same time, dependent on the commerce of the northern for the conveniences and luxuries of life.

The security our western settlements will derive against the numerous tribes of savages, who would be at the disposal of any power holding Louisiana, may be ranked amongst the most certain advantages of the acquisition. Our vicinity to the Mexican provinces will enable us to carry on a trade, which if permitted to be free, must in a short time become of incalculable value. It is ardently to be wished that these people during their present struggles may be able to throw off the foreign government, which ruled them as it were by the spells of Circe, by using every art to retain them in ignorance, and to render them debased. Could these people become independent and be regenerated by the ennobling spirit of freedom, the northern continent would be exclusively possessed by two great nations, Americans and Mexicans, united in friendship by harmonizing interests and sympathy of governments.

The intrinsic value of Louisiana notwithstanding the vast extent which may be considered almost barren, is beyond calculation. The territory of the Missouri, and the state of Louisiana, are equal in extent to any three of the largest states, containing every variety of soil and climate, and capable of producing whatever may administer to the convenience or luxury of man ; rich in minerals, fertile in soil, and favorably situated for every commerce and manufacture.

CHAPTER IV.

LAKES AND RIVERS.

In so great an extent of country, it is not surprising there should be many navigable rivers. In Louisiana there are not less than three hundred streams adapted to the purposes of navigation, and yet this section of the great valley of the Mississippi, is far from being as well watered as that on the eastern side. Springs are less abundant, and the rivers depend chiefly for their supply on rains, and on the melting of the snows. It is a remark which applies to nearly all the larger rivers on the western side of the Mississippi, which take their rise in the great mountains, where springs are numerous, and the streams clear and limpid, that while they flow through the mountainous country, they possess deep and clear channels, and are of easy navigation, but on entering the lower country, spread out, become broad and shallow, even ceasing to be navigable for a long distance. The Missouri and Mississippi, are perhaps the only exceptions. But those which rise short of the primitive mountains are navigable with scarcely any interruption to their sources, which are often in lakes.

In upper Louisiana there are but few lakes except those near the heads of the Mississippi. The lake of the Woods, the lesser Winipec, Leech lake, Red Cedar lake (supposed to be the source of the Mississippi) lake De Sable, &c. are the most considerable of these. There are several lakes between the Missouri, and the N W. chain, but the country is yet but little known. It is supposed that lake Winipec, perhaps the largest of all those inland seas, comes within the territory of the United States.— Even if in our limits of Louisiana we should be bounded by a line due west, from that one which terminates the line of the United States, it is probable that the source of the Mississippi is further north than the southern side of lake Winipec. This lake receives a number of very considerable rivers, and is discharged into Hudson's Bay by Nelson's river; it is connected with other lakes to the north-west, and has from the rivers emptying into it, an inconsiderable portage to the waters of lake Superior.

In lower Louisiana, there are a great number of lakes from the refluent waters of the Mississippi, and from the upland streams which lose themselves in the level. These will be enumerated and more particularly described, in the account of the state of Lou ana, as also the lakes Pontchartrain, and Maurepas, on the east side of the Mississippi; which although usually known under the name of lakes, might with more propriety be considered as bays, as they are immediately connected with the sea.

In this place I shall give some detailed account of the great rivers; reserving the less considerable for the place where I shall speak of the sections of country which they traverse.

THE MISSISSIPPI.

To enter into all those particulars respecting this noble river, which writers have deemed worthy of notice, would far exceed the bounds to which I am confined. Besides, it is so well known from the writings of many intelligent persons, that by entering into such detail, my task would be little more than that of compilation. The Mississippi (or Mitchasippi, the father of streams) justly ranks amongst the most magnificent rivers in the world; whether we consider its extent, the astonishing number and magnitude of its tributary rivers, or the amazing scope of fertile lands which it traverses; watering at least a fourth of the habitable part of North America. The comparison to the Nile not unfrequently made, is far from giving just conceptions of its magnitude and importance.* It is only with the equally noble and vast rivers of the New World, it can be properly assimilated. It differs from these in one particular; instead of a channel proportioned to its extent and magnitude, it gives its tribute to the ocean by innumerable out-lets and natural canals. The *Delta* of this river is said to extend several degrees of longitude, the whole formed with earth brought down by the stream. Perhaps at one period of the world, this river gave its waters to

---

* A striking difference is, that the inundation of the one is regarded as a blessing, and of the other as a misfortune; the thin sandy soil of Egypt requires the fertilizing slime deposited by the Nile, while the alluvions of the Mississippi are of exhaustless fertility.

the great reservoir with as much majesty as the Amazon, or the La Platte, but the Mississippi may challenge any of those rivers for the extent of its navigation and the quality of habitable and fertile soil on his border, and on the borders of his " thousand sons."

The alluvions, or rather immense tracts of country formed by this river, constitute its most remarkable feature; proving incontestably an antiquity equal at least to that of the old world. These constitute a valley on an average thirty miles wide from the mouth of the Ohio, to Red river, where I consider the Delta as commencing on the western side. This valley is confined by what may be termed, as distinguished from the alluvions, primitive ground. The river is thought to be approaching in its general course the upland or primitive ground, on the eastern side; it is certain that it washes the upland in ten or twelve places, in the distance before mentioned, and seldom or ever recedes from it more than ten miles: on the western side it approaches the upland but in one place, a few miles below the river St. Francis, and that within a quarter of a mile: it afterwards in no place comes nearer than twenty miles. The water which issues from it, on this side, during the floods, returns into it again by the St. Francis, Arkansas, and Red river, with more ease than on the eastern side above Iberville and Manchac; but immense quantities of water on both sides remain stagnant in swamps and lakes. Below this, the water is carried off to the sea, by the numerous out-lets on both sides; the primitive ground diverging on either hand and leaving a larger space, eighty or ninety miles in width. There are the most evident proofs that the Mississippi has at different periods meandered in a thousand channels, still visible, in the valley between the primitive ground on either hand. There are lakes of considerable extent which have much the appearance of the river, and the ridges of high ground every where through this alluvion shew that they once constituted its banks; these ridges, from the accumulation of vegetable matter, have become even higher than the present banks, and are very rarely inundated.* The banks of what are called

* It is a common idea that the Mississippi *runs upon a ridge;* but this is easily explained when we recollect, that the alluvions even of the

bayoux, (out-lets from the river) are generally higher than those of the river from the same reason; they were undoubtedly at one period the channels of the Mississippi.

It is exceedingly difficult to give an idea of the country bordering on the Mississippi below the mouth of the Ohio. Some have represented the river as running through a swamp, others, that during the season of floods it may be considered as a river thirty miles wide; the whole country in this extent being under water. It cannot properly be called a *swamp* according to the understanding of the word; that is, an almost irreclaimable morass, or marsh; there are certainly large tracts during the floods completely inundated, particularly below Red river, but are again dry when they subside. If the reader were to conceive an idea that the valley or alluvion of the Mississippi, is at those times covered by a continued sheet of water, he would be deceived: but when the flood is at its height, the whole valley or alluvion country, is replenished with water, every where in motion, through the innumerable canals and lakes scattered through it, making its way towards the sea, leaving, however, large tracts perfectly dry. Above Red river the ground is rising every year by the accumulation of vegetable substance, and by the deposition of earthy matter where the ground overflows—the period is not distant when the greater part will be entirely above the reach of inundation. Above this river several settlements had been formed on the rivers and bayoux between the Mississippi and upland, and for five or six years were not affected by the rising of the waters; it was not until the extraordinary flood of 1811, that most of them were abandoned, yet such a quantity of sediment was deposited that year, that it will require a flood of considerably greater height to affect them. It may be worthy of remark, that the alluvial banks are generally highest on the western side; there are many places where the river does not break over them in the highest floods, by twelve or eighteen inches, though the ground is overflowed in the rear, leaving on-

most trifling rivulet will be higher on the bank than at some distance from it; the grosser and more weighty matter brought down by the stream being deposited first, and the lighter and finer at a greater distance, and the last,

ly narrow strips fifty or an hundred yards wide. The settlements from the mouth of the Ohio to Natchez are chiefly on this
side; on the eastern, there are scarcely any improvements except on the upland.

Above the mouth of the Ohio to the Missouri, the valley is
not more than half the width it possesses below, and the high
land, or bluffs, generally on the western side, but of different
character; instead of high clay banks they are faced with limestone, in places rising in precipices to two or three hundred
feet in height. This perhaps constitutes one half of the western bank. The proportion of land subject to inundation on
either side is inconsiderable, nor are there many out-lets, but
there are still large lakes scattered through the bottom, which
was formerly the bed of the river.

It has been suggested by some, that there was formerly an
out-let from Lake Mitchigan, to the Mississippi by the Illinois.
This is supported by the well known facts, that the water of
nearly all the lakes drained by the St. Lawrence, has sunk several feet, and the evident marks in the present channel of the Illinois, of having once contained a stream of much greater magnitude. This opinion might be strengthened by another fact within my own observation. The bluff which encloses the alluvion on
the eastern side, at present distant several miles from the river,
appears in places, in bare precipices of limestone rock, similar to
that immediately on the river, and what is singular, bears evident marks of attrition by the waters, to the height of at least
ten feet above the highest floods. The same thing may be also
observed on the western side. Possibly the river may have been
once six or seven miles wide at this place, and included between the bluffs. Or there may have been a lake, which by
the operation of various causes may have been drained. This
idea suggested itself to me from the examination of a remarkable place on the Mississippi, eight or ten miles above the village of Cape Girardeau, called the Grand Tower, which, though
scarcely known, may be justly considered one of the greatest curiosities of the river. At this place the bluffs on the western side
are close to the river; and on the eastern, a narrow bottom lies
between it and the bluffs; the hills on both sides at this point, seem

to converge, and from the appearance of huge fragments of rock, one is led to believe that here was formerly a cataract. The tower is one of these fragments, about sixty yards from the western bank, (which is a steep rock) and is about fifty feet in height; its form nearly circular, some handsome cedars growing on the top: on the opposite side of the river there is another huge detached rock, but round which the water does not flow except in extraordinary floods;* between this and the bluffs there are several other fragments of rock, possessing every appearance of once having formed a regular chain, through which the Mississippi, by the aid of time, or some convulsion of nature has made itself a channel. It is a dangerous place and difficult to ascend, as well as to descend in safety. Between this, and the mouth of the Ohio, there are to be seen in various places, detached rocks on the shore, and on the heads of islands, evidently rolled down by some mighty and unusual current.

It is the opinion of many persons, that the Mississippi is a continuance of the Missouri; of this there can be little doubt. The Mississippi after its junction with that river assumes its appearance and character in every particular except the general course; the colour of their waters can be distinguished for sixty miles; but in the alluvia, sand bars, islands, rafts, current, and the timber on its borders, the Missouri is preserved. Perhaps it might have been more proper to have given a new name to the river which has been the result of this junction.

Above the Missouri, the Mississippi is clear and limpid, like the Ohio, and bordered by a country extremely beautiful, with many fertile spots, but is not to be compared to that on the Ohio for settlements. The greater part consists of naked plains, which promise little to the husbandman. Excepting the cataracts of St. Anthony; this river has but one or two serious interruptions in the navigation for at least sixteen hundred miles above St. Louis: but its channel generally abounds with shoals, and sand bars, the current, however, gentle. It is not an easy matter to point out exactly its source, several of the branches

---

* There is a remarkable cave in this rock, called by the Americans the Devil's Oven; stories are related of persons having gone in and never returning.

into which it divides near its head, might claim this honor. It does not take its rise in a mountainous country, and yet it must be of considerable height, from the number of important rivers which flow from the same neighbourhood. The country abounds in lakes and extensive marshes, among which the Mississippi takes its rise. A narrow ridge of high land separates it from the waters of lake Winipec. Red Cedar lake, in lat. 47° 38' is considered by Pike as its source, this is but a few miles from Red lake in which Red river takes its rise; here is therefore an easy communication with the waters which discharge themselves into Hudson's bay.

The appearance of the Mississippi in descending, varies but little. On entering from the Missouri we find ourselves in a more spacious river : in places where large islands divide the current, it spreads to a great width, sometimes of several miles ; yet when this is not the case the channel of the river is but little wider than at the Mandan villages, though at that place it is only filled in the season of high water. The navigation is considered dangerous from the Missouri to the mouth of the Ohio, on account of the great number of sawyers and rafts. Below this fine river, no perceptible difference takes place in point of magnitude, and from the St. Francis to Red river, the general width scarcely exceeds that of the Missouri. At Point Coupeé it assumes a more majestic appearance, and from this place continues a course, uninterrupted by islands and sand bars, with a current gradually diminishing.

The adjacent scenery is as little varied. The banks are covered with cotton wood trees, of enormous size, the tops apparently as level as if made so by design. Scarcely any other tree grows on the island. Below the mouth of the Ohio, the cypress makes its appearance in the bends, where the ground is lower than on the points and subject to be overflown. The *arundo gigantica*, appears about the same place, on the spots of ground least subject to inundation. It grows to the height of twenty feet, forming an impervious thicket. The long moss, or Spanish beard begins to be seen below the Arkansas, and gives a gloomy appearance to the woods. The falling in of the banks is amongst the most remarkable features of this river; sometimes whole acres with the trees growing on them are precipitated into the stream, creating frightful impediments to the navigation, and not unfrequently overwhelming boats moored near the shore. In time, the trees thus fallen in, become sawyers and planters; the first so named from the motion made by the top when acted upon by the current, the others are the trunks of trees of sufficient size to resist it. There are also frequently seen at the heads of islands, immense collections of drift wood, piled up to a great height, thrown confusedly together and closely matted : here are found, boats, canoes, planks, and a great variety of timber, brought down by the rivers of a hundred climates and soils, and heaped together in chaos. These are amongst the most dangerous places in the course of the navigation.* The current rushes towards them with amazing velocity, and it is with great difficulty and the exertion of skill, that they are avoided. It is therefore dangerous to float after night.

The Mississippi is remarkable for the muddiness of its waters, a quality altogether derived from the Missouri, but is less turbid than that river; the waters above the junction, being clear, the accession of the Illinois, Ohio, and other clear streams tending also to render it more limpid than the Missouri. It is not from the falling in of the banks, as is supposed, that this muddiness proceeds; this is scarcely sufficient to supply what is deposited by the river on sand bars, islands, &c. between the upper Missouri, (from whence the earth forming it is carried) and the mouth of the river.

There is a surprising difference in the navigation of this truly noble river, in the ordinary stages of water and during the continuance of the floods. There have been instances of persons descending from St. Louis to New Orleans, in ten days; the distance, however, is much shortened by being able to cut off points, and to go through channels impracticable in low water. The usual time in low water is from four to six weeks. In ascending, fifty days to the mouth of the Ohio is considered a good voyage, but two months is the most usual time; oars and poles are al-

---

* For a more minute account of the difficulties of the navigation, and for many interesting details, I refer the reader to the Ohio and Missis. sippi Navigator:

ways used for the purpose of navigating the boats, but the cordelle, and sails, are also of great importance. In the course of a
voyage it is rare that there are not six or eight days of sailing,
which is a great relief to the hands, as the boat is then propel-
led against the current without their assistance, sometimes, thirty miles a day. In very light winds, the sails are hoisted and although not sufficient alone to cause the boat to ascend, yet afford considerable help. The boats usually employed are from
ten to thirty tons burthen; as high as Natchez, schooners of fifty tons often ascend. There are, besides, between the places
just mentioned, a kind of boats of a peculiar construction, muc h
in use, and carrying often eight or ten tons: they appear to be
formed of a single tree, but in reality out of three of the largest
size; two are hollowed in such a manner as to form the sides, and
a third for the bottom: they are then joined together so as to make
a very durable and strong boat, easily managed, and the most
safe against hurricanes and violent winds.

The Mississippi carries generally 15 feet water from the
mouth of the Missouri to the Ohio, from thence to the Red river, it seems to increase in depth: at this place it has as many
fathoms, and at New Orleans not less than forty. On the bar,
there are usually from twelve to fourteen feet, although the water rises at the mouth of the Ohio fifty feet, and but little diminution is experienced before we pass Natchez; at Bâton Rouge
it is not more than 25 feet, at New Orleans only fifteen, and at
the mouth of the river, is scarcely perceptible.

The floods of the Mississippi usually begin in April; commencing with the first flood of the Missouri which is usually
in March, on the breaking up of the ice; this is followed by the
Mississippi above the junction, afterwards by the Ohio, and
other rivers. The great flood of the Missouri begins in June,
shortly after which those of the Mississippi, in consequence attain their greatest height. It subsides in August. A very unusual occurrence took place this winter (1812) in the month of
December, the river rose to within two or three feet of the highest water and continued to be high until the latter end of the
month. The oldest inhabitants had never witnessed any thing of
the kind.

MISSOURI.

I have already observed that this is much the most considerable of any of the rivers which swell the Mississippi, and one of
the most wonderful in the world. It enters the Mississippi
nearly at right angles in lat. 38° 55′; the confluence is by no
means comparable to that of the Ohio, principally owing to an
island at the entrance. The course of the river in ascending is
little north of west to the Platte.† Above this, its course is nearly N. W. until we reach the Mandan villages, in lat. 46. From
this point the distance to the Mississippi is less than from the
Platte. From the northernmost part of the great bend, above the
Mandans, and in lat. 47° we ascend nearly west; the course of
the three forks, Jefferson, Madison, and Gallatin, is nearly S.
W. and S.

The current of this river is at least a fourth greater than that
of the Mississippi. To the Platte, it is amazingly swift, and stem-
med with great difficulty, abounding with shoals and sand bars,
sawyers, rafts projecting from the shore, and islands. It is almost impracticable to descend in flat-bottomed boats, even in the
highest stages of the water : in barges great care and dexterity
are requisite. It is far from being agreeable in appearance, unless we consider the pleasure derived from contemplating its
wonderful swiftness and force. Above the Platte, the Missouri,
though not less swift in current, is rendered more easy of navigation by the large sand bars, and clear banks, which admit of
towing: but from the scarcity of wood of a proper kind, it is
necessary to lay in a sufficient stock of oars and poles. To the
falls, two thousand miles further, it preserves the same character; the navigation however becomes less dangerous, or difficult,
excepting from the shoals, which in low water are abundant.
Above the falls or cataracts, there is a clear fine river five hun-

† About twenty miles up, each river makes a sudden turn—the Missouri S. W. and the Mississippi N. E. but, I do not know upon what
ground it is asserted, that after having descended either river for
several days, the voyager will find himself within a days march of the
other.

dred miles to the three forks, affording better navigation than
any part of the Missouri, although the channel is generally narrow and sometimes confined between lofty mountains. The three
forks are all fine rivers, and receive a great number of smaller
streams. In ascending the Missouri, sails are of more importance than on any of the western rivers. The openness of the
country gives scope to the winds, which in the spring and summer usually blow from the S. E. and suit the general course of
the river: I frequently ascended, notwithstanding the swiftness
of the current, from thirty to forty miles per day for three or
four days in succession.

The Missouri is remarkable for its large and smaller bends.
The greater we have already seen from the general course of the
river; it would therefore not be surprising that it should afterwards turn south and take the course of the Mississippi. The
small bends are where the river pursues a zig-zag course for
forty or fifty miles, constantly returning upon its steps.

The Missouri receives all its principal rivers from the S. W.
side. The extent of country to be drained on the N. E. side is to
the other, as the east side of the Mississippi is to the western.
This is owing to the vicinity of the Mississippi, and the N. W.
chain of lakes. The distance from the Mandan villages to the
British establishment on the Red river of Winipec, is but a few
days journey.

The floods of this river usually begin early in March, and
there is a continued succession of them until the last of July;
the river subsiding and again rising as the different rivers bring
down their annual tributes. It so happens, that seldom more
than two great rivers are high at the same period. Many of these
floods are never felt in the Mississippi. But the great rise of the
Missouri itself, from the melting of the snows, takes place, about
the tenth of June, and begins to subside about the latter end of
July. In some of the northern branches, the ice does not break
up until late in the season: about one thousand miles up the Missouri, I saw a large cake of ice floating in the river on the last
of May.

There is little variation in the width of this river from its
mouth to the cataracts. In some places it spreads considerably,

and in these, sandbars impede the navigation in low water : at these times the river is reduced in places to less than a fourth of its usual breadth, between sand-bars which advance into it, and a high bank. But when the channel is full, the river even at the Mandans, appeared to me not less broad or majestic, than does the Mississippi at New Orleans.

The cataracts of the Missouri, from every description, are, next to those of Niagara, the most stupendous in the world. The descent, in the distance of eighteen miles, according to the esti-mation of Lewis and Clark, is 362 feet 9 inches.

The first great pitch	98 feet	
— second -	19 —	
— third -	47 —	8 inches
— fourth -	26 —	

besides a number of smaller ones. The width of the river is about three hundred and fifty yards.

The whole extent of navigation of this river which has no other cataract or considerable impediment, from the highest point on Jefferson river, the largest of the three forks, to its en-trance into the Mississippi, is three thousand and ninety-six miles; no other tributary stream in the world possesses such a navigation.

ARKANSAS.

The Arkansas, next to the Missouri, is the most consid-érable tributary of the Mississippi. In length it is nearly two thousand five hundred miles, and navigable at proper seasons nearly the whole distance. In many places its channel is broad and shallow, at least above the rapids, so as to render na-vigation almost impracticable. Until eight or nine hundred miles from its mouth, it receives no considerable streams, owing to the vicinity of the waters of the Missouri, of the Kansas, &c. on the one side, and those of Red river on the other. The chief rivers which fall into it, are the Verdigris, the Negracka, Cana-dian river, Grand river, &c. Several are remarkable for being strongly impregnated with salt; the Arkansas itself, at certain seasons is said to be brackish.

The lands on this river for six or eight hundred miles up, are described as very fine and capable of affording settlements, though principally untimbered. For a long distance up, the flat lands on either side are intersected with numerous bayoux.— There is a remarkable communication between the Arkansas and White river, by a channel or bayou connecting the two rivers with a current setting alternately into the one or the other, as the flood in either happens to predominate.

RED RIVER

Takes its source in the Cordilleras, at no great distance north of Sta. Fé. In length it is about the same with the Arkansas. It is navigable six or eight hundred miles, with scarcely any obstruction. There is at that point a curious raft, formed of logs and earth, which entirely covers its channel; trees are growing upon it, and one might pass over without perceiving the river. Red river runs in a valley on an average fifteen miles wide, for at least eight hundred miles, which is every where intersected with bayoux, and large lakes. The navigation meets with the first impediment one hundred and fifty miles up. The falls or rapids are about two miles in length, the breadth of the river two hundred and fifty yards. They are occasioned by a soft rock of free stone: the greatest pitch in low water, not being more than eight or nine inches. This river might with much more justice than the Mississippi, be called the American Nile. A country lies on its borders more extensive than Egypt, and of a soil the richest perhaps in the world. Its waters, which are not potable, are very red, impregnated with some mineral. The river is remarkably narrow; it seldom spreads to the width of two hundred and fifty yards, and is more generally contracted to one hundred; it is also exceedingly crooked. The annual swell, which is early in the spring of the year, raises the water fifty or sixty feet, when it flows with great rapidity: but during the summer and season of low water, it is sunk within deep and ragged clay banks, of an unsightly appearance, and has not more than eight or ten feet of water. The out-lets from this river are more numerous than even from the Mississippi, and joined by streams which flow from the uplands, or pine woods. The course of the river is conslantly subject to change; many of the bayoux which at present appear inconsiderable, at no distant period constituted the bed of the principal river.

The following are amongst the most considerable tributaries of the Mississippi and Missouri, and may be noticed in this place.

R. DES CORBEAUX,

The western branch of the Mississippi, and affording the best communication with Red river of Winipec. This river is ascended one hundred and eighty miles to the Leaf river, which enters from the N. W.; the Leaf river is again ascended the same distance; there is then a portage of one half mile to the Otter Tail lake, the principal source of Red river. The other branch of the riviere des Corbeaux, bears S. W. and approaches the St. Peters.

ST. PETERS

Enters the Mississippi about forty miles below the falls of St. Anthony. It is a fine stream, and may be navigated to its source, a thousand miles; the current is gentle, and in places scarcely perceptible; in the spring and summer it is covered with wild fowl, which collect here for the purpose of breeding, and find abundant nourishment in the wild rice which grows in the river and neighbouring lakes. Its principal branches are, Blue Earth river, Red Wood river, and Yellow Wood river.

DES MOINES.

Next to the St. Peters, it is the largest of the rivers which the Mississippi receives from the west, above the confluence with the Missouri. It enters two hundred and fifty miles from their junction, and is navigable without a fall or scarcely an interruption, to the Pelican lake, where it rises, and which is not far from the Sioux river of the Missouri, a distance of about eight hundred miles. Rackoon river, the principal branch enters on the S. W. side, and is navigable several hundred miles. There are several others of some magnitude, particularly the Red Cedar river.

GRAND RIVER,

Enters the Missouri on the N. E. side, about 250 miles up; a fine river, navigable six hundred miles; general course not distant from the Missouri. Formerly, when the traders bound for the Mahas, (800 miles up the Missouri) were infested by the Kansas Indians, they ascended this river, and then crossed to the Missouri.

KANSAS,

Rises in the vast plains between the Arkansas and the Platte. It is one of the finest rivers of the Missouri, though inferior to several of them in extent. The principal branches are the Smoky Hill Fork, Grand Saline, Solomon's Fork, and the Republican Fork. It enters the Missouri 300 miles up. I have conversed with hunters who had ascended it, without meeting any considerable obstacles, more than three hundred leagues. It receives a great number of large streams, and is by no means well known. The adjacent country is generally prairie, and the cliffs on the river, are frequently solid rocks of gypsum.

THE PLATTE,

Is the longest and largest of the rivers which discharge themselves into the Missouri, being little short of two thousand miles, and yet can hardly be reckoned a navigable stream. The channel is extremely wide and abounds with ever varying quicksands. Several fine navigable rivers, however, discharge themselves into it; the ElkHorn, and the Wolf river, and the Padoncas Fork.

THE YELLOW STONE (OR ROCHE JAUNE,)

Has considerable resemblance to the Missouri in extent and difficulty of navigation, and is the most considerable of those rivers which discharge themselves into it. The Missouri, undergoes a perceptible change after the junction. In seasons of high water it is more properly a torrent; the descriptions of its rapidity are almost incredible. It enters the Missouri 1880 miles up. The principal branches are, Big Horn, Tongue river, and Clark's river.

WHITE R.—CHIENNE R.—R. A. JAQUE—SIOUX R.

Might be reckoned the largest rivers any where else. The Little Missouri, (90 leagues above the Mandan villages) is remarkable for the quantity of mud which it carries down. At the *Maria river*, a large stream which enters the Missouri two thousand miles up, the muddiness of the Missouri in some measure ceases.

There are several considerable rivers, between the Missouri and the N. western lakes. Red river is the principal; the Assineboin is its principal branch. The Mouse river, or Saskashawin, which flows into the Assineboin, is remarkable for taking its rise from the very bank of the Missouri

The following, is a table of the navigable rivers of Louisiana; it is necessarily incomplete, but from it some rude conjecture can be formed as to the immense extent of navigation which it possesses.

TABLE OF NAVIGABLE RIVERS IN LOUISIANA—EXTENT OF NAVIGATION.

Principal R.	Tributaries	Navi.	Remarks.
MISSISSIPPI....		3,000	
	Sang Sue . . .	80	By some considered the source
	Pike R.	120	of the Miss. heads in Leech lake,
	des Corbeaux .	300	and is larger than the branch
	St. Peters . . .	1,000	which rises in Red Cedar lake;
	Turkey R. . .		considered the source of the a-
	Catfish R. . .		bove mentioned river.
	des Moines . .	800	About 250 miles above the mouth
	Wayaconda .		of the Missouri, not much known.
	Jauflione . . .		
	Salt R.		
	Buffaloe . . .		
	Cuivre	150	
	Missouri . . .	3,096	
	Maramek . .	350	
	St. Francis .	800	
	White R. . . .	1,100	
	Arkansas . . .	2,000	
	Red R.	2,500	
		15,296	
DES CORBEAUX	Leaf R.	180	There is a portage of one mile
			from the head of this river to the
ST PETERS....	Blue Earth R.		Otter Tail lake, the principal
	Red Wood R.		source of Red River of Winipec.
	Yellow Wood R		
DES MOINES...	Rackoon R		
	Red Cedar R.		

Principal R.	Tributaries.	Navi.	Remarks.
MISSOURI........	Gasconnade .	100	S. W. side
	Mine R. . . .	40	id.
	G. Osage . .	600	id.
	1 Charlatans .	50	id.
	2 Charlatans .	100	N. E side
	Grand R . . .	600	N. E side
	Kansas	1,200	S. W. side
	Little R. Platte	40	N. E. side
	Nodawa	60	N E side
	Platte		S. W upwards of 2,000 miles
	F.oyd's R. , .		in length, but affords little or no
	Big Sioux . . .	200	navigation.
	White Stone .		
	River á Jaque	300	N. E. A point of rendezvous for the traders, and the Yankton band of Sioux.
	Qui Courre . .		S. W. A handsome river, but not navigable any great distance.
	Poncas		S. W.
	White R. . . .	600	S. W. A large fine river; its branches not known, 300 yards at its mouth.
	Tylers R. . . .		
	Chienne R. . .	800	S W. Not better known than White river; 400 yards wide at its mouth.
	Ser-war-ser-na		S. W side
	Win-i-pen-hu		S W.
	Cannon-ball R.		S. W. 140 yards wide
	Knife R. . . .		S. W. Near the Mandan villages.
	Little Missouri		S W. 134 yards wide, but not navigable.
	Goose R . . .		N E 300 yards wide.
	White earth R.		N. E.
	Yellow Stone .		S. W 855 yards wide at the mouth; a very large river, equal in length to the Platte; affords much better navigation, but is astonishingly rapid.
	Porcupine R. .		N. E 112 yards wide.
	Dry R. . . .		S W 100 do.
	Big Dry R. . .		S. W. 400 do.
	Muscle Shell R.		S. W. 100 do.
	Big Horne . .		S W 100 do.
	Manoles . . .		S. W. 100 do.
	Fancy R. . . .		S. W. 180 do.
	Dearborne . .		
	Maria		N. E. At this place the Missouri is observed to have nearly all its turbidness.
	Jefferson Fork	96	
	Madison . . .	80	
	Gallatin	60	

Principal R.	Tributaries.	Navi.	Remarks.
YEL. STONE....	Big Horne . .		
	Tongue R. . .		
	Clark's R. . .		
	Lewis's R. . .		
MARAMEK........	Big R.	150	
ST. FRANCIS...	Western branch	150	This river is not perfectly
	Penusco . . .	50	known.
WHITE RIVER	Aux Cashe . .	80	
	Black R. . . .	400	
	James R. . . .	150	
	Rapid John . .	100	
	Red River . .	300	
ARKANSAS......	Verdigris . .	200	
	Nagraca . . .	150	
	Canadian R. .	100	
	Grand R. . . .	200	
	Grand Saline .		
	Strong Saline .		
RED RIVER.....	*Black R.* . . .	50	This river is formed by the junction of the Tensa, Washita and Little river—There are numerous navigable bayoux and streams from Red river, but no considerable branches except the one just mentioned.
Q. OSAGE.........	Nangira . . .		
	Grand R. . . .		
	The Fork . . .		
	Cook's R . . .		
	Vermillion R.		
KANSAS..........	Smokey hill F.		These rivers are navigable from 150 to 300 miles.
	Grand Saline .		
	Soloman's Fork		
	Republican do.		
PLATTE..........	Elk-horn . . .	400	
	Wolf R. . . .	600	Heads in a lake.
	Padoncas . . .		
BLACK R. (w.)	Spring R. . . .	50	Rises in a lake, and is navigable from the very source.
	Current		
	Eleven		
BLACK R. (M.)	Washita . . .	1,000	
	Riviere au Bœuf	400	This is a long river which flows
	Tensa	150	between the Mississippi and the
	Catahoula . .	50	Washita, and said to communi-
	Little River .	100	cate with the St. Francis, by
RED RIVER.....	Little Missouri		means of a lake, with which the
of Winipec	Assineboin . .		waters of that river are connected.
	Saskas hawin .		
TECHE............			Called a bayou, but more pro-
		150	perly a river.
SABINE...........		400	
Chaffallaya......		300	A continuation of Red river.

I have not attempted to enumerate the different navigable bayoux and lakes, but these are very numerous : and doubtless many rivers equal in size to the Schuylkill, have not been placed in this table, the country being still but imperfectly explored.

CHAPTER V.

NATURAL OR INDIGENOUS PRODUCTIONS—ANIMAL, VEGETA BLE, AND MINERAL.

NOT being a naturalist, I shall only attempt to give some idea of the extensive field which lies open to the learned. Were I to attempt, upon a slender knowledge, to give a scientific account, I might lead the reader into error.

I am informed that the western side of the Mississippi, to the eye of the naturalist, has a character altogether different from any part of the United States, and that except New Holland, the world does not afford a more interesing field.

Mr. Bradbury* has made an extensive collection of specimens, and some very interesting discoveries. The indefatigable research of this gentleman, and that heart-engaged enthusiasm, which the student of the great book of nature, has ever been observed to possess, promise a valuable acquisition to pleasurable and useful knowledge. The discoveries of Lewis and Clark, even in this department, are said to be very important; but, from the expedition necessary in the movements of the exploring parties, and the necessity of a continual watch, for their own safety, they could not posses the opportunity and leisure, necessary for the examination of objects more minute.

The forest trees, and plants and animals, described by Mr. Jefferson, and other writers, are found in some part or other of this territory; but there is also a great variety, peculiar to itself. The subject of its mineralogy remains untouched Mr. Bradbury has discovered nearly one hundred and fifty *non-descript* plants; near twenty of which, cannot be assigned to any known genera, and may therefore be considered as forming new ones.

* About the time of writing the following view of the *natural productions, &c.* I became acquainted with Mr. Bradbury, and submitted the sketch to him, he was good enough to make some corrections, and to annex several interesting notes. Mr. Bradbury is a naturalist of eminence, a fellow of the Linnean Society, and engaged to come to this country to pursue his researches.

His discoveries with respect to the animated part of the creation, and the subterraneous riches of the country, are not less important.

ANIMALS.

Agreeably to what I have already said, I shall not attempt to give any catalogue of animals, plants, &c. but merely notice those most remarkable.

The Grizzly Bear—First claims our attention. This animal, is the monarch of the country which he inhabits. The African lion, or the tyger of Bengal, are not more terrible or fierce. He is the enemy of man; and literally thirsts for human blood. So far from shunning, he seldom fails to attack; and even to *hunt* him.* The Indians make war upon these ferocious monsters, with the same ceremonies, as they do upon a tribe of their own species: and in the recital of their victories, the death of one of them, gives the warrior greater renown than the scalp of a human enemy.

The Grizzly bear, is a *non-descript*, and much the largest of the species. He is three times the size of a common brown bear, and six times that of an European one. One of them, killed by Lewis and Clark, near the Porcupine river, about two thousand miles up the Missouri, measured as follows:

Round the head   3 feet 5 inches
Round the neck   3 feet 11 inches
Length   8 feet $7\frac{1}{2}$ inches
Round the fore-leg   1 foot 11 inches
Talons—in length $4\frac{3}{8}$ inches

Mr. Manuel Lisa, the first who ascended to this country for the purpose of trade, and who spent nine months in it, informed me that they sometimes exceed 1,200 lbs. in weight, and that one full grown, will commonly weigh eight or nine hundred. He possesses an amazing strength, and attacks without hesitation and tears to pieces the largest buffaloe. The color, is usually such as the name indicates, though there are varieties, from black to silvery whiteness The skins are highly valued for muffs and tippets; and will bring from twenty to fifty dollars each.

---

* I am credibly informed that he has been known to pursue the track of a hunter an hour after his having passed.

This bear is not usually seen lower than the Mandan villages. In the vicinity of the Roche Jaune, and of Little Missouri, they are said to be most numerous. They do not wander much in the prairies, but are usually found in points of wood, in the neighbourhood of large streams. The Indians hardly ever venture into the fringe of wood, which borders the rivers, in that great extent of open country, without first setting up a loud and continued shout, in order that the bears, if there be any, may either come forth to attack them, or retire, if they happen not to be so disposed.

In shape, he differs from the common bear in being proportionably more long and lank. He does not climb trees, a circumstance which has enabled hunters with whom I am acquainted, to make their escape. The Indians complain that some of their best warriors, have fallen victims to this animal. Lewis and Clark's men, on several occasions, narrowly escaped from their attacks. The Grizzly bear is sufficient to disprove, the idle theories of Buffon or Raynal, as to the impotency of the NEW WORLD in the production of animals.

Antelope, was thought to be a non-descript species of deer, it is a beautiful little animal, and is found on the Missouri above the Platte. The antelope goes in flocks of several hundreds; the Indians frequently take them, by driving them into the water and attacking them with clubs.

Grosse Corne, so called from the large size of the horns, some of them being two feet in length, and four or five inches in diameter; they are extremely shy, and climb without difficulty to the pinnacle of the highest mountain, and sport upon the giddy verge of precipices. They have been called also *mountain sheep*, but have little resemblance to sheep, except in the head, horns, and feet. On the rump, they are white, but every where else of a dun color. In size they exceed the deer, and have a fine soft hair: the horns of the male are larger than those of the female. This animal is thought to be the *Agalia*.

The Buffaloe, may be said to have retired north of the Illinois, and west of the Mississippi. The plains of Indiana and Illinois, were once his places of favorite resort, and he loved to frequent the banks of the beautiful Ohio; but encroaching settlements have driven him away. His proper country appears to be the plains of the Missouri; those of Indiana and Illinois, are miniatures of these. Here the buffaloe is found in immense herds; frequently covering the plain as far as the eye can reach. Some of these herds, have been estimated at fifty thousand heads. In the dry season, they are found in the neighbourhood of the great rivers, but there are also regular migrations of them from north to south, when they are seen passing the Missouri, for several days in succession, like the march of Xerxes' army.

The wool* of the buffaloe has a peculiar fineness, even surpassing that of the merino. I have seen gloves made of it, little inferior to silk. But for the difficulty of separating the hair, it might become a very important article of commerce. Should any means be discovered of effecting this, or should it be found, that at certain seasons, there is less of this mixture, the buffaloe wool must become of prime importance in manufactures.

Elk and Deer, are found in great numbers in this territory. In the neighbourhood of the settlements deer are very abundant; the poor animals enjoy some respite from their cruel persecutors, on account of the low state of the peltry trade, and for some time past have been observed to increase. Two varieties of deer are discovered high up on the Missouri. The black tailed, or mule deer ; remarkable for very long ears, and tails almost without hair, except at the end where there is a small tuft of a black color. The other kind is distinguished by very small horns, and a tail of unusual length—eighteen or twenty inches.

There is a species of wolf different from the wolverin, and a curious one of the fox. The braireau or badger, is found on the Mississippi and on the Missouri. The changeable hare *(lepus variabilis)* a beautiful animal, gray in summer, and white in winter is seen in this country.

* It is curious to observe, that in the instruction to Iberville by the king of France, two things were considered of the first importance, the *pearl fishery*, and the *buffaloe wool.* Charlevoix observes, that he is not surprised that the first should not have been attended to, but he thinks it strange that the second should be neglected even to his time.

The Prairie dog, or *Squirrel*, is a great curiosity. It lives in burrows, or as they are commonly called *towns*, and is about a third larger than the fox squirrel. The head is thick and clumsy, it has large jaws, full, large eyes, but the ear is not prominent, consisting of little more than the orifice. The body is long, and legs short, the tail not much larger than that of a common ground squirrel, and very delicate; the hair short and sleek, of a light grey, excepting on the belly, where it is white. It is without doubt a species of squirrel, though it has a cloven lip like the rabbit. It makes a noise very similar to that of the ground squirrel, though much louder; and resembling in a slight degree the barking of a very small dog. When at some distance from its hole, which, however, seldom happens, it may be easily caught, but is exceedingly fierce in the first instance; yet in a few days, it becomes perfectly domesticated, and is pleased with being caressed. It seldom drinks; it feeds on the grass which grows around its hole, and remains torpid during winter. These towns are to be found in the large prairies about three hundred miles west of the Mississippi, and are frequently more than a mile in length. The situation chosen, is generally dry, being on the slope of a hill, and at a distance from any water course. When a person approaches, he is assailed by the whole village, with a noise, which as I have mentioned, bears a resemblance to the barking of small dogs. The animals are seen behind small hillocks at the side of their holes: on approaching within a few yards of one of these, the inhabitant instantly retreats to his subterraneous apartments. The wolves have declared war against these curious people, and frequently commit great havoc, in their little republics.

The *Gopher*,* is supposed to be a non-descript; it lives under ground, in the prairies, and is also found east of the Mississippi. It bears considerable resemblance to the mole, but is twice the size of that animal. It has at each jaw, a kind of bag, or purse, about one inch and a half in length, for the purpose of conveying food, or for carrying the dirt out of its hole. The

* This name is also given to a species of terrapin.

Note by Mr. Bradbury—If the Gopher is not the animal, described in the Systema Naturæ, as *mus bursorius*, by Linnæus, it is yet undescribed.

quantity of earth thrown up,' is enormous; frequently forming
mounds of three or four feet in height.

The *Alligator*, is too well known to require any thing to be
said of him. He is not considered a ferocious or dangerous animal by the inhabitants. The numbers of this animal have lessened of late years from the destruction made by the inhabitants,
who value their skins.

The *Cameleon*, is very common; and I am informed that in
the southern parts, both the scorpion and the tarantula exist.

Of the feathered tribes, something may also be said. There
is a beautiful bird called the prairie hen, which I think is not described. In winter it is found in large flocks, comes into barn-
yards, and frequently alights on the houses of the villagers. It
is somewhat larger than the pheasant of the United States, (*tetrao
umbellus*,) which it resembles somewhat in color, but in shape
is much like the guinea hen: and differs from the pheasant in being easily domesticated. The flesh is dry, black, and by no means
agreeable. There is a bird on the Missouri, which bears a strong
resemblance to the pheasant, but, is nearly as large as a turkey
hen; it is described as being a fine bird. I have seen a specimen
of the Columbia partridge, of the most beautiful plumage. The
magpie is found in abundance on the Missouri.

In the settlements, and for a considerable distance up the
Missouri, turkies stalk through the woods, in numerous flocks,
but are rarely met with where the open country commences.
Quails, *tetrao marliandica*, are found every where. In the fall
of the year all the lakes are literally covered with wild fowl,
ducks, geese, swans, cranes, and a variety of others.

VEGETABLE PRODUCTIONS.

I have already observed that an extensive field lies open to
the botanist. There are even some considerable forest trees, yet
undescribed: there is particularly one very beautiful, *bois jaune*,
or yellow wood: by some called the mock orange. In size, it
equals that of the largest peach tree, and the leaves, though
longer, are pretty nearly similar. The trunk is short, the limbs
branching out low down. The fruit has some resemblance to the

orange, but more spherical, and covered with tubercles;* the color, when at maturity, is a pale yellow. This fruit has been
deemed poisonous, but perhaps without reason : in its green
state, it gives forth when cut, a great quantity of milky fluid,
which possesses a corrosive nature, blackening the knife, with
which it is cut, like the pine apple. It would certainly be in gardens a highly ornamental tree; Mr. Choteau, of St. Louis, has
planted one in his garden, which thrives well. The tree is found
on the Osage, Arkansas, and other places west of the Mississippi;† it is said, in low, moist and swampy ground. The wood
is remarkably heavy, scarcely yielding to lignum vitæ, and of a
beautiful yellow. It might be of use in dyes, or for inlaying. The
Indians use of it for war clubs, and for bows.

There is a grape on the Missouri, found in the prairies,
which ripens in the month of June, as far north as latitude 40°.
It is very sweet and pleasant. A hundred writers, have spoken
of the vines of the Illinois, with strange exaggeration. This
forms a part of the pictures of the romancing writers, who first
described Louisiana. Father Hennepin, describes the *sugar
cane*, as growing spontaneously, on the banks of the Mississippi, and tells of purple clusters of grapes, imparting their rich
hues to the gliding wave. Notwithstanding the figure the vines
of this country have made in description, they are very little different from those of the United States. Formerly a wretched
sort of wine was made of the *winter grape*, but which is at present almost neglected. These vintages were never considered
of much importance. The wine was made by bruising the
grapes in a large tub; a heavy stone was then placed on them,
to press out the juice, which flowed through an opening at the
bottom into a vessel prepared for its reception.‡

* See the voyage of Hunter and Dunbar up the Wabash.

† I have seen one near Natchitoches, on the Red river.

‡ *Note by Mr. Bradbury.* On the Ohio and on the Mississippi, there
are two kinds of grapes, not found in the United States; *vitis æstivalis*
and *vitis riparia*; the last is a very fine grape. There are also two species on the Missouri, the one described, and a white grape, said to be
very fine. The change which all the American vines, undergo from cul-

Amongst the forest trees of this country, the cedar, (juniperus virginiana,) the cotton wood, (populus anguliscus,) and the peccanne, (juglans olivæ formus) deserve particular attention. The cedar, grows in great abundance and perfection. There are fine groves, on the Maramek, St. Francis, Missouri, and on the Mississippi. Some very large islands in the Missouri are covered with this tree. The houses in the villages are generally built of this wood, which is also used for their enclosures. The cotton wood (so called from a down which it casts off in the spring, with which the air is filled like fleeces of snow) does not appear to have attracted as much attention as it deserves. It is invariably found on the river bottoms of the Mississippi, and Missouri, and after the willow, is the first tree which springs up on alluvion soils. The more ancient islands of the rivers west of the Mississippi, as well as on that river, are covered with this tree; it adds much to the beauty of the scenery, from its lofty and uniform appearance, and the deep green of its foliage contrasted with the light color of the river. The growth of this tree is extremely rapid; it shoots up in the course of a few years, into a noble column, several feet in diameter, and forty or fifty in height, before it becomes lost in branches. It permits no part lately gained from the river to remain long without timber; and will afford wood to the settlers of adjacent prairie, which could not otherwise be settled, as it answers extremely well for rails and fuel. The peccanne,* is found on the low grounds, where it grows to most perfection; it is a large tree resembling somewhat the hickory, but has a more delicate leaf, its branches are more numerous and spreading, and it is in every respect a more beautiful tree. There were formerly beautiful groves of it in the American bottom, (Illinois) but they have been nearly destroyed in order to procure the nuts. The sugar tree *(acer saccharinus)* is found in the present limits of the settlements, but not far to the west, or to the

ture, is truly surprising; kind and bounteous nature, seems to have furnished vines suited to every climate and soil; so that no part of the human race should be denied this general blessing.

* It is one of the principal ornamental trees of the plantations on the lower parts of the Mississippi,

south.   The cypress, magnolia, ever green oak, and a number
of other trees, common in the state of Louisiana, have been amply described by Barton and Michaud.

A nongst the wild fruits of Louisiana, the plum has been
celebrated. They are in great abundance.* Several species deserve to be transplanted to our gardens ; the yellow plum is delicious. Mulberries are very abundant, both on the Mississippi,
and a considerable distance up the Missouri. The woods and
prairies are every where overrun with strawberry vines ; the
fruit is excellent. *Le Haut Missouri*, (the upper Missouri, the
name given it by the French traders) surpasses the other parts
of the territory, in the variety of wild fruits ; plums, cherries,
currants and a great variety of berries.

Of flowers, and herbaceous plants, peculiar to this country, †
there exist a great variety, but want of botanical skill, and the
plan assumed for these cursory views, prevent me from entering
into detail. White clover, grows wild in many parts of the country. In the upper Missouri, the plains are filled with hyssop ;
near the mountains there is a plant resembling flax.‡ Hunters

* Note by *Mr. Bradbury*. Amongst the species of plums in Louisiana, and particularly at some distance up the Missouri, there is none
more interesting than the prairie plum, *(prunus chickasa)* which literally covers tracts of ground, of many acres in extent, and produces
fruit so abundantly, as to bend down to the earth with its weight.

† The natural consequence of the difference of habit, arising from
the prairies, and flint knobs, which of course give birth to distinct tribes
in the vegetable kingdom ; many of which, could not exist in the um-
brageous woods of the eastern states. *Bradbury*.

‡ From the description of this plant, it seems probable, that it is a
new species of *linum ;* and although perennial, differs from *linum perenne*.
The number of plants, made use of by the aborigines, for medical
purposes, is much greater than might be supposed, by those unacquainted with the skill, in the healing art, of these untaught children of nature. But not having, as yet, had an opportunity of examining the contents of their *medicine bags*, I am not prepared to give a scientific account, nor of the plant with which they produce the beautiful dye, in
their ornaments ; it is, however, a golium, and I think a new species.
                                                            Bradbury.
[This was written before Mr. Bradbury ascended the Missouri.]

tell of some curious plants on the Arkansas, amongst which are the common sun-flower, the bean, and the simblin, which grow there in their natural state. There is no reason to think this improbable, for these plants are known to be indigenous.

MINERALS.

If we denominate parts of the United States, by their predominating characters, and qualities; this territory may be called the country of minerals.

A small quantity of gold, is said to have been found on the St. Francis, by an inhabitant of St. Genevieve; it is probable, that some of the precious metals may be found, and it is certain that nearly all the useful ones exist in great abundance. A story is related of a wonderful mass of *platina*, on the Black river; this is not sufficiently attested, to merit much attention.*— It is the prevailing opinion, that there is silver, and numerous stories are related respecting it. A hundred places, where there is said to be silver ore, are indicated from the information of Indians and hunters; on the Missouri, Arkansas, and on the waters of White river. Geographers have for a long time, agreed in placing a gold mine on the Arkansas; and, considering the precision with which it is marked on the map, it is surprising to me that some of our enterprising Americans do not avail themselves of it. Many accounts have been given of silver mines on the Red river, above the Cado nation. Du Pratz as-

---

* The story is related by Indians; it has been supposed to be *platina*, from their description, but it is most likely some other metal, as platina is only found in very small pieces. The weight of the mass, being disproportioned to its size, causes a curious deception to the Indians, who, in consequence, call it a moncton or spirit. A story similar to this, was told me by an Arikara chief, of a mass which he has frequently seen in a prairie near the Black mountains. Another mass has actually been brought down Red river, by some hunters; it is probably native iron.

This wealth in precious metals, is certainly flattering; but the experience of Spain affords a salutary lesson, that a people may possess it in the greatest abundance and be poor in every thing else. The celebrated Adam Smith, proves that it is labor and industry alone that give a nation real wealth. We should be richer in mines of iron or lead, than in those of gold and silver.

serts positively, that silver ore was brought from thence in his time.

When we view, the space between the Rocky mountains, the Cordilleras, (which pervade New Mexico) and the rivers, Missouri and Mississippi, a conjecture may be formed not alto· gether unworthy of attention. Silver mines, it is well known, have been discovered north of the Cordilleras, and between them, according to the information of lieut. (now col.) Pike, they are actually wrought by the Spaniards. From the resemblance, in the character and appearance of this country, to that which lies between the Cordilleras and the Missouri, besides the connection of the different ridges, it seems probable that the same minerals are common to both, the southern and northern side of those mountains; or at least disappear gradually towards the north and and north-east. The volcanic tract, perhaps, is the tract of precious minerals. This conjecture, however, is liable to objections, and is therefore submitted with diffidence.

With more certainty I will venture to mark the situation and extent of the mineral tracts, or at least so much of them, as traverse the territory. Nearest to the Mississippi, and beginning S. on the St. Francis and White river, with its main course and diverging dependencies, perhaps two hundred miles in width, and six hundred in length, is the tract of lead mineral; perhaps the most extensive body of any mineral, known in the world. On all the great rivers which traverse this tract, the ore shews itself, in their channels, in a variety of places; as also in ravines where the soil has been carried off. This is the case, on the Maramek, the Gasconade, the Osage, on the Mine river of the Missouri, on the Missouri itself, on la riviere des Moines, and at length on the Mississippi, below the Ouisconsing. At this place it crosses the river, and is seen, though in small quantities, in places round the Michigan. There is very little doubt but that all this extent abounds in lead ore, and may afford thousands of the richest mines.

The led mines, at present wrought and productive,* are those between the St. Francis, and the Maramek: extending over a

* The mines known by the name of Dubuques mines, thought to be equal to any in Louisiana, are not at present wrought. They are situated west side the Mississippi, 60 miles below prairie du Chien.

tract of about sixty miles in length, and twenty in breadth : and those at the Ouisconsing, on the Mississippi, above the prairie du Chien. I reserve the description of the first for a separate number. The mines of the prairie du Chien, are still in the hands of the Sacs and Foxes, and wrought by themselves exclusively ; but in a very imperfect manner. Last year (1811) they made about five hundred thousand weight, which they disposed of to traders. By some, these mines have been considered the richest yet opened. The Indians are badly provided with tools for mining ; a common hoe is almost the only instrument which they use. They merely scratch away the soil a few feet, and the ore may be said without exaggeration, to be raised, in the manner of stones in a quarry. The mode of smelting is equally rude. The ore is thrown on piles of wood, and the lead is afterwards gathered up in cakes, in the shapes and forms, assumed by melted lead, when carelessly thrown out on a hearth. It is afterwards melted by the traders, and made into pigs by the use of moulds.

West of the tract of lead mineral, is that of the salines : It runs parallel with the other, but goes further south, and not so far north. The extent is not well known. This tract affords the most numerous and best salines, of any part of North America. The number, on the Arkansas and on the Osage is surprisingly great. At the salines on the last river, there is a greater number of the enormous bones of the mammoth, and of other animals, now extinct, than at the Big Bone Lick, or in any other part of America.* I have already touched upon the extraordina-

---

* I am informed about two hundred miles west of St. Louis. No collection has yet been made from this place. The bones are found in some places on the surface of the earth, and generally a few feet under ground

A prevailing notion, the origin of which is attributed to the celebrated anatomist, Cuvier, is, that these bones belong to a creation different from the present. They are found in all parts of the world, and of a great variety of species, some even resembling those of the present creation, but of much greater magnitude. In South America, near Buenos Ayres, the skeleton of a *sloth* is said to have been dug up, nearly as large as that of an elephant. Cuvier discovered in the vicinity of Paris, bones which appertained to a race of animals now extinct. Four

I

ry body of salt, near the Arkansas. This appears to be the principal seat of the salines. The water of the Arkansas, itself, is brackish, and persons ascending, are obliged to provide themselves, from such streams and springs of fresh water, as put into it. Near the place, where this tract crosses the Arkansas, several streams enter it, which are strongly impregnated with salt; among others, the Big Saline, and the Strong Saline, both nearly one hundred yards in width. It is here that the salt rock is said to be found, and that salt prairies are known to exist. The salt rock (if there be such a thing) has not been descried by any person, who has examined it. The notion of its existence was probably suggested by the solid masses of salt, found in low places, which have formed drains, or reservoirs for the higher surrounding ground; after the evaporation of the water, a crust of good salt is left in the bottom, congealed like ice. And of this, there appear to be accumulations. The color is of the purest white; there is usually a mixture of gypsum, and I have seen some pieces penetrated with sparry matter. Considerable quantities are also scattered over the prairies, in a pulverised state, resembling sand; the Indians gather it with the wing of a turkey

I do not mean by marking off these tracts, to convey the idea, that it is only in such parts, that certain minerals exist, but merely as the predominating character, and where these minerals most abound Throughout every part of the territory, there are salines, but far below the great scale of those, in the tract which crosses the Arkansas and Osage rivers.

The volcanic tract, may be placed west of the last, in the slope, and spurs of the Rocky Ridge. It was formerly conjectured from the pumice found floating on the Missouri, that some

or five distinct species of the mammoth are perceived; the bones found at the Big Bone Lick prove the existence of a variety of animals, no longer on the earth, or not supposed to have existed in these climates.

The traditions said to prevail amongst the Indians on this subject, are easily accounted for by those, who are acquainted with the custom amongst those people of inventing and relating amusing tales, like the Arabs. The big bones would naturally furnish a hint. I have heard several on this very subject more curious than those, which have been recited, as affording evidence of the existence of the animal.

part of the country, traversed by this river, or its waters, was volcanic; this still remains uncertain.* There is no doubt but that
many of these appearances arise from the burning of coal banks.
Near the Mandans, there are places in which smoke is emitted
from the high banks of the river, and putting down a stick into
the fissure, fire is instantly communicated. I think it probable,
that a close examination of the country, will discover traces of
extinguished volcanoes. Mr. Lisa, informed me, that he had
been told by Indians, and some of his hunters, that about sixty
miles from his fort, on the Roche Jaune, at the entrance of a river, there is a mountain which emits flames. This is about two
hundred miles from the mouth of the Roche Jaune. In this
part of the country, I am well informed that great quantities of
sulphur can be procured ; it is found not only in caves, but can
be scraped off the prairies in the manner of the salt.

I have spoken of the minerals which are found in the greatest quantities, I shall now mention such, as are more thinly dispersed through the territory.

Copper, is certainly found on the Mississippi, between la
riviere des Moines and the Ouisconsing ; and several other places
in the territory are mentioned. There is iron ore on the St.
Francis, on the Maramek, on the Osage, and in great quantities
throughout the White river country. On the St. Francis there
are said to be huge masses like rocks. Several gentlemen who
have examined specimens from these different places, do not
think favorably of the ore, but I believe no proper trial of it, has
yet been made.

There doubtless exists a variety of minerals, which a better
acquaintance with the country will discover: it has not been at-
tentively examined by any skilful mineralogist. Mr. Bradbury,
on a visit to the mine à Burton, informed me that he found those
working at the mines, throwing away as useless, the *blende* ore
of Zinc. The late Dr. Elliot of St. Genevieve,† informed me

---

* A thorough examination of the causes of the late earthquake
might perhaps throw light on this subject. The seat of this convulsion
may be far to the west.

† Formerly of Connecticut. I cannot refrain from seizing this opportunity of paying a tribute to the memory of that excellent man. Possess-

that an Indian had once brought him a specimen of antimony, but that he could not be prevailed upon by any offers to shew the place where it was procured : believing, probably, from the reward offered him, that it must be something of great value.

Coal, seems to be a fossil common to every part of the valley of the Mississippi, the space between the range of mountains towards the Atlantic, and that towards the Pacific. It is found in every part of this territory. On the east side of the Mississippi, in the bluffs of the American Bottom, a tree taking fire some years ago, communicated it by one of its roots to the coal, which continued to burn, until the fire was at length smothered by the falling in of a large mass of the incumbent earth. The appearance of fire, is still visible for several rods around. About two miles further up the bluffs, a fine coal bank has been opened ; the vein as thick as any of those near Pittsburgh.

Salt-petre has been made on the Gasconade, and there is no doubt, but that great abundance may be had throughout this country, which reposes on limestone, and is consequently cavernous. In caves, from the Missouri to the St. Francis, there are immense quantities of a pure silex, adhering like solid rock ; it is as white as refined sugar, and so much like it, that the difference is not discernible to the eye. I have seen a deception practised on a stranger, by giving him a lump and passing it for sugar. It crumbles with the pressure of the fingers : in the manufacture of glass, it may undoubtedly be of use. A beautiful *serpentine** of a red color, is found about three hundred miles west of the Mississippi, near the heads of la riviere des Moines and the St. Peters, and of which the Indians make their pipes. It is soft and easily cut, into any shape in the first instance, but soon assumes the hardness of stone. A curious circumstance is connected with this and noticed by several writers. The Indians of different tribes, no matter how inveterate or fierce their animosities, meet here, always in peace. In this sa-

ed of an enlightened and philosophic mind, and the most amiable disposition ever gifted to a mortal. He was formed to instruct and to be beloved.

* So called by Pinkerton, Carver, &c.

cred spot of general rendezvous, that most ungovernable of sav-age propensities, revenge, is completely subdued.

There is marble in the territory in various places; it resem-bles that which is commonly found in Kentucky: but none of a superior quality has yet been discovered On Bon Homme creek, about fifteen miles from St. Louis, a quarry of stone was opened some time ago, said to equal the French burr. The mill stones procured here are thought by good judges to be of a su-perior quality, and it only remains for experience to decide.

Earths and clays of a rare and useful kind, have been found in different parts of the territory. Gypsum, may be had in any quantities, on the Maramek, Osage, Missouri, &c. ; on the Kan-sas, I have been informed by hunters there are whole bluffs com-posed of it. In the district of Cape Girardeau, there is a kind of clay, which in painting, answers the purpose of Ochre.

I shall here notice a phenomenon frequently observed; but without attempting a solution, which is left to the scientific. On the St. Francis and in the White river country, subterraneous explosions, have been heard, and their effects discerned. The sound is like that of cannon or distant thunder; and the earth and rocks appear to have been convulsed as though by the force of gun powder. The rocks blown up, are glazed with a shining matter, of metallic appearance.*

CHAPTER VI.

A VIEW OF THE INDIAN NATIONS OF LOUISIANA—OF THE INDIAN TRADE FOR FURS, &C. OF THE MISSOURI AND MIS-SISSIPPI.

From the fatal ravages of the small pox, the present Indian nations of Louisiana, particularly on the Missouri, have not the tenth of the numbers which they had near thirty years ago.

* I have since learned that the same phenomenon has been known on the Washita, and on the Sabine.

Within a few years past, however, they have been rapidly increasing. Notwithstanding the formidable list here presented, these people are scattered over so wide a country as scarcely to be noticed in it. One may travel for days without meeting a living soul; I descended the Missouri *one thousand miles*
without once seeing a human being that was not of our party.

The only *fixed* or agricultural villages on the Missouri, are
those of the Osage, Maha's, Poncas, Pani's, Arikara's, and Mandan's; and all on the S. W. side of the river. On the Blue earth
river, and in the forks of the Kansas, there are several villages
of the nation of that name, the Pani villages below the mouth of
Wolf river, and a village of Ollo's and Missouri's. Yet even
some of these, are abandoned for a great part of the summer season, and their inhabitants wander through the plains; generally
en masse, and carrying with them all their property, excepting
their corn, and a few bulky articles which they deposit in hiding
places. Their baggage is more cumbrous, than would be imagined, and employs a great number of dogs and horses in transporting it from place to place.

All the other nations lead a life similar to that of the shep-
herds of Asia; it is true they do not drive domestic herds to
places where the best pasturage may be found, but what
amounts nearly to the same thing, they follow the instinctive migrations of the Buffaloe, feed upon his flesh and kindle their fires
with his ordure. The great object of serious employment in
these nations, the ruling passion, is a thirst for mutual destruction. The great distance to which their war parties wander in
pursuit of this darling gratification is indeed surprising; eight
hundred or a thousand miles is not an unusual journey. It is
only, however, on women and children, and on parties taken by
surprise that their attacks prove really bloody and destructive.
In their more regular engagements, or battles, where there is
something like equality in the adverse parties, they engage, generally on horseback, in a manœuvering fight, in which they
display wonderful activity and skill on both sides so much so,
that they do each other very little harm. A battle between three
or four hundred men on each side, will continue a whole day,
and be at length terminated by the death of two or three and as

many wounded.   In this they bear a strong resemblance to the
Arabs; it is the result of the theatre of war on which they engage, the open plains, and not the want of courage.

Nearly all the nations of the N W. side, are descendants of
the Sioux, and at peace with each other, but with scarcely an exception, at war with those on the S. W. side. These nations have
considerable trade or traffic with each other.   The Sioux have
for this purpose regular fairs, or assemblages, at stated periods.
The same thing prevails with the nations on the S. W. side of
the Missouri.   Those towards the south, have generally vast
numbers of horses, mules, and asses, which they obtain in trade,
or war, from the Spaniards or nations immediately bordering on
New Mexico.   These animals are chiefly transferred to the nations N. E. of the river, by such of the southern tribes as happen to be on good terms with them, who obtain in exchange European articles, procured from the British traders.   Their stock of
horses requires to be constantly renewed by thefts or purchases:
from the severity of the climate and the little care taken of the
foals, the animal would otherwise be in danger of becoming extinct.   Their mode of trading with each other is perfectly primitive.   There is no bargaining or dispute about price;
a nation or tribe comes to a village, encamps near it, and after demonstrations on both sides of a thousand barbarous civilities, as
sincere as those which are the result of refinement, one of the
parties makes a general present of all such articles as it can con-
veniently spare: the other a short time after makes in return a
similar present, the fair is then concluded by a variety of games,
sports and dances.   They hold the mode of trading by the
whites, in great contempt; they say it displays a narrow and
contemptible soul to be weighing and counting every trifle; the
price is usually fixed by the chief and his council, and the nation as well as traders must submit.

Their arms consist principally of bows, spears, clubs, and
light fusees.   But the bow, particularly in hunting, is still the
principal weapon.   Like all savages they are superstitious.   It appeared to me that if they had any particular object of adoration
it was the buffaloe head.   They place it in every holy or sacred
spot of ground, and each lodge or tent, has one or two, to which

the whole family seem to pay the utmost reverence. I saw in the village of the Mandan chief, She-he-ke, in an open space before the temple or medicine lodge, an enclosure of about six feet square, in which were four on these heads on elevated mounds of earth.

I had not sufficient time to form any idea of their languages, but from what I was able to learn there are about six primitive ones: it is very probable that a more accurate scrutiny would discover of those, several common to other nations of the continent. It appeared to me that the Snake Indians, both in language and in appearance were different from any Indians I had e꜕ seen. In the sound of the language there is a good deal of resemblance to those of Africa which I have heard. I am informed that copious vocabularies have been made by Lewis and Clark, of nearly all the Indian languages of the Missouri. As their journal is expected shortly to appear, I shall not publish the collections made by me, which must necessarily be much inferior to theirs, they having had more time and much greater opportunities. A few primitive words of different nations will suffice in this view.

OSAGE.

They call themselves Wasashe, and are divided into three bands, 1. The Great Osage, 2. Little Osage, 3. The band of " Big Track," from a chief who left the nation some years ago and is now settled on the Arkansas Their language may be considered the primitive of several others, which are spoken by neighbouring nations, without any great difference; as the Arkansas, Kansas, and Mahas. Their trade is principally in deer skins, bear skins, beaver, otter, muskrat, and the Buffaloe.

These people have been noted for their uncommon stature; this is somewhat exaggerated, though they are undoubtedly above the ordinary size of men. The wandering or semi-wandering nations of Louisiana, may be characterised as exceeding in stature the whites. The Osages are reputed warlike, but this arises from their being at war with all their neighbours, and not from any uncommon degree of bravery. When compared with the Shawanese, and the nations east of the Mississippi, they might with more propriety be regarded as a treacherous and cowardly race.

A purchase was made a few years ago by governor Lewis, of the greater part of the country claimed by these people, reserving to them the privilege of hunting on it, until the extension of the settlements should render it inconvenient. The object of this was to fix a certain and determinate boundary for the exercise of the jurisdiction of the courts, and in order to do away all question or difficulty as to the title of the United States. But great dissatisfaction has been excited amongst them in consequence of the purchase, which they alledge not to have been fairly made. In fact, this is not a matter easily effected with strict correctness, and it is doubtful with me whether our extensive Indian purchases east of the Mississippi, were conducted in the fairest manner. A desire of doing something meritorious, may have induced some of our agents, to go rather too far in procuring the consent of the chiefs of the nation, and, perhaps of chiefs created for the express purpose. When this subject is considered, there may be more justice in the disaffection of the Indian nations than is generally supposed. The governments of the Indian nations are generally republican; the chiefs propose, and the people approve or disapprove; the proper solemnities are not so easily complied with; the consent of a few of the principal chiefs has generally been thought sufficient, but there are instances of those chiefs falling into disgrace in consequence of their unauthorised conduct. The Osage purchase was sanctioned by the government, but nothing was done in complying with the stipulations of the treaty on our part for nearly two years. Shortly before the arrival of governor Howard, the Osages were informed that the first payment of the annuity was soon to be made for their land. Thirty or forty chiefs came to St. Louis, soon after the arrival of the governor, and in council, remonstrated against the purchase, declaring it to have been unfair. The principal speaker, Le Sonneur, addressed him with great art, and some eloquence. He said, that " he was much surprised to hear of this purchase, which had been forgotten by his nation, and he supposed, had also been forgotten by his great father. The sale was made by those who had no authority; and his great father not having complied with his part of the bargain, by delaying two years the stipulated payment, and not performing the other parts

K

of the treaty, his nation ought not to be held to their part of it, even if fairly entered into. But, said he, the Osage nation has no right to sell its country, much less have a few chiefs, who have taken it on themselves to do so; our country belongs to our posterity as well as to ourselves; it is not absolutely ours, we receive it only for our lifetimes, and then to transmit it to our descendants. Our great father is good and just, will he permit his children to sell the bones of their fathers, to sell the inheritance of their children! No, my father, keep your goods, and let us keep our lands." This chief satisfied me of the talent for oratory amongst these rude men. He spoke for an hour, and as completely exhausted his subject as could have been done by the best speaker. His speech was evidently prepared with care for the occasion. Governor Howard replied to him with dignity and firmness, and informed him, that the treaty must be kept; that their great father did not compel Indians to sell their lands, but when they did sell, the bargain could not be broken; that circumstances had rendered it impossible to pay the annuities sooner, the treaty not having been approved by their great father for a considerable time. That the annuities for two years were ready for them, if they chose, they might accept, if not, it was of no consequence, the land would still be considered as purchased, and their obstinacy would have no other effect than that of displeasing their great father. Finding that opposition was useless, they finally promised to use their influence to induce their nation to accept. These purchases have a good appearance, but I question whether they are in reality more just than the French and Spanish mode of encroaching on their lands, and insinuating themselves into their country imperceptibly; taking a piece of land as they might happen to want it, without saying any thing about Indian title, and keeping those people quiet by presents, more pleasing to them than if given as the payment of a debt, for which an equivalent had been received. I fear it is not with respect to Indian purchases, that we have manifested a conduct more generous and noble than our predecessors; we must look for this in the pains and expense which we have been at, in civilizing and instructing these people, together with the uniform practice of advising them to neutrality in our wars with white nations;

and to peace amongst themselves. The establishment of trading houses and factories, though originating from the best intentions, is not in reality so praise-worthy as might appear from the first glance, otherwise than it affords protection to traders, and keeps the Indians in awe.

KANSAS,

A few years ago they were the greatest scoundrels of the Missouri, robbing traders, and ill-treating the whites, but since about two years, in consequence of a severe defeat from the Panis, in which their greatest warriors fell, they have been humbled. They are brave, and are esteemed great warriors. They have their villages on the Kansas river. The country which they inhabit abounds with beaver, but they do not hunt much. They speak the Osage language with some difference of dialect.

OTTOES (Wa-dook-to-da.)

They are the descendants of the ancient Missouris, and speak their language, which is remarkably lofty and sonorous.—They are not numerous, but esteemed brave and warlike. They reside fifteen leagues up the river Platte, and live in community and friendship with the Panis.

MISSOURIS,

The remnant of one of the most numerous nations of the Missouri, and who have given their name to the river. They were reduced to about eighty warriors. They reside with the Ottoes. Their village was formerly at the mouth of the Grand river.

PANI PROPER,

A much more friendly and civilized people than those just described, they treat their traders and the whites generally with remarkable hospitality, have frequent intercourse with the Spaniards, and live about thirty leagues from the mouth of the river Platte, and in two villages. The Council Bluffs on the Missouri would be a good place for a trading establishment for these people. They have but faint ideas of the exclusive right of soil, and have no fixed boundary; in which, they resemble the greater part of these nations. They hunt on the rivers Platte and Kansas; their country very little wooded, but of a beautiful surface, consisting of open plains.

The Pani Loups, reside on the Wolf river, thirty six leagues from its mouth. There is said to be a good deal of timbered land between this river and the Corne-de-Cerf, or Elk horn, principally pine and shrubby oak. The two rivers just mentioned, afford excellent navigation; the Wolf river rises in a lake, or rather a large fountain.

The Pani, Republican, a small band which seceded from the nation a few years ago, reside on the Republican fork of the Kansas river.

MAHAS, *(or Oo-ma-ha)*

Reside on the Maha creek, about eighty leagues above the Platte, in their village, and raise corn. A friendly and industrious people, and have a considerable trade. Their language originally Osage. All the Sioux bands, except the Yanktons, make war upon them. Their numbers have been much reduced within the last ten years.

PONCAS,

Originally Maha; village a short distance below the Qui-Courre. They were almost destroyed by the Sioux, their village broken up, and they were compelled to be altogether wandering; but within a few years, they have re-established their village, and are increasing rapidly.

ARIKARA

Live 1440 miles up the Missouri, in two villages, an industrious people, but from the attacks of their neighbours, are unable to hunt any other but the buffaloe, though their country abounds in game. They are at present on very friendly terms with the whites, though guilty a few years ago of an outrage on a party commanded by lieut. Prior. In my Journal I have dwelt a good deal on the customs and character of these people, which in many respects are peculiar and highly interesting. They were originally Pani.

MANDANS, OR GROS VENTRES,

The remnants of a number of villages, according to their account, seventeen. They claim only the small portion of country which they actually occupy; in this, resembling the Arikaras. They still consist of seven villages, five of Gros Ventres, and two of Mandans, in the distance of about fifteen miles. They are generally on good terms with each other, but at present there exists considerable dissentions, and even open rupture. There is not the least affinity in their languages, but the Gros Ventre is spoken by all the Mandans. According to the tradition of these last, who were originally of the Crow nation, owing to a quarrel between two chiefs, over the carcase of a buffaloe which they had slain, a separation took place of the followers of each.

CHIENNES

Are a wandering nation, on the heads of the Chienne river. Trade with the Arikaras—speak a different language from any nation I know. Their complexion very fair. They trade also with the Spaniards, and have a great number of horses, &c.

SIOUX TRIBES.

On an ancient map I have seen them named Naddouwessi-oux; the Noddouwessces of Carver, are probably a band of Si-oux—Are nearly all wandering tribes, and may be considered as divided into four nations, the Sioux, Teton, Assineboin and Black-feet.

YANKTONS,

Wander in an agreeable country, a considerable portion of which is woodland—trade on the St. Peters, and on the Missouri at the riviere à Jaque. Their trade is not valuable, chiefly buffaloe robes and deer skins: they are the most friendly and peaceable of the Sioux bands.

YANK-TONS OF THE NORTH.

On Red river of lake Winipec, and trade with the British establishments.

WAH-PA-TONE.

On the N. W. side of the river St. Peters, to the mouth of the Chippoway river.

MINDA-WAR-CARTON,

The only Sioux band which attends to the cultivation of the earth ; but this not to any great extent. They live on the Mississippi above the river St. Peters. Their country is represented as tolerably fertile, and well watered.

WAH-PA-COO-LA,

On the S. W. side of the river St. Peters, from a place called Hardwood, to the Yellow Medicine river, some traffic with the Yanktons and Tetons west of them

SESSATONE,

On the upper part of Red river and the St. Peters. This country abounds with small lakes, and is valuable for animals, beaver, otter, muskrat, martin, &c. They meet the Tetons, &c. on the riviere à Jaque, about the months of May and June to trade. They supply the Yanktons with articles of European manufacture, and receive in return, horses, &c.

TETONS, BOIS BRULE, ARKANDADA, MINI-KINIAD-ZA, SA-HONE.

These are the pirates or marauders of the Missouri, their country without timber, and not good for hunting, except as to the buffaloe, they have therefore hardly any thing but buffaloe robes to trade.

The Sioux bands claim as follows; " beginning at the confluence of the riviere des Moines and the Mississippi, thence to the river St. Peters, thence on both sides of the Mississippi to Crow Wing river, and upwards with that stream, including the waters of the upper part of Red river of lake Winipec, and down to the Pemberton river ; thence a S W. course to intersect the Missouri, at or near the Mandans, and with that stream, down to the Warricon river, thence, crossing the Missouri, it goes to include the lower part of the Chienne river, all the waters of White river, and Teton river, including the lower portion of the Qui Courre, and returns with that stream downward to the Missouri, thence eastward to the beginning."

ASSINEBOIN,

Divided into the following bands—

Manelopec, (gens de Canot,) wander on the Mouse river, between the Assineboin and the Missouri. *Osee-gah,* about the mouth of the little Missouri, to the Assineboin river.

Mah-to pa-na-to, on the Missouri, about the mouth of the White earth river, and on the head of the Assineboin and Copelle rivers.

These bands trade with the Hudson's Bay Company, who have establishments on the Assineboin and Copelle rivers; occasionally also on the Saskashawin. Their country has little or no timber.

BLACKFEET.

They wander on the heads of the Missouri, Maria river, and along the Rocky mountains, they are also Sioux. They trade at the same establishments with the Assineboin, and are at war with the Crow nation. They have been very troublesome to our traders, to whom they have conceived a deadly hatred. Their country the most abundant in beaver and other furs.

GROS VENTRES OF THE PRAIRIE,

Speak the Crow language, and wander on the south fork of the Saskashawin.

Nations on the Lakes, and upper part of the Mississippi.

CHIPPOWAYS,

Are divided into three bands, one in a village on an island in Leech lake; another about the head of the Mississippi, and around Red lake, and the third on Red river, of lake Winipec, and about the mouth of Pemberton river. They wander along the lakes, however, to a grea distance. They are the inveterate enemies of the Sioux; with whom they have been at war time immemorial. Their country is tolerably well covered with wood, but abounds with morasses and lakes.

ALGONQUINS

Speak the same language with the Chippoways, and live in two bands, one on the south side of Rainy lake, Rainy Lake river, and the Lake of the Woods; the other about the mouths of the Assineboin and Red rivers.

KNISTENAUS,

Descendants of the Chippoways—on the head of the Assinc boin, thence towards the Saskashawin. They might be induced to trade at an establishment on the Missouri, at the mouth of the Yellow Stone river.

Indians south of the Missouri and Arkansas.

AYUTAN BANDS, OR SNAKE INDIANS,

A very numerous race, who have as yet but little intercourse with the whites. They are badly armed, and much at the mercy of the other Indians, by whom they are made slaves when taken prisoners. They are also called Camanches. They wander about the heads of the Platte, and in the vast plains bordering on New Mexico and New Spain, south of the Arkansas; and are divided into many bands. They possess an immense number of horses, asses, and mules.

CROW INDIANS,

On the Yellow Stone, and heads of the Missouri; they are divided into a number of small bands.

PAUNCH INDIANS

Wander along the Rocky mountains, and sometimes venture across. Probably a band of the Snake Indians. The *Padoncas*, *Kioways*, &c. are probably bands of nations already enumerated; inhabit an arid, unproductive country.

CADDOQUIS.

Thirty-five miles west of the main branch of Red river, 120 miles by land above Natchitoches, formerly lived 375 miles higher up, at a beautiful prairie, which has a lake of clear water. The nation is small, but the warriors greatly celebrated for their courage, and as much respected by their neighbours, as the Knights of Malta were in Europe.

YATTASCES.

Fifty miles above Natchitoches on Bayou Pierre, there is a small French settlement. They are but a remnant, but live in a fixed village.

NAU-DO-QUES,

On the Sabine, sixty or seventy miles from the Yattasces. The French had formerly a factory here—language Caddó.

ADDAIZE,

Forty miles from Natchitoches—below the Yattasces; language peculiar—extremely difficult to speak.

EYISH,

Near Nacogdoches—nearly exterminated a few years ago by the small-pox—language peculiar, but speak Caddó.

KYIS,

On the Trinity river, near where the road to St. Antonio crosses it.   Language peculiar.

TACHEES,

On a branch of the Sabine—language Caddó—gave their name to the province of Texas—*Nabadaches*, in the same neighbourhood.

BEDDIES,

On the Trinity, about sixty miles S. of the Nacogdoches, speak Caddó, but have a peculiar language.

ACCOKESAUS,

Two hundred miles S. W. of Nacogdoches, on the W. side of the Colerado—speak a peculiar language—wander about the bay of St. Bernard.

MAYES,

On the bay of St. Bernard, near the Guadaloupe—hate the Spaniards, and are attached to the French—have a tradition of the landing of La Salle in this neighbourhood—speak Attakapas.

CARANKOUAS,

On an island or Peninsula in the bay of St. Bernard, 10 miles long and 5 broad—at war with the Spaniards—a peculiar language.

CANCES,

A very numerous nation; consisting of a number of tribes, who occupy the country from the bay of St. Bernard, across Grand river, towards la Vera Cruz.—On bad terms with the Spaniards—speak a peculiar language.

TANKAWAYS,

A wandering people, near the Rio Grande.

TAWAKENOES,

On the Brassos de Dios—for some months at the prairie of the Tortuga—usual residence 200 miles west of Nacogdoches, towards Sta. Fee—speak Pani, or *Towiache.*

PANI, OR TOWIACHE,

Eight hundred miles above Natchitoches, 340 by land. Much diminished six or eight years ago by the small-pox.

NATCHITOCHES,

Formerly resided where the town of Natchitoches is now sit-uated— Have always been friendly to the whites. They have dwindled away to a few warriors.

BOLUXAS,

Emigrants from Pensacola—they came with a few French families—are not more than thirty in number. There are, be-sides several small bands or parties, originally from Florida, the *Appalaches*, on Bayou Rapide—*Alibamas*, in Oppelousas—*Conchatas*, of the same nation with the *Alibamas*, emigrated to the Sabine about fifteen years ago—*Pacanas*, a small tribe who live on the Qulequeshoe river, which heads S. W. of Natchitoches. *Pascagolas*, live in a small village 60 miles above Natchitoches. *Tunicas*, at Avoyall, emigrants from Bayou Tunica. All these nations speak the Mobilian, which was formerly the court lan-guage amongst the Indian nations of Lower Louisiana. There are besides, a number of small bands of *Chactas*, on Bayou Boeuf, on the Teche, and on the Sabine.

OPPELOUSAS,

In the Indian language means black head, or black scull.—
They are aborigines of this district.

ATTAKAPAS,

Signifies man-eater. They at present reside with the Caran-
kouas on an island in the bay of St. Bernard. They have the
reputation of being to this day anthropophagi. A French writer,
who published a book on Louisiana in 1713, of the name of Dumont, relates a fact of two white men who fell into their hands,
one of whom was killed and eaten, the other made his escape.

TENSAS,

Emigrants from the Tensa, and Bayou Boeuf.—*Washas*, formerly a considerable nation, now extinct, lived near New Orleans, and were the first with whom the French became acquainted.

ARKANSAS,

South of the Arkansas village, descended from the Osage.
—The Houmas and Avoyall extinct.

*Indians on the Mississippi, between the Missouri and the Falls
of St. Anthony.*

AYUWAS,

Descended from the Missouris, and claim the country west
of them. Have a village on the riviere des Moines, S. E. side,
but are generally wandering.

SAUKEES,

One hundred and forty leagues above St. Louis. Trade with
the merchants from Michilimackinac, and St. Louis. Live with
the Foxes, and may be considered as identified with those people. The country which they claim lies principally on the east
side of the Mississippi. On the west side, they claim the country of the ancient Missouris by right of conquest, without de-
fining any portion to the Ayuwas. To them may be ascribed the
destruction of the Piorias, Kaskaskias, Cahokias, Missouris,
and Illinois.

Lower Louisiana, when first discovered, was inhabited by very numerous nations; the accounts given by early writers are almost incredible. Charlevoix states that about the year 1560, there were many powerful nations in what was then called Florida. Outina. Timogoa, and Saturiora, the neighbours of Mons. Ribaut, could each command eight hundred or a thousand warriors. Onothaca, and Calos, one on the eastern, the other on the western side of the Peninsula, were still more powerful. In 1565, M. Laudamère sent thirty men to assist Outina, against another chief, named Patanow, whom they encountered and defeated, his force consisting of two thousand men. The *Baya goulas* who were situated near the mouth of the Mississippi, when visited by M. D'Iberville, are described as having seven hundred families in their principal town. Charlevoix gives a curious description of their temple.

In Upper Louisiana (Ter. Missouri) there are several small bands scattered through the settlements, and in the White river country. Near Apple creek there are two villages of Shawanese, a sober orderly people, and another of the same on the Maramek. In the White river country, there have been of late considerable emigrations of Cherokees, who are said to claim it.— Straggling families may be seen at all seasons of the year, encamped near the villages, and on the banks of the Mississippi, who subsist by vending the produce of their hunting to the whites. These stragglers are usually a miserable and degraded race, lazy, and filthy in the extreme.

A TABLE OF THE INDIAN NATIONS OF LOUISIANA...THEIR TRADE, &c.

NOTE.—The 1st column contains the names of the different nations---2nd, the number of warriors---3d, the number of souls---4th, the country which they occupy---5th, estimate of the value in dollars of the merchandise required for their trade---6th, value of returns---7th, remarks.

1	2	3	4	5	6	7
1 Big Osage 2 Little Osage 3 band of Big Tracks	1,500	5,500	on the Osage, Missouri & Arkan.	20000	30,000	...trade at the Factory at Fort O-
Kansas	300	1,500	on the Kansas river	3,000	5,000	sage, and on the Osage river.
1 Panis Loup	400	2,000	hunt on the Platte and Kansas	6,000	10,000	...Council Bluffs would be a pro-
2 Panis Republican	35.	1,600	on the Kansas			per place for a trading establish-
3 Panis Loup	30.	1,500	on Wolf river, of the Platte	2,400	3,500	ment.
Mahas	250	800	eighty leagues above the Platte	4,000	7,000	
Poncas	80	450	on the Missouri at the Qui Courre	500	1,000	
Ottos and Missouris	80	450	on the Platte near the Elk horn			
Chiennes	500	1,600	a wandering tribe on the heads of the Chienne river			...trade at the Arikara village.
Arikaras	800	3,000	1,400 miles up the Missouri	500	1,000	
Mandans	350	2,000	,600 miles up the Missouri	1,500	3,000	
A-wa-ha-ways	50	300	3 miles above the Mandans			
Minetares	600	2,500	on Knife R. 6 mi. from Mandans			...the value of their trade very inconsiderable.
Wate-pana-toes and Ryuwas	200	900	on the Padoncas fork			...these nations have little in-
Padoncas	300	1,000	on the Padoncas			tercourse with the whites; but
Kan-ne-na-wish	1,500	5,000	a wandering people, on the heads of Yellow Stone river			inhabit a country abounding in game.

TABLE OF THE INDIAN NATIONS OF LOUISIANA....THEIR TRADE, &c.

1	2	3	4	5	6	7
Pasta-now-nas	400	1,500	between the Padoncas fork and the Platte			
Crow Indians	2,000	7,000	divided into numerous tribes and scattered over the country on the heads of the Missouri and Yellow Stone	1,000	3,000	....a trading establishment at the 3 forks of the Missouri would suit these people provided peace could be made with the Black feet Indi. ..trade with the British establishm.
Paunch Indians	800	2,500	N. E. of the Missouri near the head			
Assineboin	900	3,500	3 tribes living near the Missouri			..trade with British—inimical to Americans—their trade might be rendered valuable in case of peace
Black-foot Indians	2,500	5,500	in different tribes, near the heads of the Missouri			
Gros Ventres of the Prairie	500	2,000	N. E. side of the Missouri			...have some trade with New Mexico.
Ayutans, or Camanches	2,000	8,000	s. w. of the Missouri			
Snake Indians	900	5,500	near the heads of the Arkansas, Platte and Yellow Stone			...trade with New Mexico.
Blue mud, and Long hair'd Indians			numbers unknown, supposed to reside somewhere on the heads of the Columbia			
Flat heads			chiefly on the west side of the Rocky mountains			...Lewis & Clark, first whitemen who passed thro' their country.
Knistenoos	300	1,000	on Assineboin, & along the lakes		15,000	..trade with the British establishments—might be induced to come on the Missouri.
Algonquins	1,000	5,000				
Chippoways	900	4,000	on the Red river of Winipec, and on the heads of the Mississippi		30,000	
Saukees	500	2,500	on the Mississippi, below the falls of St. Anthony	2,000	3,000	

TABLE OF THE INDIAN NATIONS OF LOUISIANA....THEIR TRADE, &c.

	1	2	3	4	5	6	7
Foxes				with the Saukees . . .	1500	2500	...trade at Prairie du Chien; principally in lead.
Shawanese . .		36.	800	on the Mississippi & St. Francis	1000	3000	...trade in their villages, or come to the settlements for the purpose.
Ayuwas . . .		20.	600	on the riviere des Moines.	500	1000	
Sioux bands .				on the N. E. side of the Missouri and on the Mississippi .	5000	20000	...these bands occupy a very extensive country, but which does not abound in valuable furs.
Chickashs&Cherokees		500	2000	on White river . . .	4000	10000	...trade chiefly at the Arkansas post, or with people descending the Mississippi
Arkansas . . .		200		on the Aarkansas river . .	1000	2000	...at the Arkansas post.
Coddoques . .		10.	50	on a branch of Red river .			
Nanda-koes .		40	180	on the Sabine . .			
Addaize . .		20	100	40 miles from Natchitoches .			
Alishes . .			25	live near Natchitoches . .			
Keyeshees .		60	200	east branch of the Trinity river			
Tachees . .		80	250	on a branch of the Sabine .			....these nations trade principally with the public factory at Natchitoches, in the frontier villages; and those tribes beyond the Sabine, chiefly with the people of Mexico.
Nabedoches .		80	250	s. w. of the Sabine . .			
Bedees . .		100	320	on the Trinity . .			
Aco-ke-sas .		80	240	west of Colorado of St. Bernard			
Mayees . .		200		near the mouth of Guadaloupe			
Karan-koo-as		500	1800	on a peninsula in the bay of St. Bernard . . .			
Cances . . .		2000	5500	inhabit the country from the bay of St. Bernard, to Vera Cruz			

TABLE OF THE INDIAN NATIONS OF LOUISIANA....THEIR TRADE, &c.

1	2	3	4	5	6	7
Tanks	200	700	....wander on the Colerado and Trinity			
Tawakenoes	200	700	200 miles west of Nacogdoches towards Sta. Fee			
Tawa-ke-noes or Panis	500	2500	south of the Red river above the Caddoques			These are generally wretched creatures, who are diminishing daily; they cultivate a little corn, and hunt.
Natchitoches	.	.	almost extinct			
Boluxas	25	100	about sixty miles below Natchitoches			
Appalaches	14	50	Bayou Rapide	.	.	
Alibamas Conchatas Pacanas Atta-ka-pas Oppe-lou-sas Tunicas Tensas Washas	.	.	These are scattered remnants of tribes, who reside in the state of Louisiana; in the whole they do not exceed 400 warriors			
Chactas	2000	5500	Scattered over every part of the state of Louisiana, from Mobile to the Sabine	.	.	I am unable to form any estimate of the value of their trade.

Before the change of government, the mode of carrying on the Indian traffic, like all other colonial trade, was by monopolies, in which the interest of the governor or intendant was alone consulted. The traders obtained the exclusive privilege of trading to a particular tribe, or upon a certain river. But they were cramped in their enterprise by the narrow views of the government, who established no forts for the protection of the trade, nor would sanction the establishment of companies capable of protecting themselves. Since the change, a more extended theatre has been opened, both on the Mississippi and Missouri; and enterprising individuals have ventured up those rivers with great prospects of advantage. The merchandise consumed in this trade, was chiefly brought from New Orleans or Michilimakinac. The place of rendezvous on the Mississippi, was at prairie du Chien, but there were no fixed trading establishments. It was usual for the traders to ascend the rivers in the autumn, remain during the winter at a spot considered most convenient for the resort of the Indians, and return to St. Louis on the breaking up of the ice in the spring, with the produce of their traffic. The only permanent trading establishments on the waters of the Missouri, were those of Choteau's, on the Osage river Others, wintered with the Mahas, Poncas, and at different points on the river. A trader of the name of L'Oiselle, had a fort on Cedar island, in the country of the Sioux, nearly twelve hundred miles up. This trade could not have been considerable; and besides, the traders were exceedingly harassed by vagabond Indians, who frequently pillaged, carried away in captivity, or even murdered them and their men.

Notwithstanding the freedom of trading was open to all, on possession being taken by the United States, it was not until after the return of Lewis and Clark from their expedition that any perceptible change took place. Mr. Manuel Lisa, an enterprising gentleman of St. Louis, was the first to venture towards the source of the Missouri for the purpose of trading. His own capital not being adequate to the undertaking, he was joined by two or three gentlemen of St Louis. A brief account of his expedition, as it may be considered somewhat connected with

M

the fur trade of Louisiana, may not be uninteresting in this place.

He set off in the spring following the return of Lewis and Clark. Besides his own boats there were two others in company, which constituted a tolerable force. This trading expedition was very different from a journey of discovery. The difficulties would necessarily be much greater. A party of men well armed and equipped, and under proper submission to their officers, with presents to bestow to the different tribes, and not incumbered with goods or effects, might, with prudence, pass through with much less difficulty. The case is different where the trader has unruly hands to manage, who think themselves perfectly at liberty when once out of the reach of law: without discipline, badly armed, and coming to the nations, not for the purpose of making presents, but of trade. All these obstacles were encountered by Lisa and the traders who accompanied him.

At the river Platte, Lisa met one of Lewis and Clark's men, of the name of Coulter, who had been discharged at the Mandan villages, at his own request, that he might make a hunt before he returned. Coulter was persuaded to return: his knowledge of the country and nations rendered him an acquisition. Lisa passed the country of the Sioux, without finding any of that nation. On his arrival at the Arikara villages, his reception was such as to require the exhibition of prudence and courage. Two or three hundred warriors were drawn up, and on his approach, such as had fire arms fired a volley before his boat, to indicate the place where he should land. He accordingly put to shore, but instantly made it known, that no one of them was to enter his boat: the chiefs at the same time appointed warriors to stand guard and keep off the crowd. The women, who always trade amongst these nations, came to the beach with bags of corn, which they offered: an Indian rushed forward, cut open the bags with his knife, while the women took to flight. Lisa, who was perfectly acquainted with the Indian character, knowing that the least appearance of alarm would be dangerous, instantly called his men to arms, pointed a couple of swivels which were fixed on his boats, and made every preparation for defence. The Indians perceiving this, dispersed in confusion; and after some time, the chiefs approached with pipes of peace, extended before them in their hands. Lisa making signs of reconciliation, they came to him, and according to their custom, stroked him on the shoulders, begging him not to be displeased, declaring that the Indian who had offended him was considered a bad man. This had a good effect, and enabled him to proceed on his voyage without further molestation.

On his arrival at the first Mandan village, he determined to proceed through these villages, which are situated at intervals along the river, in the distance of about twenty miles, while his boats continued to ascend. At this village, he held the usual council with the chiefs, and presented them a few rolls of tobacco, and other articles, and was permitted to continue his journey. At the third village, his presents were rejected, and the chief demanded some powder, which was refused : Lisa, knew that his life was in no danger while his death could not procure them his goods, and resisted their repeated solicitations in a bold and firm manner ; he told them that they might kill him, but that his property would be safe. They were finally compelled to accept of such presents as he offered.

A few days after, having passed the Mandans, he espied the Assineboin nation approaching, in a body of four or five thousand souls. These wandering people had learned from their scouts, the approach of the traders. The whole prairie, to use his expression, was *red with them ;* some on horseback, others on foot, and all painted for war. His situation required the utmost boldness and intrepidity. He charged his swivels and made directly across to the savages, and when he had come within an hundred yards, the match was put, while there was at the same time, a general discharge of small arms. This was intended to strike them with terror ; the effect was ludicrous, they fell back, tumbled over each other, and fled to the hills with precipitation. A few of the warriors and chiefs only remained. The pipe of peace was presented, and matters concluded amicably. He continued his voyage to the Yellow Stone river, which he ascended about one hundred and seventy miles, to the Big Horn river, where he built a trading fort. He shortly after despatched Coulter, the hunter before mentioned, to bring some of the Indian nations to trade. This man, with a pack of thirty pounds weight, his gun and some ammunition, went upwards of five hundred miles to the Crow nation; gave them information, and proceeded from thence to several other tribes. On his return, a party of Indians in whose company he happened to be, was attacked, and he was lamed by a severe wound in the leg; notwithstanding which, he returned to the establishment, entirely alone and without assistance, several hundred miles. Yet such instances of intrepidity would not be regarded amongst those people, as any way extraordinary. How should those blush, who are continually whining about the little inconveniences and privations of common life! Lisa remained nine months at this place. He returned to St. Louis, having indemnified himself for his voyage, by considerable benefits. But he had not chosen the proper country, as the north side of the Missouri was much more abundant in furs, and of a more valuable quality.

After the return of Lisa, the favorable reports which he made, induced a number of gentlemen to turn their attention to this trade, and in a short time a company was formed under the name of "the Missouri Fur Company;" of this association Lisa became a member, and has been one of the most active and useful. The company was composed of ten persons; but the capital was greatly inadequate, not exceeding forty thousand dollars. Having collected about two hundred and fifty men, they ascended the Missouri; left trading establishments with the Sioux, the Arikaras, and Mandans, but the principal part proceeded to the three forks of the Missouri, the country most abounding in beaver, for their intention was to hunt as well as trade, and the greater number of the men were hunters. But they had not been long here until they found their hopes entirely frustrated by the hostilities of the Black-feet Indians, a numerous tribe, who had unfortunately been rendered inimical to the Americans by an unlucky affair, in which Lewis and Clark, on their return, had killed two or three of their nation; besides, probably instigated by the jealousy of the British companies. A party of fifteen or twenty American hunters were attacked by surprise, and nine killed. The greatest precaution was found necessary in going out to hunt, they were at length so much harassed by the savages, as to be compelled to remain altogether at their fort, or to venture but a short distance from it. It is supposed that in the different rencounters with these savages, at least twenty of the whites were killed, and nearly twice that number of the others. Thus a most implacable enmity has been unfortunately excited, which will for a long time, exclude our traders and hunters, from that part of the western country by far the most favorable for their pursuits. It is supposed that had they continued unmolested, the company would have brought down the first year, three hundred packs of beaver alone. Instead of which there were scarcely twenty. The following spring a considerable number of the party descended the river; the remainder continued until autumn, when, fearing a general attack, and finding the situation otherwise exceedingly irksome, Mr. Henry, one of the company, who now commanded the party, resolved to cross the mountains, and winter on some of the branches of the Columbia; this he accordingly effected, but not without suffering every possible hardship, from hunger, cold, and fatigue. In the mean time, the company suffered considerable loss from the accidental burning of one of their factories; this was estimated at fifteen thousand dollars. The establishments at the Mandans and Arikaras, brought no profit. In the spring of the year 1811, the third, and by the time fixed for the duration of the association, the last, an expedition was fitted out by the company, the command of which was given to Lisa, whom I accompanied. By his prudence and good management, the affairs of the company were in some measure retrieved. After remaining sometime at the Mandan villages, he was joined by Mr. Henry and all his party, who brought about forty packs of beaver. Leaving trading establishments at the Mandans, Arikaras, and with the Sioux, he descended to St. Louis. It appeared that at the termination of the third year, notwithstanding all these unforeseen difficulties and misfortunes, the company had saved the capital, and had besides the establishments before mentioned. I have been informed that the company has been renewed, and its capital considerably enlarged.

Such is the present situation of the Indian trade. Besides the Missouri company, there are many individuals, who trade with nations on the Mississippi, or on the Missouri, as high as the Mahas. There are few of the Indian tribes who hunt; they have hitherto had little encouragement; and besides, the continual wars which prevail amongst them, renders it impracticable.

A well regulated company, with sufficient capital, would in a very short time draw immense profits from the Indian trade of the Mississippi and Missouri. A very great proportion of the North West Company's trade, would find its way down those rivers. The city of New York is highly interested; its situation may render it the rival of Montreal in this trade; the climate of New Orleans is unfavourable to furs and peltries. Near the heads of all the western rivers, tributary to the Mississippi and Missouri, there are immense numbers of the beaver, muskrat, otter, and other furred animals. An extensive company, well established, might count upon a thousand packs annually, besides a vast number of buffaloe robes, which will be found of much use in the slave states, as a cheap and comfortable bedding for negroes. The buffaloe would furnish other articles of trade, wool, horns, tongues, &c. which would also be considerable. Wolf, bear, elk, and deer skins, might be had in immense quantities. It requires no gift of prophecy to tell, that such a company will not be long in forming. Should Canada, in the present struggle, be wrested from Britain, it would be immediately established.

The establishment of factories by the United States, in the Indian country, have had good effects where they are accompanied by forts, with a small number of soldiers; they keep those nations in awe, and enable the traders or hunters to traverse the country in security. The factory highest on the Missouri, is at fort Osage, three hundred miles from its entrance: two more might be established advantageously on this river; one at the Council Bluffs, and another at the little Cedar island.

CHAPTER VII.

VIEW OF THE COUNTRY ON THE COLUMBIA.

BUT little is yet known of this extensive section of our continent; it is certain, that it is on a much larger scale than the tract east of the Alleganies to the Atlantic, but it must be admitted, that its relative position with the rest of the world, (except as to the East Indies) is much less advantageous. Its remoteness from any European country or settlement, will discourage the establishment of colonies. Before its colonization can be effected, the same obstacles as were encountered by nearly all the colonists in America, must be overcome, and perhaps still greater.

This tract differs from that east of the Allegany in one respect, and which is of considerable moment; it does not open to the ocean by fine bays, and by large navigable rivers, crossing it parallel to each other. The cause of this difference principally arises from a chain of mountains, which runs with the coast, seldom receding more than sixty miles. The Columbia, and the Multnomak, its southern branch, are both confined between this ridge and the principal mountains, until after flowing towards each other, the one, a thousand, and the other, nearly fifteen hundred miles, they break through the ridge before mentioned, and find their way to the sea, uniting their waters about sixty miles from it. The other rivers which rise in the Rocky mountains, instead of falling into the sea, become tributary either to the Multnomak or the Columbia.

Next to the Mississippi, this river and its tributaries, water a greater extent of country than any river of our continent, not even excepting the St. Lawrence. The distance from the source of the Columbia, to that of the Multnomak, which rises with the Colerado of California, is not less than two thousand miles. The Multnomak was not discovered by Lewis and Clark when descending the Columbia, its entrance being concealed by an island; on re-ascending the Columbia, those celebrated travellers were astonished at the sight of a noble river little inferior to the principal stream.

The lands immediately in the vicinity of the Columbia, are represented as rich and highly susceptible of cultivation; but the country in general is too open, and deficient in wood. The climate is more temperate than the same latitudes in the United States. Near the sea, however, there prevails almost continued fog, and drizzling showers of rain, which renders it extremely disagreeable.

The natives on the Columbia and its branches are very numerous. Gen. Clark informed me that their numbers might be safely estimated at eighty thousand souls.

The route taken by Lewis and Clark across the mountains, was perhaps the very worst that could have been selected. Mr. Henry, a member of the Missouri company, and his hunters, have discovered several passes, not only very practicable, but even in their present state, less difficult than those of the Allegany mountains. These are considerably south of the source of Jefferson river. It is the opinion of the gentleman last mentioned, that loaded horses, or even wagons, might in its present state, go in the course of six or eight days, from a navigable point on the Columbia, to one on the waters of the Missouri.— Thus, rendering an intercourse with settlements which may be formed on the Columbia, more easy than between those on the heads of the Ohio, and the Atlantic states. Mr. Henry wintered in a delightful country, on a beautiful navigable stream.

An attempt is now making to form establishments on the Columbia, with what success, is not yet much known. This has been undertaken by a company in the city of New York, at the head of which we find Jacob Astor. Two vessels were despatched for the mouth of the river, we are informed, with orders to commence an establishment. A party of about eighty men under the command of Wilson P. Hunt, and a brother of Sir Alex. M'Kensie, who was formerly in the employment of the N. W. company, has proceeded across the mountains. The principal object of the company at present, seems to be the establishment of a fur trade direct with China. The valuable sea-otter, and the fine furs which may be obtained in this country in great quantities, will undoubtedly produce considerable profits. Whether the returns could be introduced into the United States across the Rocky mountains, to any advantage, might be worthy of experiment. A shortening of the distance, by more than a thousand leagues, will certainly make it an object, to lessen the the expense and difficulty of transporting goods across the mountains, and down the Missouri. It is worthy of consideration, that articles usually imported from the East Indies are not of great bulk, or weight, that a small compass will include goods of great value. Hence this transportation will be attended with much less difficulty.

There can be little doubt but that the United States have the best claim to the country watered by the Columbia, at least of the greater part. If not as a part of Louisiana, yet by the right of discovery, universally acknowledged by European nations, with respect to this continent. We have besides exercised various acts of ownership over it, and the colony at present forming, is under the protection and license of our government.

N

BOOK II.

VIEWS OF LOUISIANA.

IN TWO BOOKS.

TERRITORY OF THE MISSOURI.

CHAPTER I.

BOUNDARIES....EXTENT....RIVERS....GENERAL VIEW.

ALTHOUGH the executive exercises authority out of the
Indian boundary, the territory itself cannot properly be considered as extending beyond it; the territorial governor, acts as
well in the capacity of a general agent for the United States, as
in that of civil magistrate. The judiciary has determined that it
possesses no jurisdiction over the Indian country.

The territory of the Missouri is bounded on the south by the
33° of lat. which strikes the Mississippi about one hundred and
fifty miles below the Arkansas, and constitutes the northern
boundary of the state of Louisiana. On the west, it may be considered as bounded by the Osage purchase;* this line runs from
a place called the Black rock, about three hundred miles up the
Missouri, due south to strike the Arkansas. On the north, a line
was agreed upon in a treaty between governor Harrison, and the
Sacs and Foxes, which begins at a point opposite the Gasconade river, and strikes the Mississippi at the Jaufloine river. It
is unnecessary to observe, that the Mississippi bounds on the
east.

---

* Except on the south of the Arkansas, where there is no western
boundary.

This embraces an extent of country nearly three times as large as the state of Pennsylvania, and which contains a much greater proportion of tillable land. The section north of the Missouri, and the one south of the Arkansas, are each sufficient to form a considerable state; but the Osage Purchase, constitutes the principal body of the territory, and may be justly considered, next to the state of Louisiana, the most valuable tract in the great valley of the Mississippi.

A description of the principal rivers, with some account of the portions of country watered by them, will give some view of this tract: reserving the tract including the settlements for a more minute description.

WHITE RIVER.

This fine river was little known until lately; it is one of the most considerable in the western country, and will one day be important. It was thought to be a stream of very inconsiderable magnitude, until explored by capt. Many, of the U. S. army, and rendered known from settlements made on it, and from wandering hunters. It rises in the Black mountains, which separate the waters of the Arkansas from those of the Missouri and Mississippi. Several of its branches interlock with those of the Osage river, the Maramek, and the St Francis. It is navigable, according to the computation of several hunters with whom I have conversed, about twelve hundred miles, without any considerable interruption; eight hundred of these may be made with barges, the rest with canoes, or smaller boats. The waters of this river are clear and limpid, the current gentle, and even in the driest season, plentifully supplied from the numerous and excellent springs which are every where found. It is not less remarkable for the many considerable rivers which it receives in its course. Black river is the largest of these; it enters on the N. E. side, about four hundred miles up, and is navigable nearly five hundred miles, receiving a number of handsome rivers, as the Current. Eleven Point, and Spring rivers. The last merits a more particular description. It issues forth, suddenly, from an immense spring, two hundred yards in width, affording an uninterrupted navigation to its mouth, contracting its width;

however to fifty or sixty yards. It is about fifty miles in length.* This spring is full of the finest fish; bass, perch, pike, and others common in the western rivers. Besides this river, White river receives several others from one hundred and fifty to three hundred miles in length; as *Eaux Cache'*, James river, *Rapid John*, and others known by various names.

The country watered by this river has only been traversed by Indians and hunters, and may be considered as still unexplored. It is spoken of with rapture by those who have seen it; it is described as being generally well wooded, and uncommonly abundant in springs and rivulets. The soil is said to be rich, though there are some places hilly and broken; some of the hills might be more properly termed mountains. A hunter described to me three high and remarkable hills, about eight hundred miles up the river, standing on a plain, and perfectly unconnected with any ridge. They are each about a quarter of a mile in length, their form oblong; two stand parallel and the third across; at a distance, giving the appearance of three walls of some immense building. It has been called Jupiter's Palace. Hunters agree in declaring that on the waters of this river, a country may be chosen, at least one hundred miles square, not surpassed by the best parts of Kentucky, and one of the best for settlements in the western world.

ST. FRANCIS,

Discharges itself into the Mississippi seventy-five miles above White river, and would be navigable but for rafts which impede its course, for nine hundred miles. The western branch rises with the waters of White river, and the eastern, which is the principal, interlocks with Big river, of the Maramck. It is very erroneously laid down on the common maps; its general course is much further east: the principal branch in fact, runs nearly parallel with the Mississippi in its whole length, and seldom recedes more than fifty miles. It is a beautiful and limpid stream, passing through a charming country, but afterwards, though increased in size, by its junction with several other ri-

---

* A town or village has been lately commenced at the mouth of this river.

vers, it flows with a slow and lazy current. The St. Francis communicates with a number of lakes which lie between it and the Mississippi, formed by the streams which flow from the upland country, and lose themselves in the low grounds commencing at Cape Girardeau. This river receives several considerable streams, which rise between it and the Mississippi; the Pemisco has its source near the Big prairie, eight or ten miles N. W. of New Madrid; but generally, the St. Francis in high water overflows its banks on that side to a great distance. A person, at such times may easily lose the channel, unless well acquainted with its course. The western bank is generally higher and much less subject to inundation.

MARAMEK,

Is forty miles below the mouth of the Missouri, and heads with the Gasconade and the St. Francis. Passes generally through a broken country, the flats mostly narrow. It affords excellent navigation to its source, a distance of more than three hundred miles. The source of this river is considered a curiosity; it is a small lake formed from fountains issuing immediately around the spot. Big river, which winds through the Mine country, is the principal branch.

THE GASCONADE,

Enters the Missouri about one hundred miles up, can be ascended in small boats nearly one hundred miles, but the navigation is not good on account of shoals and rapids. It passes through a hilly country, in which there probably exist mines.

OSAGE R.

Navigation about five hundred miles, though considerably impeded in places by shoals. Enters the Missouri 133 miles up. Principal navigable branches are Nangira, Grand river, the Fork, the Cooks river, Vermillion river. Country bordering, generally high prairie, but the bottoms are fine and sufficiently timbered for settlements. On the Nangira, about twenty miles from its mouth, there is a curious cascade of more than one hundred and fifty feet fall in the distance of four hundred yards; the water issues from a large spring and is precipitated over three different ledges of rocks, and falling to the bottom, is collected into a beautiful basin, from whence, it flows into this river, a considerable stream. A few miles below this place there is a great abundance of iron ore.

———

CHAPTER II.

SOIL—FACE OF THE COUNTRY, &c. FROM NEW MADRID TO THE MISSOURI—THE FORKS OF THE MISSOURI.

ABOUT twenty miles below Cape Girardeau, and thirty-five from the mouth of the Ohio, the limestone rock terminates abruptly, and there commences an immense plain, stretching with scarcely any interruption, to the Balize. There is but one place in which the hilly country, on that side, can be seen from the Mississippi.* It is successively traversed by the St. Francis, White river, Arkansas, Washita, and Red river. This flat may be considered, on an average, about thirty miles wide, and with hardly an exception, is without a hill, or a stone. The soil, is generally rich, and has the appearance of being alluvial, though there is a greater proportion of sand, than is usual, in the neighbourhood of the rivers. It is a common idea, but very erroneous, that this is a continued swamp, or rather low land, subject to inundation. There are doubtless a great many swamps, and lakes, interspersed with the plains; but there are also extensive bodies of land fit for cultivation. The swamps, and wet lands, I think, might be drained without any great difficulty. At some future day, this will be the Flanders of America.

It is worthy of observation, that from the Maramek, to the mouth of the St. Francis, upwards of five hundred miles, no river of any consequence, empties into the Mississippi; the considerable rivers, as the St. Francis, Black river; and Osage, fall to the S. W. or to the Missouri. It is therefore probable, that

---

* A few miles below the St. Francis, the hills approach within a quarter of a mile of the river. The S. W. side of the Arkansas, the highland comes within eight or ten miles of the Mississippi.

when these countries, become settled, the produce, fifty or sixty miles west of the Mississippi, will be carried to market by those channels. In the summer floods, there is an almost continued connection, between the lakes east of the St Francis, by means of these; at that period, a person may go from this river, to New Madrid.

In leaving the upland country, at Cape Girardeau, we enter what has been called the *great swamp:* though it does not properly possess this character. The timber is not such as is usually found in swamps, but fine oak, ash, olive, linn, beech, and poplar of enormous growth. The soil a rich black loam. In the fall, it is nearly dry; the road which passes through, being only muddy in particular spots: but during the season of high water, it is extremely disagreeable crossing it. The horse sinks at every step, to the belly in water and loose soil; and in places entirely covered, the traveller, but for the marks on the trees, would be in danger of losing the road altogether. This swamp is sixty miles in length, and four broad, widenning as it approaches the St. Francis. In the season of high water, the Mississippi and the river just mentioned, have a complete connection by means of this low land.

After crossing the swamp, there commences, a ridge of high land, running in the same course, and on the Mississippi, bounding what is called Tywapety bottom: this ridge, in approaching the St. Francis westward, subsides. In passing over it, we appear to be in a hilly country, possessing springs and rivulets; the soil, though generally poor and sandy, is tolerably well timbered, and not altogether unfit for tillage.

After passing this high land, we enter again the level plain. The road crosses two lakes, one of which, forms the Bayou St. John, at New Madrid; the other is connected with lakes to the westward. They are four or five feet deep, and several hundred yards wide, with clean sandy bottoms. These lakes are formed by the rivulets of the upland before described; they rise or fall but little. During the fall season, they are the resort of vast numbers of wild fowl, and are full of fish.

The traveller, now enters a perfect level, alternately prairie, and beautiful woods of tall oak, walnut, mulberry, sassafras, honey locust, perfectly open, as though planted by art. Those of the shrubby kind, are usually on tracts of ground, apart from the groves of larger trees. They are the plum tree, catalpa, dogwood, spice wood, and the different species of the sumack.— The prairies, or natural meadows, are covered with grass and a profusion of flowers. Herds of cattle, of two or three hundred, are seen, and contribute to the pleasure of viewing these natural meads. The *Big prairie*, through which the public road passes, is a delightful spot; it is about eight miles long, and four broad, enclosed by woods, and interspersed with beautiful groves, resembling small islands. It is not surpassed in beauty by the artificial meadow, improved with the greatest care. In passing through these prairies in the spring, the traveller may stop under the shady trees, by the road side, and suffer his horse to feed, while he feasts on strawberries of a superior size and flavor.— A number of good farms are scattered round the edges of the prairie, and a few within.

This description, may give some idea of the country to the S. W. as far as the Arkansas. Except, that the prairies are more extensive, the lakes and the inundations towards the Mississippi, more considerable, and every thing on a larger scale. But, it is extremely difficult, to give a correct notion of the topography of a country, from bare description; a well executed map would be indispensably necessary.

The soil of the prairie, is more light and loose than in the woods, and has a greater mixture of sand: but, when wet, it assumes every where, a deep black color, and an oily appearance. Judging from the borders of the lakes, and the wells which have been dug, this soil does not seem to be more than three feet deep. But after digging through a stratum of sand, there appears a kind of clay, of a dirty yellow, and of a saponaceous appearance; this is the substratum of the whole country, and is perhaps a kind of marle, the deposit of very ancient alluvia. No stones are met with in any of these wells, that I have heard of.

The greatest objection to this country is the want of fountains and running streams. Water is procured in wells of the depth of twenty-five or thirty feet; but the taste is not agreeable;

owing most probably to their being lined with mulberry, which
soon decays, and gives its taste to the water. Mr. Rawle, near
New Madrid, has erected a mill on the lakes, on a new construction, requiring no natural fall ; the wheel runs horizontally, and
entirely under water.

On the other side of the Big prairie, as we advance to the
Mississippi, the soil appears to be stronger, and the vegetation
exceedingly luxuriant. Trees are seen of the most towering
height, thick underwood, and enormous vines, binding, as it
were, those sturdy giants, to the earth, and to each other. To
clear those forests, requires an immense labor, but the American settlers, usually prefer them, from the superior quality of
the land. The creole, on the contrary, generally makes choice of
the open ground or prairie. The one, whom scarcely any consideration will persuade to remain long in the same place, choos-
es a soil which promises to last for ever, while the other, who is
seldom induced to change, sits down on land that may wear out
in a few years.

Notwithstanding the variety of beauties, which attract the attention of the traveller, in passing through these low lands, yet
one who has been accustomed " to the pleasant vicissitude of
hill and dale," becomes at length wearied with the sameness of
the scenery, and experiences a relief, on emerging to the high
land at Cape Girardeau. From this place, to the Missouri, the
country may be called hilly and broken, but with excellent flats,
or bottoms, on the creeks and rivulets, of a width usually proportioned to the size of the stream. The river hills of the Mississippi, perhaps from five to ten miles out, are in many places
far from being prepossessing. They are badly watered, have many
rugged and abrupt acclivities ; and considerable precipices on the
river. A strange appearance is also given by the number of fun-
nels, or *sink holes*, formed by the washing of the earth into fissures
of the limestone rock, on which the country reposes. In other
places, flint knobs present themselves, strewed with rude masses of horn stone, and affording a scanty nourishment to a few
straggling black jacks, or groves of pine. But it is not to be
understood that this forms the greatest proportion of the lands,

a more minute description of particular parts will prove the contrary. Even in these places there is abundance of fine grass, affording excellent pasturage.

For thirty miles above Cape Girardeau, (with the exception of some places near the Mississippi) and extending back to the St. Francis, there is a country not unlike that around the head of the Ohio; though not quite so hilly. The timber nearly the same, hickory, oak, ash, walnut, maple, and well supplied with springs and rivulets.

North of Apple creek, there is a tract on the river, of very unpromising aspect, extending to the Saline, within nine miles of St. Genevieve. It is scarcely fit for tillage, badly watered, with woods of a poor and straggling growth; but to make amends in some degree, for the sterility of the upland, there is a fine bottom (Bois brulé) terminating just below the Saline, of twenty miles in length, and on an average three in width. In the neighbourhood of the Saline creek the land is exceedingly broken and hilly, though tolerably well timbered, and not altogether unfit for cultivation. On the á Vase,* there are many fine tracts, and extensive platts.

From St. Genevieve to the Maramek, and extending back, the same description will apply, except that the country is more rough and broken, but generally better watered, being traversed by la riviere Habitation, Big river, the Mineral Fork, the Platin, and the Joachin. In some places the country is exceedingly wild and romantic. Ledges of limestone rock frequently shew themselves on the sides of hills, forming precipices of twenty or thirty feet high, and have much the appearance of regular and artificial walls. What is somewhat singular, they are generally near the top of the hill, which gradually slopes down to the vale of some rivulet: a view of great extent and magnificence is presented to the eye; rocks, woods, distant hills, and

---

* Apple creek—the Saline—and the A' Vase, are considerable streams, which rise, as well as Big river (a branch of the Maramek) and some other streams, in a high ridge, about fifty miles west of the Mississippi, which separates these waters from those of the St. Francis.

a sloping lawn of many miles.* The whole, forming prospects, the most romantic and picturesque.

North of the Maramek there are fewer rugged hills; the land is waving. Towards the river, nearly to St. Louis, the country is not well watered, it is also thinly timbered, and the soil but indifferent. On Gravé, and in the Bon Homme settlement, between the Maramek, and the Missouri, the land is good, and generally well adapted to cultivation. Between St. Louis and the Missouri, with but trifling exceptions, the lands are of a superior quality; there are some beautiful spots, as the village of Florissant, and the environs. No description can do justice to the beauty of this tract The Missouri bottoms, are covered with heavy timber, and by many are preferred to those of the Mississippi or of the Ohio.

The tract of country north of the Missouri, is less hilly, than that on the south, but there is a much greater proportion of prairie. It has a waving surface, varied by those dividing ridges of streams, which in Kentucky, are called *knobs*. These prairies, it is well known, are caused by repeated and desolating fires,† and the soil is extremely fertile. Such woods as remain

* Near col. Hammond's farm, there is a natural curiosity worth noticing. A hill, commanding a most extensive prospect, embracing a scope of fifteen or twenty miles, and in some directions more, is completely surrounded by a precipice of the sort described. It is called Rock Fort, and might answer the purpose of fortification; it is nearly two hundred feet higher than any of the surrounding hills, and on the top there is a level space of ten acres, overgrown with trees, the soil is good. The Platin, which winds at the base of the hill, and whose meandering course, can be traced by the sycamore and other trees peculiar to river bottoms, render the prospect still more agreeable. The fort is accessible only by two narrow passes up the precipice or wall, and a fine fountain issues out from the rock.

† The plains of Indiana and Illinois have been mostly produced by the same cause. They are very different from the savannas on the sea board, and the immense plains of the Upper Missouri. In the prairies of Indiana, I have been assured, that the woods in places have been known to recede, and in others to increase, within the recollection of the old inhabitants. In moist places, the woods are still standing, the fire meeting here with obstruction. Trees, if planted in these prairies, would doubtless grow. In the islands, preserved by accidental causes,

are fine, but the quantity of adjoining prairie is usually too great. There are large tracts however admirably suited for settlements: a thousand acres or more of wood land, surrounded by as much of prairie. It is generally well watered with fine streams, and also interspersed with lakes. There is an extensive strip of land along this side of the Missouri, of nearly thirty miles in width and about one hundred and fifty in length, altogether woods, and of excellent soil. An old gentleman who has seen Kentucky a wilderness, informed me, that the appearance of this tract is similar, with the exception of its not being covered with cane, and a forest so dark and heavy. The "Forks of the Missouri," (such is the name given to the northern angle, formed by the two great rivers,) daily increases in reputation, and is settling faster than any part of the territory.

The Missouri bottoms, alternately appearing on one side or other of the river, are of the finest kind for three hundred miles up, generally covered with heavy timber; the greatest part of which is cotton wood of enormous size. The bottoms are usually about two miles in width, and entirely free from inundation. A-bove this, in many places, after a small border of wood on the bank, the rest, to the hills or bluffs, is entirely bare. The bottoms of the Mississippi are equally extensive and rich, but not so well wooded. They are in fact a continued succession of the most beautiful prairies or meadows. The tract called *Les Mamelles*, from the circumstance of several mounds, bearing the appearance of art, projecting from the bluff some distance into the plain, may be worth describing as a specimen. It is about three miles from St. Charles; I visited it last summer, and ascended the mounds to have a better view. To those who have never seen any of these prairies, it is very difficult to convey any just ide

the progress of the fire can be traced; the first burning would only scorch the outer bark of the tree; this would render it more suscep‑ tible to the next, and the third would completely kill. I have seen in places, at present completely prairie, pieces of burnt trees, proving that the prairie had been caused by fire. The grass is usually very luxu‑ riant, which is not the case in the plains of the Missouri. There may doubtless be spots where the proportion of salts, or other bodies, may be such, as to favor the growth of grass only.

of them. Perhaps the comparison to the smooth green sea, is the best. Elevated about one hundred feet above the plain, I had a view of an immense extent. Every sense was delighted, and every faculty awakened. After gazing for an hour I still continued to experience an unsatiated delight, in contemplating the rich and magnificent scene. To the right, the Missouri is concealed by a wood of no great width, extending to the Mississippi; the distance of ten miles. Before me, I could mark the course of the latter river, its banks without even a fringe of wood; on the other side, the hills of the Illinois, faced with limes one, in bold masses of various hues, and the summits crowned with trees: pursuing these hills to the north, we see, at the distance of twenty miles, where the Illinois separates them, in his course to the Mississippi. To the left, we behold the ocean of prairie, with islets at intervals. The whole extent perfectly level, covered with long waving grass, and at every moment changing color, from the shadows cast by the passing clouds. In some places there stands a solitary tree of cotton wood or walnut, of enormous size, but, from the distance, diminished to a shrub. Fifty thousand acres of the finest land, are under the eye at once, and yet on all this space, there is but one little cultivated spot to be seen!

When the eyes are gratified, with the survey of this beautiful scene, the mind naturally expatiates on the improvements of which it is susceptible, and creative fancy, adorns it, with happy dwellings and richly cultivated fields. The situation in the vicinity of these great rivers, the fertility of the soil, a garden spot, must one day yield nourishment to a multitude of beings. The bluffs are abundantly supplied with the purest water; those rivulets, and rills, which at present, are unable to reach the great father of waters, and lose themselves in lakes and marshes, will be guided by the hand of man into channels fitted for their reception, and for his pleasure and felicity.

CHAPTER III.

CLIMATE—DISEASES.

WHAT is generally remarked respecting the climate of the U. States, is particularly applicable to this territory; to wit, variableness. In the spring and winter, during the continuance of S. W. winds, it is agreeably warm; but by the change of the wind to N. W. the most sudden alteration of weather is produced. The winters of St. Louis are usually more mild than in the same latitudes east of the Allegany mountains, but there are frequently several days in succession of greater cold than is known even in Canada. Last January (1811) after several weeks of delightful weather, when the heat was even disagreeable, the thermometer standing at 78°, a change took place, and so sudden, that in 4 days it fell to 10° below 0°. This winter was also remarkable for a circumstance, which the oldest inhabitants do not recollect to have ever witnessed; the Mississippi closed over twice, whereas it most usually remains open during winter.

The settlements of this territory, have in some measure obtained the character of being unhealthy. There is no doubt, but that, as in other parts of the western country, which have not been properly put under cultivation, autumnal fevers will prevail. The vicinity of the lakes has not been remarked as more unhealthy than at a distance: convenience generally induces the settler to choose this situation. It is a prevailing notion, that to be sick the first summer, is what every settler must expect. This is not generally true. In some parts of the territory, the district of New Madrid, and immediately on the Mississippi, this *seasoning* is severely paid : but in other parts of the territory, I can say with confidence, that not more than one tenth undergo it, and that in a slight degree. From the first of August to the last of September, is considered the most unhealthy. Much depends upon the care which the settler takes in avoiding whatever may tend to produce sickness. The scorching heat of the sun is universally agreed to be unfavorable to health. Night dews and exhalations are not less so. The food of most of the settlers, is calculated to generate bile ; great quantities of

fat pork, seldom any fresh meat, or vegetables, and large quan‑
tities of milk and coarse corn bread are used.   The mephitic
exhalations from putrid vegetables, and from enormous masses
of putrifying trees, in the new clearings, also contribute to this
insalubrity.   The fields of corn, with which the settler surrounds
his cabin, are thought by many. to be another cause; the foliage
of the corn is so rich and massy, that it shades the earth, and
prevents the action of the sun from exhaling unwholesome
damps.

The last season was uncommonly unhealthy throughout the
western country, and this territory experienced it in a degree
not less than many other places.   The natives, and the oldest in‑
habitants, were attacked, as well as strangers.   The Missouri,
which had never experienced it, did not escape.   This season
did great injury to the commencing emigration to this country;
many who had suffered, retired from it, and others who had
determined to come, changed their minds.

CHAPTER IV.

POLITICAL DIVISIONS—INHABITANTS—SETTLEMENTS— POPULATION.

SHORTLY after the taking possession of this territory,
it was divided by proclamation of governor Harrison, into six
districts:

1 St. Charles,	4 Cape Girardeau,
2 St. Louis,	5 New Madrid,
3 St. Genevieve,	6 Arkansas.

The territorial legislature has again subdivided these districts
into townships.   The term " district" corresponds with the
county of the states.

The inhabitants are composed of whites, Indians, metiffs, a
few civilized Indians, and negro slaves.

The whites, consist of the ancient inhabitants, and of those
who have settled since the change of government.   The former,

are chiefly of French origin; there were scarcely more than three or four Spanish families in this province, and the citizens of the United States, although advantageous offers were held out to them, rarely settled on this side of the river. The French inhabitants resided in villages, and cultivated common fields adjacent to them; in the manner of many parts of Europe: it was here, also, rendered in some degree necessary from their situation. There were always good reasons to apprehend the attacks of Indians; of which, on some occasions, they had a fatal experience. The small number of Americans settled here, is also owing to the tide of emigration having set in for the western states. Kentucky, Ohio and Tennessee, were yet unpeopled. Besides, until it was transferred to the United States, there was no security against the depredations of Indians.

For these three last years, the settlements have been increasing rapidly. The American mode, of living on detached farms, has been adopted by a number of the French inhabitants of villages, and the settlements, in larger or smaller groups.

The frontier, at least below the Missouri, may be said to have retired, sixty miles west of the Mississippi, and the settlements on the rivers, are perfectly safe from the attacks of a savage enemy, should any be apprehended. Within the last two years, farms have been opened, from the Missouri to the Arkansas, on the Mississippi; and on this river, above the Missouri, they extend, at distant intervals, to the Prairie du Chien.* On the Missouri, they extend upwards of two hundred miles from the mouth of the river. Near Fort Clark, there are a few farms, which have lately been opened.

Next to the banks of the navigable rivers, the public roads, form the greatest inducement for making settlements. There are consequently establishments on nearly all the roads which traverse the territory; seldom at a greater distance than five or six miles from each other.

* In case of Indian war, these remote and feeble settlements will have to be broken up. But there is very little to be apprehended from incursions into the more populous parts of the territory south of the Missouri. This is as secure as the interior of Kentucky.

An enumeration of the principal settlements will not be un-interesting—I shall therefore begin with those of the district of St. Louis. That of Bon Homme is amongst the most noted—It is on a creek of that name, about fifteen miles from St. Louis: at this place, the Maramek and Missouri come within eight miles of each other. The land is said to be good, and there are in this settlement some very respectable farmers. La riviere des Peres, and a branch of it, called Gravé, are also tolerably well in-habited; from its vicinity to Bon Homme, it may be considered a part of the same settlement. La rivere des Peres, is a hand-some stream which enters the Mississippi between St. Louis and the Maramek. On the Missouri, from the junction to the mouth of Bon Homme, there is a continued and excellent set-tlement. Immediately on the Maramek the land is broken, but well adapted to the culture of grain : the river bottoms, I have already observed, are of small extent, and but few farms have yet been opened. Between the Maramek and the Platen, there are a considerable number of scattered settlers ; and in the neigh-bourhood of the Joachin, numerous and extensive improve-ments.

In the district of St. Genevieve, the principal compact settle-ments are on Big river, which passes through the tract of lead mines : the largest, that of Belle Vue, is about fifty miles west of the town of St. Genevieve. There is also a settlement on the St. Francis, within this district, perhaps not inferior to any. In the neighbourhood of the mines, there are usually a number of farms. On la riviere Habitation, the a Vase, on the Saline, and on Apple creek, there are a number of small settlements, and all over the district there are scattered farms. Bois brulé bot-tom, has also a number of good plantations.

Cape Girardeau, contains some of the best settlements in the territory. Burd's is the principal ; it is a few miles from the Mississippi, on excellent land ; the improvements extensive.—There is also a large settlement of Germans, about thirty miles west of the town. They live well, and are becoming easy in their circumstances: there are also a number of good farms in Ty-wapety bottom. In general, the settlements are much scatter-ed in this district.

In the district of St. Charles, the settlements are also considerable. They extend up the Missouri, nearly two hundred
miles. Though between the more considerable groups, the plantations are thinly scattered. Charrette, is the next village after
St. Charles, about fifty miles above; it is composed of ten or
twelve French families, who live close together, after the ancient
custom. There are about forty families on Salt river, above this,
who live in the American mode. At the Otter island, there is a
settlement, large enough to afford a company of militia. Below
the Osage river, but within sight, on the opposite side of the
Missouri, there is a French village of about twenty families; it
is called Côte sans Dessein. But far the best settlement on the
Missouri, is that near the Mine river, on the N. E side of the
river, and extending about six miles along the bank. There are
here about eighty families; some engaged in working salines on
the river before mentioned. Several of them have slaves. They
will be completely able to defend themselves against any Indians
that may be dreaded in this quarter. There are some good settlements on the riviere de Cuivre, near the mouth; but they are
much scattered in the forks of the Missouri. A man who was
up through that country last summer, for the purpose of looking at the land, told me, that he found five families near the heads
of the Cuivre; sixty or seventy miles distant from any other settlement: he happened on this group when he had not the most
distant expectation of meeting with any one. In case of Indian
war, these poor stragglers will most probably be butchered, unless fortunate enough to escape into the settlements.

The district of New Madrid is but thinly inhabited, considering the great proportion of fine land, which it contains. There
are some good farms in the neighbourhood of the village. There
are also some settlements on the St. Francis, on the banks of the
Mississippi, and through the prairies towards Cape Girardeau:
particularly on the public road. I travelled over it when it was
a wilderness; the contrast even now, is pleasing: some one who
passes here at a future day, will find still greater cause of won-

der. Little Prairie, thirty miles below New Madrid, on the river, is a considerable settlement.*

The settlements of the Arkansas, are principally in the neighbourhood of the Arkansas Post, or extend up the river, and are the least considerable of the territory.

There are besides, a number of small groups through the White river country ; but so scattered and remote, that it is difficult to obtain any information respecting them. A number of families in the course of the present year, have removed to Spring river, and others are preparing for it. Several families who arrived at St. Genevieve from the District of Maine, have actually set out for the same place. A village has been commenced at the mouth of Spring river, and consists already of a store, tavern, &c. There seems to prevail a rage amongst the frontiers-men, for emigration to that quarter.

The emigrants to this territory, are chiefly from North Carolina, and Kentucky ; of late, the western part of Pennsylvania contributes considerably to its population. The excellence and cheapness of the lands, besides the permission of holding slaves, will cause this territory to be preferred by emigrants from the southern states, to any part of the western country, unless it be on the lower parts of the Mississippi, whose unhealthy climate, independant of the high price of lands, will counterbalance many other advantages.

It is perhaps good policy in our government, circumstances considered, to thicken the frontier, and to suffer the intermediate space to fill up gradually. But it is scarcely necessary to hold out inducements for this purpose ; it has already taken a start, which it will be almost impossible to arrest. The uncertainty in a great number of the land titles, particularly of the large claimants, presents an obstacle to the torrent of emigration ; but I should not be surprised, if in five years, this territory should contain sixty thousand souls.†

* At present entirely under water, by the earthquake.

† A combination of the most unexpected events have contributed in checking this emigration ; the uncommon unhealthiness of the last season, the dread of Indian war, and the *earthquake.*

The manners of the first settlers, are not such as writers usually represent them. A principal cause of their removal to the frontier, is the want of wild pasturage, or *range*, as it is called, for their cattle; and those who have been accustomed to the greater ease and freedom of this half shepherd life, naturally desire a continuance. These people, advancing westward, into the vast plains which do not admit of compact settlements, may come still nearer to the pastoral state. The remote settlers, contrary to what would be supposed, from their situation, are not only shrewd and intelligent, but also far from illiterate.— The most trifling settlement, will contrive to have a school master, who can teach reading, writing, and some arithmetic. Very different from the good natured, but unenterprising creole, who does not know a letter of the alphabet. A lady, who had resided with her husband two years at fort Osage, three hundred miles up the Missouri, told me, that descending the river, on her return from that place, she observed on the very spot, where, on ascending she had seen a herd of deer, several children with books in their hands, returning from school! The settlement had been formed, while she was at the fort.

The frontier is certainly the refuge of many worthless and abandoned characters, but it is also the choice of many of the noblest souls. It seems wisely ordered, that in the part which is weakest, where the force of laws is scarcely felt, there should be found the greatest sum of real courage, and of disinterested virtue. Few young men who have emigrated to the frontier, are without merit. From the firm conviction, of its future importance, generous and enterprising youth, the virtuous unfortunate, and those of moderate patrimony, repair to it, that they may grow up with the country, and form establishments for themselves and families. Hence in this territory, there are many sterling characters. Amongst others, I mention with pleasure, that brave and adventurous North Carolinian, who makes so distinguished a figure, in the history of Kentucky, the venerable col. Boon. This respectable old man, in the eighty-fifth year of his age, resides on Salt river, up the Missouri, at the settlement I have before mentioned. He is surrounded by about forty families, who respect him as a father, and who live under a kind of

patriarchal government, ruled by his advice and example. They
are not necessitous persons, who have fled for their crimes or
misfortunes, like those that gathered unto David, in the cave of
Adullam; they all live well, and possess the necessaries and
comforts of life, as they could wish. They retired through
choice. Perhaps, they acted wisely in placing themselves at a
distance from the deceit and turbulence of the world. They enjoy an uninterrupted quiet, and a real comfort in their little society, beyond the sphere of that larger society, where government
is necessary; where, without walls of adamant, and bands of iron,
the *Anarch Fiend*, or the *Monster Despotism*, would trample
their security, their happiness, and their dearest possessions under foot. Here they are truly free; exempt from the vexing du-
ties and impositions, even of the best of governments; they are
neither assailed by the madness of ambition, nor tortured by the
poison of party spirit. Is not this, one of the most powerful in-
centives, which impels the *wandering Anglo-American*, to bury
himself in the midst of the wilderness?

The following is an abstract of the population of the territory, according to the last census:

St. Charles	3,505
St. Louis	5,667
St. Genevieve	4.620
Cape Girardeau . . .	3.888
New Madrid	3,103
Hope Field ⎫ St. Francis ⎭	183
Arkansas	874
	21.845

Allow for the troops at the military posts in this territory	200
Hunting and trading parties up the Missouri and Mississippi . . .	300
Families settled in remote places, and not found by the sheriff . . .	300
	22.645

Of these. 8.011 are slaves; the number of civilized Indians
and of metiffs, not known, but cannot be considerable.

CHAPTER V.

TOWNS AND VILLAGES.

AMONGST the Americans, every assemblage of houses, no matter of how small a number, is denominated a *town;* in this country every place except New Orleans, however considerable, or extensive, is called a village. This is right in both cases; the occupation of villages, is principally, the cultivation of the soil. In the states, those who follow the plough, are scattered over the country; while the mechanics, and retailers of merchandise, gather in a cluster. Hence the difference in the appearance of the towns or villages of this country, from those of the states. Although there is something like regularity of streets, and the houses are built in front of them, they do not adjoin, while the gardens, orchards, and stables, occupy a considerable extent of ground. Each house with its appurtenances, has the appearance of one of our farm-yards. All kinds of cattle, cows, hogs, sheep, mingle with the passengers, in the streets. These tenements are generally enclosed with cedar pickets, placed in the manner of stockades, and sometimes with stone walls. The houses are built in a very singular form, and it is said, copied after the fashion of the West Indies. They do not exceed one story in height, and those of the more wealthy are surrounded with spacious galleries; some only on one or two sides, while the poorer class are obliged to put up with naked walls, and a poor habitation. These galleries are extremely useful; they render the house cool and agreeable in summer, and afford a pleasant promenade in the heat of the day.

In building their houses, the logs, instead of being laid horizontally, as ours, are placed in a perpendicular position, the interstices closed with earth or stone, as with us. This constitutes a more durable dwelling, and it retains its shape much longer. The roof is extremely broad, extending out with a gradual slope, for the purpose of affording a covering to the gallery. Within these two years, some alteration is perceptible in the general appearance of the villages, from the introduction of a new mode of building by the Americans of frame, stone, or brick, and in the use of what was before unknown, signs and boards, to indicate the residence of persons following different trades or occupations: although a trifling circumstance, it is a characteristic.

In none of the villages or towns is there a market house; the reason I have already mentioned, the inhabitants raised their own provisions, and were all cultivators of the soil.

ST. LOUIS

Is the seat of government of the territory, and has always been considered the principal town. It was formerly called Pain Court, from the privations of the first settlers.* It is situated in latitude 38° 23' N. long. 89° 36' W.

This place occupies one of the best situations on the Mississippi, both as to site and geographical position. In this last respect, the confluence of the Ohio and Mississippi, has certainly much greater natural advantages, but the ground is subject to inundation, and St. Louis has taken a start, which it will most probably retain. It is perhaps not saying too much, that it bids fair to be second to New Orleans in importance, on this river.

The ground on which St. Louis stands is not much higher than the ordinary banks, but the floods are repelled by a bold shore of limestone rocks. The town is built between the river and a second bank, three streets running parallel with the river, and a number of others crossing these at right angles. It is to be lamented that no space has been left between the town and the river; for the sake of the pleasure of the promenade, as well as for business and health, there should have been no encroachment on the margin of the noble stream. The principal place of business ought to have been on the bank. From the opposite side, nothing is visible of the busy bustle of a populous town; it appears closed up. The site of St. Louis is not unlike that of Cincinnati. How different would have been its appearance, if built in the

---

* Judging from many of the names of villages, one might suppose that they had not been settled under the most happy auspices; there are *Misere*, *Creve-coeur*, and *Vuide poche !*

same elegant manner: its bosom opened to the breezes of the
river, the stream gladdened by the enlivening scene of business
and pleasure, compact rows of elegant and tasteful dwellings,
looking with pride on the broad wave that passes!

From the opposite bank, St. Louis, notwithstanding, appears
to great advantage.   In a disjoined and scattered manner it extends along the river a mile and an half, and we form the idea of
a large and elegant town.   Two or three large and costly buildings (though not in the modern taste) contribute in producing
this effect.   On closer examination, the town seems to be composed of an equal proportion of stone walls, houses, and fruit
trees: but the illusion still continues.

On ascending the second bank, which is about forty feet above
the level of the plain, we have the town below us, and a view of
the Mississippi in each direction, and of the fine country through
which it passes.   When the curtain of wood which conceals the
American bottom shall have been withdrawn, or a vista formed
by opening farms to the river, there will be a delightful prospect into that rich and elegant tract.   The bottom at this place
is not less than eight miles wide, and finely diversified with prairie and woodland.

There is a line of works on this second bank, erected for defence against the Indians, consisting of several circular towers,
twenty feet in diameter, and fifteen in height, a small stockaded
fort, and a stone breast work.   These are at present entirely unoccupied and waste, excepting the fort, in one of the buildings of
which, the courts are held, while another is used as a prison.—
Some distance from the termination of this line, up the river,
there are a number of Indian mounds, and remains of antiquity;
which, while they are ornamental to the town, prove, that in former times, those places had also been chosen as the site, perhaps, of a populous city.

Looking to the west, a most charming country spreads itself
before us.   It is neither very level nor hilly, but of an agreeable
waving surface, and rising for several miles with an ascent almost imperceptible.   Except a small belt to the north, there
are no trees; the rest is covered with shrubby oak, intermixed

with hazels, and a few trifling thickets, of thorn, crab apple, or plum trees. At the first glance we are reminded of the environs of a great city; but there are no country seats, or even plain farm houses: it is a vast waste, yet by no means a barren soil.—— Such is the appearance, until turning to the left, the eye again catches the Mississippi. A number of fine springs take their rise here, and contribute to the unaven appearance. The greater part fall to the S. W. and aid in forming a beautiful rivulet, which a short distance below the town gives itself to the river. I have been often delighted in my solitary walks, to trace this rivulet to its sources. Three miles from town, but within view, amongst a few tall oaks, it rises in four or five silver fountains, within short distances of each other: presenting a picture to the fancy of the poet, or the pencil of the painter. I have fancied myself for a moment on classic ground, and beheld the Naiads pouring the stream from their urns.

Close to the town, there is a fine mill erected by Mr. Choteau, on this streamlet; the dam forms a beautiful sheet of water, and affords much amusement in fishing and fowling, to the people of the town.

The common field of St. Louis was formerly enclosed on this bank, consisting of several thousand acres; at present there are not more than two hundred under cultivation;* the rest of the ground looks like the worn common, in the neighbourhood of a large town; the grass kept down and short, and the loose soil in several places cut open into gaping ravines.

St. Louis was first established in the spring of 1764. It was principally settled by the inhabitants who abandoned the village of Fort Chartres, on the east side of the Mississippi. The colony flourished, and became the parent of a number of little villages on the Mississippi and Missouri; Carondelet, St. Charles, Portage des Sioux, St. Johns, Bon Homme, St. Ferdinand, &c.

From that abominable practice, of urging the northern Indians against the settlers, this place suffered an attack which still excites bitter recollections. In 1779, a combination of the Indian tribes, prompted by the English, attempted a general inva-

* From the American mode of farming having been adopted.

sion of the French villages on both sides of the river, and accordingly descended in considerable force, but were checked by
gen. Clark, who commanded the American troops on the other
side.   An attack was, however, made upon a small settlement,
commenced within a few miles of the town, and the inhabitants
were nearly all butchered: others, who happened to be out of St.
Louis, were killed or pursued within a short distance of the
town.   It is said that upwards of eighty persons fell victims to
their fury. Happily, this will be the last time that St. Louis will
ever have any thing to dread from the Indians ; the frontier has
extended so far north and west, that a complete barrier is formed against future incursions.   They may come here in peace,
and for the purpose of trade, but it will be far hence that they
will dare to raise the tomahawk.

St. Louis contains according to the last census 1,400 inhabitants. One fifth Americans, and about 400 people of color.
There are a few Indians and metiffs, in the capacity of servants,
or wives to boatmen. This town was at no time so agricultural
as the other villages ; being a place of some trade, the chief town
of the province, and the residence of a number of mechanics,
It remained nearly stationary for two or three years after the
cession ; but it is now beginning to take a start, and its reputation is growing abroad. Every house is crowded, rents are
high, and it is exceedingly difficult to procure a tenement on any
terms. Six or seven houses were built in the course of last season, and probably twice the number will be built the next. There
is a printing office, and twelve mercantile stores. The value of
imports to this place in the course of the year, may be estimated at two hundred and fifty thousand dollars. The outfits for
the different trading establishments, on the Mississippi or Missouri, are made here. The lead of the Sac mines is brought to
this place ; the troops at Belle Fontaine put sixty thousand dollars in circulation annually. The settlers in the vicinity on
both sides of the river, repair to this place as the best market
for their produce, and to supply themselves with such articles
as they may need.

The price of marketing does not differ much from the towns
of the western country ; every thing appears to be approximat-

ing to the same standard. Game of all kinds is brought in by the neighbouring Indians, or the poorer inhabitants, and sold for a mere trifle; as venison, turkeys, geese, ducks, swans, prairie hens, &c. Upon the whole, provisions are no higher than in the towns of the Ohio.

The manners of the inhabitants are not different from those in other villages: we distinctly see the character of the ancient inhabitants, and of the new residents, and a compound of both. St. Louis, however, was always a place of more refinement and fashion, it is the residence of many genteel families, both French and American

A few American mechanics, who have settled here, within a short time, are great acquisitions to the place; and there is still ample room for workmen of all kinds. There is a French school and an English one.

St. Louis, will probably become one of those great reservoirs of the valley between the Rocky mountains and the Alleghany, from whence merchandise will be distributed to an extensive country. It unites the advantages of the three noble rivers, Mississippi, Illinois and Missouri. When their banks shall become the residence of millions, when flourishing towns shall arise, can we suppose that every vender of merchandise, will look to New Orleans for a supply, or to the Atlantic cities? There must be a place of distribution, somewhere between the mouth of the Ohio and the Missouri. Besides a trade to the northern parts of New Spain will be opened, and a direct communication to the East Indies, by way of the Missouri, may be more than dreamt: in this, St. Louis will become the *Memphis* of the American Nile.

ST. GENEVIEVE,

Is next in consequence to St. Louis. It is at present the principal deposit of the lead, of Mine la Motte, the Mine á Burton, New Diggings, the mines on Big river, with several others; and is the store-house, from whence those engaged in working the mines are supplied with a variety of articles. This town was commenced about the year 1774.

It is situated about one mile from the Mississippi, between the two branches of a stream called Gabourie, on a flat of about

one hundred acres, and something higher than the river bottom.
There is a second bank about twenty feet higher than this, upon which the town begins at present to extend; this is merely a
slip, however, and bounded by a third bank, eighty feet above the
level of the river: there are also scattered houses for some distance up each branch of the Gabourie. West of the town, and also
north of the Gabourie, the country is high and somewhat broken.
The soil is a yellow clay; in places strewed with horn stone, but
produces good wheat. The timber, has been nearly all destroyed for the use of the inhabitants. In front of the town, on the
Mississippi, there is a fine bottom, commencing from the Gabourie, and extending eight or nine miles down the river; and
for the greater part of that distance, three miles in width. The
common field under fence, contains seven thousand acres.—
There are six stores, and in the course of the present year, the
imports might amount to one hundred and fifty thousand dollars.
St. Genevieve is a rising town; a greater number of buildings
have been erected here than at St. Louis, and preparations are
making for building a number more in the course of the next
season. There are two brick yards. A very handsome edifice
has been erected of limestone, on the hill, commanding an elegant prospect of the river, the American bottom, and of the hills
on the other side of the Kaskaskia. This building is intended
as an academy, but unfortunately, those gentlemen who gener-
ously undertook this work, have not been able fully to succeed,
from the want of proper support.

The population of St. Genevieve including New Bourbon,
amounts to 1,400. There is about the same proportion of slaves,
as at St. Louis; the number of Americans is also about the same.
There was formerly a village of Piorias below the town, but
they abandoned it some time ago.

This appears also to have been one of those spots pitched upon by former and numerous nations of Indians as a place of residence. In the bottom there are a number of large mounds.—
Barrows, and places of interment, are every where to be seen.

The mouth of the Gabourie is about one mile and an half
above the town; it is the landing place and harbor of boats; and

when the water is high, they can come up to the town, of every size.

In the neighbourhood, there are several remarkable fountains, which send forth copious streams of water. One about a mile distant, affords a considerable accession to the Gabourie, and turns a mill a short distance below. The fountain itself, is truly beautiful; after wandering for some time over arid and dry hills, we come all at once into a thick grove of oak, hickory and other trees, and descending a declivity, we discover the fountain, fifteen or twenty feet square, and as many in depth, enclosed on all sides, except the one from whence the stream issues, by masses of living rock, and its glassy surface, shaded with young trees and shrubs. Various beautiful creeping vines, with their flowers, soften the severity of the frowning rock, and sport in festoons woven by the fantastic hand of nature. I recollect a trifling incident, which occurred in one of my visits to this fountain, but which made an impression on my mind. I found a party of about sixty Shawanese warriors encamped near it; after some coversation with the chief, a good old man, and of a remarkable fine figure; why said he, does not some white man build a house and settle himself near this place? but, continued the old chief, seemingly recollecting himself, perhaps some Manitou (spirit) resides here, and will not permit it! How similar is the action of the human mind in all countries, and in all ages. It seems to be a natural sentiment to attribute to whatever is extraordinary, the agency or control of some superior being. The ancient Greeks and Romans, in their highest stage of refinement, carried it so far, as to have divinities for every fountain and river.

St. Genevieve was formerly built immediately on the Mississippi, but the washing away of the bank, and the great flood of 1782 (l'anne' des eaux) caused the inhabitants to choose a higher situation. The ruins of the old town may be still seen, and there are several orchards of fine fruit yet remaining.

The principal employment of the inhabitants is agriculture; but the greater part, are also more or less engaged in the lead mines. This is a career of industry open to all, and the young, in setting out to do something for themselves, usually make

their first essay in this business. A number of the inhabitants
are also employed as boatmen, for the purpose of conducting
voyages. There is some Indian trade, from the neighbouring
Shawanese, Piorias, and Delawares. There are but few mechanics, and these but indifferent. A chapel is erected here, at which
the Rev. Mr. Maxwell officiates.

As the agriculture of St. Genevieve, is carried on more extensively, than in any of the other villages, I shall take this opportunity of giving a description of it. One fence encloses the
whole village field, and this is kept up at the common expense.
The river side is left open, the steepness of the bank rendering
any enclosure unnecessary. This field is divided into a number
of small lots, of an equal size; a certain number of arpents in
front, and a certain number in depth. The more wealthy possess and cultivate several of these lots, while some of the poorer
class do not own one entire. But nearly all the inhabitants have
a share in them; they were ceded by the Spanish government, as an appendage to the possession of every resident-
er in the village. This mode has been practised from the earliest settlements on both sides of the Mississippi, and perhaps
had its origin from necessary precaution against the Indians.
Their agricultural labors commence in the month of April,
when the inhabitants, with their slaves, are seen going and returning, each morning and evening, for eight or ten days, with
their ploughs, carts, horses, &c. The ground is broken up with
a kind of wheel plough, which enters deep into the soil. Corn,
pumpkins, and spring wheat, compose the usual crop. It is now
left entirely to nature, and no further attention is paid to it until
harvest, when each villager, but without that mirth and jollity,
which usually takes place on such occasions, in other countries,
quietly hauls in his own crop. There is a great contrast between the lots cultivated by the Americans, and those of the
creoles; pains are taken to keep them clear of weeds, and this
is rewarded by a crop of at least one third greater. In the
rich alluvia, it is thought, that wheat sowed in the spring is
best; it does not grow so rank, and is less apt to lodge or mil-
dew. There is a kind of weed here resembling hemp, having a
coarse, vigorous stalk, and a strong but not disagreeable smell;

this, the inhabitants cut during summer, to feed their horses. It grows in the rich bottoms, and in great abundance through the common fields; cattle are extremely fond of it. After the harvest is completed, the barriers of the fields are opened, and all the cattle of the village permitted to be turned in. Horses put into the field before this period, (for each one has generally a part of his lot in grass) are tied to long ropes, which are fastened to stakes.

Besides the lots, in the great field, the principal inhabitants, have of late years, opened plantations, within some miles of the town; and the greater part of the stock formerly seen about this place, has been removed to the country farms: in consequence of which, the passengers are enabled to go through the streets without danger of being jostled by horses, cows, hogs, and oxen, which formerly crowded them.

ST. CHARLES.

As well as the two places before described, is the seat of justice of the district bearing its name. It contains three hundred inhabitants, a considerable proportion of them Americans. There are two or three stores, which, besides supplying the country people of the neighbourhood, have some trade with Indian or white hunters, in furs and peltries. But this is in a great measure, the residence of that class of French inhabitants, whose occupation is that of *engagees*, or boatmen. Several genteel families also reside here.

The village is situated on the north side of the Missouri, twenty miles from the junction. It is built on a very narrow space, between the river and the bluff, admitting but one street a mile in length. A short distance below, the bottom becomes wide; the hills behind the village are extremely rough, and scarcely susceptible of tillage. The Missouri is yearly washing away the ground on which this place stands. The common field is situated two miles lower down.

NEW MADRID,*

The seat of justice of the district, and formerly called, *l'Anse a'la gresse*. It is situated in 36° 34 N. long. 89° 20 W. Though in a low state of improvement at present, it ought to become important. It will be the store-house of the produce of an extensive and fertile country ; and from the St. Francis and the lakes which lie S. W. it may derive important advantages. New Madrid was laid out twenty-four years ago, by col. Geo. Morgan, on an extensive scale, and an elegant plan. It was chosen as one of the best situations on the river. The town contains four hundred inhabitants, one third Americans, living in a scattered way, over a great space of ground. It is the residence of several amiable and genteel families, from whom, I acknowledge with pleasure, to have received much kindness and hospitality. There is, however, a due proportion of the worthless and despicable part of society.

At New Madrid, the Mississippi has assumed the shape of a half moon, in the hollow of which, the town stands. The bank is high, but the washing away has been astonishingly great, at least three hundred yards have disappeared. Three forts, and a number of large and spacious streets have been taken away, within these fifteen years. From the course which the river has now assumed, it is probable that this will cease, and such is the character of this wonderful stream, that in a few years, New Madrid may be left far from its bank.

* It might appear useless to insert this description ; the town having been nearly destroyed by the earthquake† ; but it may be curious to record what it once was.

† We are informed that the shocks at this place have entirely ceased, and that this town, which had been almost depopulated, is again beginning to be re-established. Where the town stood, the ground has sunk so much, that in the last flood it was entirely overflowed ; but, a short distance below, the ground which was before low, is now at least five feet above the highest water. Several lakes are now cornfields.— There are hopes that this beautiful district will soon regain its former advantages.

At the upper end of the town there is a considerable stream, of which I have already spoken, and might, at most seasons, be navigated to its source; at New Madrid it is called the Bayou St. John, and affords an excellent harbor. Below the town there is a beautiful lake, six or eight feet deep, with a clear sandy bottom, and communicating with the St. Francis, and the Mississippi, in high water. On the bank of this lake, about four miles from New Madrid, there is one of the largest Indian mounds in the western country: as near as I could compute, it is twelve hundred feet in circumference, and about forty in height, level on the top, and surrounded with a ditch five feet deep and ten wide. In this neighbourhood there are traces of a great population.

The country in the vicinity of New Madrid, is a vast plain of the richest soil, handsomely diversified with prairie and woodland. There is not much business done at this place; two or three mercantile stores are established, but not extensively; yet I should think this, a situation extremely eligible for a person of enterprise.

New Madrid is considered healthy, and from my own experience, I am convinced of the justice of this character. There is nothing more delightful than a promenade in a summer evening, on the smooth green along the bank. The climate is mild and agreeable; in the hottest days of summer, a cool and refreshing breeze is felt from the river. The spring is comparatively early. I ate strawberries here the twentieth of April, and at St. Louis in June. New Madrid deserves to be noted for having the first gardens in the territory.

ARKANSAS.

This place is situated sixty miles up the river, and contains four hundred and fifty inhabitants; it has a few stores, and seems to be improving. There is a considerable trade with the Osages up the Arkansas, and with the Indians, who live in the White river country. This is also a French establishment, and with about the same proportion of Americans as in the other towns.

CAPE GIRARDEAU,

The seat of justice for the district of that name, and situated thirty-five miles above the mouth of the Ohio. This town is entirely American, and built in their fashion. It is thriving fast: there are a number of good houses, several of them of brick. It contains about thirty dwellings, and three hundred inhabitants.

The town is situated on a high bluff, but the descent to the river is not difficult. From its situation, and the excellence of the surrounding country, this town bids fair to become a flourishing place. Two stores are established here, though on a small scale. I have the pleasure of being acquainted with several amiable families.

HERCULANEUM,

On the Mississippi, half way between St. Louis, and St. Genevieve.

The situation of this place is extremely romantic; at the mouth of the Joachin, and on a flat of no great width, between the river hill and second bank, while at each end, perpendicular precipices, two hundred feet high, rise almost from the water's edge. It appears to be an opening for the admission of the Joachin to the Mississippi. On the top of each of these cliffs, shot towers have been established. The town contains twenty houses, and two hundred inhabitants; here is a store, an excellent blacksmith, and a hatter. The country behind the town is hilly, but well timbered, and land good. Several fine mills have been erected in the neighbourhood of this place, and boat building is carried on here.

Carondelet, or Vuidepoche, is situated six miles below St. Louis—218 inhabitants. Florissant on the Missouri, 270. Mine La Motte, 250—and a number of other small villages. A village has lately been commenced at the mouth of the St. Francis.

CHAPTER VI.

THERE is scarcely any thing more difficult, and consequently more rare, than correct delineation of character:—This task is usually undertaken by friends or enemies, and the result is either panegyrick or satire.—Even amongst such as are unbiassed, how few the happy copyists, who can paint nature with her own colors, so as to be recognized by every beholder!

Conscious of this difficulty, I entertain humble hopes of success, in being able to satisfy the expectation and inquiries of the intelligent reader. And, particularly where there are no striking and prominent features, but the traits of an infant colony delicately marked.

A colony will not remain long separated from the parent stock, until it exhibits a peculiar and distinct character. Climate, situation, and country, although not exclusively the agents in forming this character, must nevertheless, be admitted to have great influence. Nor do the manners of the parent country continue invariable ; other times, other men, other circumstances, produce the most surprising changes, while the colony, beyond the sphere of their influence, retains its pristine customs and manners. The Spaniards of Mexico, are said to bear a stronger resemblance to their ancestors of the fifteenth century, than to their present brethren of Old Spain:—The French inhabitants of the Mississippi, have little resemblance to the gay, and perhaps frivolous, Frenchmen of Louis the fifteenth and sixteenth, and still less to those who have felt the racking storm of the revolution.

To the country on both sides of the Mississippi, the general name, *Les Illinoix*, was given. It was inhabited by a powerful Indian nation of that name, at present reduced o a handful of miserable creatures. After the discovery of the Mississippi, by Mons. Joliet and the priest Marquette, from Canada, a number of Canadian traders, about the year 1680. settled in Kaskaskia, a large Indian town. By degrees, a number of families were induced to quit Canada, for a country represented as much more desirable. A monastery of Jesuits was established here, which succeeded in converting a number of the Indians to christianity. I am credibly informed, that they had at one time, five hundred catechumens In time, these people, as it has ever been the case, were found to degenerate and diminish, from their intercourse with the whites : and the French were left the possessors and proprietors of their village.

About the beginning of the last century, the celebrated scheme, of *Law, and Company*, was set on foot, and supported by the high reputation for wealth and fertility, which Louisiana had already required. To further this delusion, it was represented in still more glowing colors, and it became the paradise of Frenchmen. The Illinois was regarded as of immense importance ; the attention of the nation was turned towards it, and notwithstanding the failure of Law's project, this remote colony flourished surprisingly. Besides Kaskaskia, which became a considerable place, there were several large villages, a lucrative fur trade was carried on, and an extensive agriculture.— These settlements sent to New Orleans in one year, (1746) eight hundred thousand weight of flour. But, at this time there was not one permanent establishment on the west side of the Mississippi, although resorted to by traders, and the lead mines were known and worked. Twenty-five or thirty years after the failure of Law, the French, with something more substantial in view, had formed the plan of securing the great valley of the Mississippi, and of connecting it with Canada ; immense sums of money were expended. Fort Chartres, which is said to have cost the crown, nine millions of livres, was built, and the village of Fort Chartres rose by its side ; but alas ! such are the reverses of fortune, even in this newly peopled region, the gay and sprightly village has disappeared forever, and the fort is but a noble ruin. This fort was deemed an important one, at which there was stationed an officer of rank, with a suitable command. Much of the elegance and refinement of the officers was communicated to the susceptible inhabitants.

The war between France and England, which broke out about the year 1754, deprived France of her possessions in this part of the world. In consequence of this, les Illinoix experi-

enced a sudden and rapid decay; which was again accelerated
by the conquest of general Clark for the United States, in
1779.   The greater number of the wealthy and respectable
inhabitants descended the Mississippi, and settled in New Orleans, and the lower country.   Others crossed the Mississippi,
and established St. Louis and St. Genevieve.   Scarcely any but
natives of the country remained.   The foreigners chiefly returned to the countries from whence they first emigrated.

Such then, is the origin of the greater part of that class of the
population of this territory, which I have denominated the ancient inhabitants.   They are chiefly natives of the country; but
few families are immediately from France, or even from New
Orleans or Canada.

In the character of these people, it must be remembered, that
they are essentially Frenchmen; but, without that restlessness,
impatience and fire, which distinguishes the European.   There
is, even in their deportment, something of the gravity of the
Spaniard, though gay, and fond of amusements.   From the gentle and easy life which they led, their manners, and even language, have assumed a certain degree of softness and mildness:
the word *paisible*, expresses this characteristic.   In this remote
country, there were few objects to urge to enterprise, and few
occasions to call forth and exercise their energies.   The necessaries of life were easily procured, and beggary was unknown.
Hospitality was exercised as in the first ages, for there were no
taverns.   Ambition soared far hence, for here there was no prey.
Judges, codes of law, and prisons, were of little use, where such
simplicity of manners prevailed, and where every one knew how
far to confide in his neighbour.   In such a state of things, to what
end is learning or science?   The schools afforded but slender
instruction; the better sort of people acquired in them reading,
writing, and a little arithmetic.   The number of those who were
lovers of knowledge, and made it a profession, was small.   From
the habits of these people, it would naturally be expected, that
they would have been unaccustomed to reason on political subjects; they were in fact, as ignorant of them, as children are
of life and manners.   These inhabitants were as remarkable for
their tame and peaceable disposition, as the natives of France are
for the reverse.

Amongst their virtues, we may enumerate honesty and punctuality in their dealings, hospitality to strangers, friendship and affection amongst relatives and neighbours. Instances of abandonment on the female side, or of seduction, are extremely rare. The women make faithful and affectionate wives, but will not be considered secondary personages in the matrimonial association. The advice of the wife is taken on all important, as well as on less weighty concerns, and she generally decides. In opposition to these virtues, it must be said, that they are devoid of public spirit, of enterprise or ingenuity, and are indolent and uninformed.

They are catholics, but, very far from being bigoted or superstitious, as some travellers have said. They were perhaps more strict observers, formerly, of the rules and discipline of their church, and of the different holy days in the calendar. Their *fetes*, or celebration of these days, were considered, as the most interesting occasions; the old and young engaged in them with the greatest delight, and they doubtless contributed to their happiness. Of late, this attention to the ceremonies of their religion is considerably relaxed, since other objects of pursuit and interest have been opened to their view. The catholic worship is the only one yet known in the territory, except in private families, and in a few instances of itinerant preachers.

There was scarcely any distinction of classes in the society. The wealthy or more intelligent, would of course be considered as more important personages, but there was no difference clearly marked. They all associated, dressed alike, and frequented the same ball room. They were in fact nearly all connected by the ties of affinity or consanguinity: and so extensive is it, that I have seen the carnival, from the death of a common relation, pass by cheerless and unheeded. The number of persons excluded was exceedingly small. What an inducement to comport ones self with propriety and circumspection! The same interest at stake, the same sentiments that in other countries influence the first classes of society, were here felt by all its members. Perhaps as many from unmerited praise have been formed into valuable characters, as others from having been unjustly despised have become truly despicable.

Their wealth consisted principally in personal property, lands were only valuable when improved. Slaves were regarded in the light of *bien foncier*, or real property, and in fact, as the highest species. Lead and peltry were frequently used as the circulating medium.

There was but little variety in their employments. The most enterprising and wealthy were traders, and had at the same time trifling assortments of merchandise for the accommodation of the inhabitants, but there were no open shops or stores, as in the United States. There were no tailors or shoemakers; such as pursue these occupations at present, are from the United States. The few mechanics, exercising their trades, principally carpenters and smiths, scarcely deserved the name. The lead mines, I have already observed, engaged a considerable number. The government gave employment to but few, and those principally at St. Louis. By far the greater proportion of the population was engaged in agriculture; in fact, it was the business of all, since the surplus produce of the country was too inconsiderable to be depended upon. A number of the young men for some time, embraced the employment of boatmen, which was by no means considered degrading; on the contrary, it was desirable for a young man to have it to say, that he had made a voyage in this capacity: and they appeared proud of the occupation, in which they certainly are not surpassed by any people in dexterity. It is highly pleasing to see them exerting themselves, and giving encouragement to each other, by their cheering songs—

> —— adductis spumant freta versa lacertis.
> Infindunt pariter sulcos ; totumque dehiscit
> Convulsum remis, rostrisque tridentibus aequor.

But this occupation, amongst many other changes, has been reduced to the same footing as with the Americans. Arising probably from the simple cause, of there having arisen objects of more generous emulation.

What is somewhat strange, there were no domestic manufactures among them; the spinning wheel and the loom were alike unknown. So deficient were they in this respect, that al-

though possessed of numerous herds, they were not even acquainted with the use of the churn, but made their butter by
beating the cream in a bowl, or shaking it in a bottle.

Their amusements, were cards, billiards, and dances: this
last of course the favorite. The dances, were cotillions, reels,
and sometimes the minuet. During the carnival, the balls follow in rapid succession. They have a variety of pleasing customs, connected with this amusement. Children have also their
balls, and are taught a decorum and propriety of behavior,
which is preserved through life. They have a certain ease and
freedom of address, and are taught the secret of real politeness,
self-denial; but which by the apes of French manners, is mistaken for an affected grimace of complaisant regard, and a profusion of bows, scrapes and professions.

Their language, every thing considered, is more pure than
might be expected; their manner of lengthening the sound of
words, although languid, and without the animation which the
French generally possess, is by no means disagreeable. They
have some new words, and others are in use, which in France
have become obsolete.

In their persons, they are well formed, of an agreeable pleasant countenance; indicating cheerfulness and serenity. Their
dress was formerly extremely simple; the men wore a blanket
coat, of coarse cloth or coating, with a cape behind, which
could be drawn over the head; from which circumstance it was
called a *capote.* They wore a blue handkerchief on their heads:
but no hats, or shoes, or stockings; moccasins, or the Indian
sandals, were used by both sexes. The dress of the females was
likewise simple, and the variations of fashion, few: though they
were dressed in a much better taste than the other sex. These
manners will soon cease to exist, but in remembrance and description: every thing has changed. The American costume is
generally introduced, amongst the first families, and amongst the
young girls and young men universally. I never saw any where
greater elegance of dress than at the balls of St Louis. We still
see a few of both sexes in their ancient habiliments; capots,
moccasins, blue handkerchiefs on the head, a pipe in the mouth,
and the hair tied up in a long queue. These people exhibit a

striking difference when compared with the unconquerable per-
tinacity of the Pennsylvania Germans, who adhere so rigidly to
the customs, manners, and language of their fathers. A few
years have effected more change with the inhabitants of this
territory than has been brought about amongst the Germans in
fifty years.

The *government*, of the province, though a mixture of the
civil and military, was simple. Each district had its commandant,
or syndic. These were the judges in civil matters under a certain amount, and had also command of the militia. They received their appointment from the intendant at New Orleans, to
whom there was an appeal, from their decisions, and where were
also referred such matters as exceeded their jurisdiction. Arbi-
trators under the direction of the commandant, in some degree
obviated his want of authority. The mode of proceeding is singular enough; the party complaining obtained a notification from
the commandant to his adversary of the complaint, accompanied by a command from the commandant, to render the com-
plainant justice. If this had no effect he was notified to appear
before the commandant on a particular day, and answer the complaint; and if this last notice was neglected, a sergeant, with a
file of men, was sent to bring him.

The lieut. governor, who resided at St. Louis, was the commander of the militia, and had a general superintendance of the
public works and property, but I do not know the exact extent
of his powers. The laws of Spain were in force here: but it
does not appear that any others had been in practice, besides
those, which related to lands and the municipal arrangements.
Laws regulating civil contracts, are so intimately interwoven
with the manners of a people, that it is no easy task to separate
them: here *la coutume de Paris*, the common law of France,
was the system by which their contracts were governed. The
judges, in administering justice according to the American jurisprudence, are often perplexed by the article of Session, which
provides, that respect should be paid to the usages and customs
of the country. A few troops were kept up in each district,
throughout the province, but too inconsiderable to afford much
protection to the inhabitants. This country being so remote

from the main possessions of Spain, was not regarded with much
attention, when we consider its natural importance. The rod of
government was so light as scarcely to be felt; the worst of the
governors, were content, with imposing on their king, by exor-
bitant charges for useless fortifications, or for supplies never furnished. I have heard of some oppressions practised on strangers, but I have been informed by a number of Americans settled here before the change, that the Spanish government treated them with particular attention and respect. I believe, instances of individual oppressions on the part of the governors, were
few: but this is to be attributed, not to the government, but to
the state of society.

The present government appears to be operating a general
change: its silent but subtle spirit is felt in every nerve and vein,
of the body politic. The United States, acting upon broad principles, cannot be influenced by contemptible partialities between
their own sons and their adopted children. They do not want colonies—they will disdain to hold others in the same state, which
they themselves so nobly despised. They are in fact, both natives
of the same land, and both can claim *Freedom* as their birth right.

It requires many hands to work the complicated machinery
of our government; the object of which, is to enable men, as
much as possible, to govern themselves. Each of the principal
towns, has its officers, its legislature, in which the ancient inhabitants have the principal voice. They have been placed on
the bench, they are jurors and magistrates; commissions are
distributed, which, although not regarded of much importance
in time of peace, yet they make a man feel that he counts something in his country; for instance, in the militia, there are gene-
rals, colonels, majors, captains, &c. Thus, one might suppose
that their manners and habits of thinking were gradually preparing for the reception of a free government. The Americans
have communicated to them, their industry and spirit of enterprise, and they in turn, have given some of their more gentle and
amiable customs. Upon the whole, the American manners, and
even language, begin to predominate. The young men have already been formed by our government, and those growing up
will have known no other. A singular change has taken place,

which, one would think, ought not to be the result of a transition from a despotism to a republican government: luxury has increased in a wonderful degree, and there exists something like a distinction in the classes of society. On the other hand, more pains are taken with the education of youth ; some have sent their sons to the seminaries of the United States, and all seem anxious to attain this desirable end. Several of the young men have entered the army of the United States, and have discovered talents. The females are also instructed with more care, and the sound of the Piano is now heard in their dwellings for the first time.

Personal property, a few articles excepted, has fallen on an average, two hundred per cent. in value, and real property risen at least five hundred. But the prices of merchandise had no proportion to the price of produce. Five bushels of corn were formerly necessary for the purchase of a handkerchief, which can now be had for one. The cultivators raised little produce beyond what was necessary for their own subsistence, it was therefore held at high prices, but fell far short of the present proportion to the price of imported articles ; the petty trade was the principal dependence for these supplies. Their agriculture was so limited, that instances have been known, of their having been supplied by the king, on the failure of their crops from the inundation of the Mississippi. The low value of lands naturally arose from the great quantities lying waste, and unoccupied, in proportion to the extent of the population, or of its probable increase, and the consequent facility with which it could be obtained. Rent was scarcely known.

It may be questioned, whether the poorest class has been benefited by the change. Fearless of absolute want, they always lived in a careless and thoughtless manner ; at present the greater part of them obtain a precarious subsistence. They generally possess a cart, a horse or two, a small stock of cattle, and cultivate small plots of ground. At St. Louis they have more employment than in the other villages ; they make hay in the prairies, haul wood for sale, and are employed to do trifling jobs in town ; some are boatmen or patrons. At St. Genevieve, they depend more upon their agriculture, and have portions in the great field, but this will probably soon be taken from them by the greater industry of the American cultivators, who are continually purchasing, and who can give double the sum for rent; they are sometimes employed in hauling lead from the mines, but it will not be sufficient for their support. A number have removed to the country, and, in imitation of the Americans, have settled down on public lands, but here they cannot expect to remain long. Those who live in the more remote villages, are less affected by the change, but there is little prospect of their being better situated. But few of them have obtained permission, from the commandant, to settle on lands; in fact, there was no safety from the depredations of the Indians, in forming establishments beyond the villages. Land was only valued for what it could produce, and any one could obtain as much as he chose to cultivate.

Until possession was taken of the country by us, there was no safety from the robberies of the Osage Indians. That impolitic lenity, which the Spanish and even the French government have manifested towards them, instead of a firm though just course, gave rise to the most insolent deportment on their part. I have been informed by the people of St. Genevieve, who suffered infinitely the most, that they were on one occasion left without a horse to turn a mill. The Osages were never followed to any great distance or overtaken; this impunity necessarily encouraged them. They generally entered the neighbourhood of the villages, divided into small parties, and during the night, stole in and carried away every thing they could find, frequently breaking open stables, and taking out the horses. After uniting at a small distance, their place of rendezvous, they marched leisurely home, driving the stolen horses before them, and without the least dread of being pursued. They have not dared to act in this manner under the present government; there have been a few solitary instances of robberies by them, within these three or four years, but they are sufficiently acquainted with the Americans to know, that they will be instantly pursued, even into their villages and compelled to surrender. The following well attested fact, will serve to show the insolence of the Osages under the former government. A young couple on their way

from the settlement, just then formed on Big river, to St Genevieve, accompanied by a number of their friends, with the intention of having the matrimonial knot tied by the priest, were
met by sixty Osages, robbed of their horses, and the whole party actually stripped! What serves, however, to lessen the atro-
city of these outrages, it has been remarked, that they are never
known to take away the lives of those who fall into their hands.
The insolence of the other nations who came openly to their
villages, the Piorias, Loups, Kickapoos, Chickasas, Cherokees,
&c. is inconceivable. They were sometimes perfectly masters
of the villages, and ex;ited general consternation. I have seen
the houses on some occasions closed up, and the doors barred by
the terrified inhabitants; they were not always safe even there.
It is strange how these people have entirely disappeared within a few years, there are at present scarcely a sufficient number
to supply the villages with game.

The historical epocha of this territory, are few and simple.
Shortly after the first formation of the settlement, it was ceded
by the treaty of '63; the secret treaty between Spain and
France of 1762, was not known, and perhaps never would have
been, if France had proved successful in her contest with Britain. The history of Louisiana, generally, until it came into
the hands of the United States, is the history of this territory.
By the treaty of Ildefonso, of Oct 1800, this country was receded by Spain to France; the situation of France at that period
not permitting her to take possession, she ceded it to the U.
States. The fear of its falling into the hands of her enemy was a
strong inducement.

On the part of the United States, possession was taken of this
territory in 1804, by capt. (now major Stoddard) who was our
first civil commandant. In pursuance of the act of congress,
which separated it from the district of Orleans, with the name
of the district of Louisiana, it was placed for the moment, under
the government of the territory of Indiana. Governor Harrison,
of that territory, accordingly, organized the government, and
put it in motion In 1805, it was erected into a territorial government similar to that of the other territories, by the name of

the *Territory of Louisiana*.* For these things I must refer the
reader to the different acts of congress on the subject. Two
important treaties were formed with the Indians, one with the
Sacs and Foxes, and the other with the Great and Little Osages.

If I am asked, whether the ancient inhabitants are more
contented, or happy, under the new order of things, or have reason to be so, I should consider the question a difficult one, and
answer it with hesitation. It is not easy to know the secret
sentiments of men, and happiness is a relative term. It is true,
I have heard murmurings against the present government, and
something like sorrowing after that of Spain, which I rather attributed to momentary chagrin, than to real and sincere sentiment; besides, this generally proceeds from those who were
wont to bask in the sunshine of favor. Yet I have not observed those signs which unequivocally mark a suffering and unhappy people. The principal source of uneasiness arises from the
difficulties of settling the land claimed by the commissioners on
the part of the United States. The principal inhabitants have
lost much of that influence which they formerly possessed, and
are superseded in trade and in lucrative occupations by strangers; their claims therefore constitute their chief dependence.
The subject of those claims embraces such a variety of topics,
that it is not possible to give any correct idea of them in this
cursory view. It is a subject on which the claimants are feel-
ingly alive. This anxiety is a tacit compliment to our government, for under the former, their claims would be scarcely worth
attention. The general complaint is, the want of sufficient liberal-
ity in determining on the claims. There is perhaps too great a
disposition to lean against the larger concessions, some of which
are certainly very great, but when we consider the trifling value
of lands under the Spanish government, there will appear less
reason for this prepossession against them. For many reasons,
it would not be to the honor of the United States, that too
much strictness should be required in the proof, or formalities

* The territory of Orleans has now become the " state of Louisiana"
and the " territory of Louisiana" has been changed to the "territory of
the Missouri.

of title, particularly of a people who came into their power with
out any participation on their part, and without having been
consulted. Six years have passed away without the final adjust-
ment of the claims, and even those that have been decided upon,
will give rise to lawsuits; it is probable there will be as copious
a harvest of these as ever was furnished by any of the states.

The lower class have never been in the habit of thinking beyond what immediately concern themselves; they cannot therefore, be expected to foresee political consequences. They were
formerly under a kind of dependence, or rather vassallage, to the
great men of villages, to whom they looked up for their support
and protection. Had they been more accustomed to think it
possible, that by industry it was in their power to become rich,
and independent also, the change would have been instantly felt
in their prosperity. But they possess a certain indifference and
apathy, which cannot be changed till the present generation shall
pass away. They are of late observed to become fond of intoxicat-
ing liquors. There is a middle class, whose claims or possessions were not extensive, but sure, and from the increased value
of their property, have obtained since the change of government,
a handsome competence. They, upon the whole, are well satisfied; I have heard many of them express their approbation of the
American government, in the warmest terms. They feel and
speak like freemen, and are not slow in declaring, that formerly
the field of enterprise was occupied by the monopolies of a few,
and it is now open to every industrious citizen.

There are some things in the administration of justice, which
they do not yet perfectly comprehend; the trial by jury, and the
multifarious forms of our jurisprudence. They had not been
accustomed to distinguish between the slow and cautious advances of *even-handed justice*, and the despatch of arbitrary power.* In their simple state of society, when the subjects of litiga-
tion were not of great value, the administration of justice might
be speedy and simple; but they ought to be aware, that when a

* Some of the more important lawsuits, however, where more extensive bribery could be carried on, are known to have slept for fifteen
years.

society becomes extensive, and its occupations, relations and interests, more numerous, people less acquainted with each other,
the laws must be more complex. The trial by jury, is foreign
to the customs and manners of their ancestors; it is therefore
not to be expected that they should at once comprehend its util-
ity and importance.

The chief advantages which accrued from the change of government, may be summed up in a few words. The inhabitants
derived a security from the Indians; a more extensive field,
and a greater reward was offered to industry and enterprise;
specie became more abundant, and merchandise cheaper.—
Landed property was greatly enhanced in value. In opposition,
it may be said, that formerly they were more content, had less
anxiety; there was more cordiality and friendship, living in the
utmost harmony, with scarcely any clashing interests. This perhaps, is not unlike the notions of old people, who believe that in
their early days every thing was more happily ordered.

The idea of their becoming extinct, by dissolving before a
people of a different race, and of losing their *moeurs cheries*,
might excite unhappy sensations. Already the principal villages look like the towns of the Americans. Are not the customs and manners of our fathers, and of our own youth, dear
to us all? Would it not fill our hearts with bitterness, to see
them vanish as a dream? Sentiments like these, doubtless,
sometimes steal into their hearts. They awake, and their HOME
has disappeared.

But is it likely that this state of society could have been of
long continuance? The policy which had been commenced of
encouraging American settlers, would by this time have over-
whelmed them with a torrent of emigration. Isolated as they
were, they could not have withstood this accumulating wave of
population. Had they been transferred to France, they would
have suffered from exactions and conscriptions; had they remained attached to Spain, what miseries might not have assailed them from the convulsed state of the Spanish monarchy!—
And is it nothing to exchange the name of colonists, creoles, for
that of AMERICANS, for that of a citizen of an independent state,
where they can aspire to the highest employments and honors?

T

There are some, who can feel what it is to be exalted to the dignity of freemen; to the base and ignoble mind which cannot appreciate this blessing, my writings are not addressed. Louisiani-
ans, you have now become truly Americans; never will you
again be transferred from one nation to another; IF YOU ARE
EVER SOLD AGAIN, IT WILL BE FOR BLOOD.

At the same time, let us allow, for those emotions which must
naturally be felt. Like two streams that flow to each other from
remote and distant climes, although at length, included in the
same channel, it is not all at once that they will unite their con-
tributary waters, *and mingle into one.*

CHAPTER VII.

LEAD MINES IN THE DISTRICT OF ST. GENEVIEVE—MODE OF
MINING—PRODUCE, &c.

THE different mines, or *diggings*, as they are commonly
called, are scattered over the greater part of this district. It is
not known with certainty, to what distance the mineral extends
west and south, or towards the Mississippi.* The Mine à Burton, about forty miles west of St. Genevieve, may be considered
the centre of those which are profitably worked.

These mines have been known for a great many years; for
the discovery would be made, as soon as the country could be
traversed; the ore being visible in the ravines washed by
rains, and in the beds of rivulets. The first diggings were made
by a man of the name of Renault, and so extensively, that the
present are only following up the old one.†

---

* On the Osage river, and in the country watered by White river, I
am informed by hunters, that lead ore is found in surprising quantities, even on the surface of the ground.

† See Abby Raynal—"To give the greater weight to this false report, which had already gained so much credit, a number of miners
were sent over to work these mines, which were imagined so valuable
with a body of troops to defend them."

The famous Mississippi Company, was founded principally
upon the supposed wealth, in minerals of the more precious
kinds, in Louisiana; and it was necessary to do something, to
give it an appearance of seriousness. Renault was therefore
sent, it is said, with five hundred men to search for minerals. The
number and great extent of these diggings attest the assiduity
of his researches. Perhaps, Renault not being able to find gold,
or silver ore, sufficient to reward his labor, turned his attention
to smelting lead; and there is reason to believe that very great
quantities were made.

But after the failure of the company before mentioned, it
does not appear that the lead mines were much attended to; nor
even after the crossing of the French settlements to the western side of the Mississippi, and the establishment of St. Genevieve. The lead made before the change of government, was
not a tenth of what is smelted now, and the value scarcely a third.

The object of this view, is to give some account of the different mines, the manner of working them, their produce, &c.

1. What is called a *discovery*, by those engaged in working
the mines, is, when any one happens upon an extensive body of
ore. This is made, by digging several holes or pits, five or six
feet deep, in some spot supposed to contain ore, and if a considerable quantity is at once found, the place is called a discovery; but
if only a few pounds, it is abandoned. But the fact is, that there
are few places, throughout the mine tract, in which such discoveries cannot be made, though perhaps, with different degrees
of labor. Several are made every season, and each continues
for a time in vogue, and the miners flock to it from all the others,
until the report spreads of the discovery of some new spot,
where the ore is found in still greater abundance, and procured
with more ease; to this place they are again attracted. A *discovery* is at length fixed upon, which obtains the preference
throughout the rest of the season. A discovery is sometimes
published when there is not much to warrant it, but the number
of persons drawn to the place, make one in reality.

2. The ore is most commonly found in the slopes, near rivulets, in a clay of a deep red color; frequently but a few feet from
the surface of the ground, and in huge masses, of sometimes a

thousand and even two thousand lbs. but most usually in lumps from one to fifty lbs. weight. The rock which is either a primitive limestone, or a kind of sandstone, is struck at the depth of eight or ten feet. Various kinds of clay are often found in these pits, and amongst some other substances, the *blende ore* of zinc has been discovered. The ore contains a considerable proportion of sulphur, arsenic, and it is believed, of silver; though in respect to the last, it has not been sufficiently tested by experiments, to know whether the proportion would repay the trouble and expense of separating it. It is highly probable that the ore of some of the mines, may yield it sufficiently The ore of the Maramek, which, I am informed, has been partially essayed, gave the most flattering result. Above the rock, the ore is found in enormous masses, in strata, apparently horizontal, and often two feet thick, and several of these are passed before the rock arrests the progress of the miner. I have seen pits ten or twelve feet deep where the strata of ore had only been dug through, the digger intending to strike the rock before he attempted to undermine; perhaps, gratifying his vanity with the pleasing contemplation of the shining mineral, his riches. In the rock there appears to be no regular veins; the ore occupies the accidental fissures, as is the case generally in lead mines. Leads, (or loads) are the smaller fissures that connect with the larger, which are called by the miners, *caves.* The ore is what is called potter's ore, or galena, and has a broad shining grain; but there is also, what is called gravel ore, from being found in small pieces in gravel; and that kind of ore called *floats,* being formed in large irregular, but unconnected masses. The first kind is the most to be depended on: the uncertainty of the floats, and the trouble of smelting the gravel ore, render both of less consequence.— The potter's ore, or galena, has always adhering to it, a sparry matter, which the miners call tiif, and which requires to be separated with small picks made for that purpose: this operation is called *cleaning* the ore. The floats have no tiif, and are the most easily smelted.

3. The mode of working the mines is exceedingly simple. The word *diggings,* by which they are known, very well designates the appearance of these places; pits, and heaps of clay

thrown out of them, covering sometimes fifty acres or more.—
With two or three exceptions, there is scarcely any place
which might be termed mining. There is but one shaft,
which is at the Mine à Burton, and sunk by Moses Austin. The
miners usually work them upon their own account, and dispose
of their ore to the smelters: there are some, however, who hire
hands by the month, or employ slaves. But experience has
shewn that it is best for the interests of both the digger and
the smelter to pursue the first mode; from the chance to the
one of falling upon a good body of ore, and to the other of the
general uncertainty; the keeping a number of persons in constant pay for a length of time before he would be remunerated
by a profitable discovery. If mining were carried on in a proper
manner, the case would be different; the profits might then be
susceptible of calculation, but this scratching the surface of the
earth cannot be attended with certainty. To find a large body of
ore, so near the surface, although not unfrequent, yet cannot be
depended upon; it is little better than a lottery. The miners
have a variety of rules amongst themselves, to prevent disputes
in diggings. Each one takes a pole, and measures off twelve
feet in every direction from the edge; the pits seldom exceed
eight or ten feet in diameter. He is not permitted to undermine
farther than his twelve feet, but must dig a new pit if the ground
be not occupied. The only instruments are a pick, wooden sho-
vel, and a sledge hammer, to break rocks. The ore delivered
at the pit, sells from twenty to twenty-five dollars per thousand
lbs. A digger will sometimes raise two thousand in one day, but
notwithstanding, these people do not grow rich faster than their
neighbours. What is easily earned is carelessly spent; and besides, it often happens that the miner will work for months without making a cent, before he has the luck of lighting on this
treasure. It sometimes happens that he will quit in despair, a
pit at which he has been laboring for months, while another
leaps in, and after a few hours work, falls upon a body of ore that
would have rewarded the labors of the first. The appearance
of ore in a pit which has been the work of a few days, is frequently such as to enable him to sell it for four or five hundred
dollars. This kind of gaming, for it scarcely deserves any other

name, gives rise to great industry and satisfaction in the miners. The constant stretch of expectation in which the mind is kept, gives a zest to their labors.

4. The careless mode of smelting in use proves the great a-bundance of the ore. There is but one regular furnace, the rest are of a temporary and simple construction. The most common are built on the declivity of some hill, with stones, open at the top, and with an arch below. Three large logs about four feet wide, so as to fit the furnace, are rolled in, smaller pieces of wood placed round, and the ore then heaped up in large lumps: fire is set to it in the evening, and by the next morning there will be a sufficient quantity of the melted lead in the little reservoir or hole, scratched in the earth before the arch, to commence the operation of pouring it into moulds to form pigs. There are usually several of these furnaces joined together. About six thou-sand lbs. of ore are put into each, and the first smelting produces 50 per cent, besides leaving a quantity of scori or scorched ore. The ashes, which contain particles of ore and scori, are wash-ed, and smelted in a furnace of a different construction, and often yield twenty-five or thirty per cent more. The ore smelted in this rude way, may be safely considered as yielding seventy-five per cent. There remains a dark green substance called slag, which on late examination, is thought still to retain a proportion of lead worth pursuing. There is no process of pounding or washing, except at the air furnace. The three modes of smelt-ing, to wit, the *open furnace*, the *ash furnace*, and the air furnace, (belonging to Mr. Austin,) have all been introduced since the Americans took possession of the country. The creoles never smelted any other way than by throwing the lead on log heaps. Each of the diggings has its smelting furnace, and the ore is smelted on the spot. The business of smelting is considered unhealthy, but that of mining remarkably the reverse. This un-healthiness arises from the fumes of the furnace, in which there are quantities of arsenic and sulphur. Animals raised about the furnace are frequently poisoned, by licking the ore, or even the stones. Dogs and cats, and even poultry, are seen to fall down suddenly and die.

Having taken this general view, of the mines, their produce, &c. I shall proceed to describe the different *diggings*, more minutely. I have elsewhere observed, that they are scattered over a tract of country about sixty miles in length and twenty-five in breadth, many of those in vogue a few years ago, are now abandoned, for new discoveries. The appearance of the diggings which I have before partly described, is like that of small villages, consisting of a collection of little cabins or huts. The distance from Mine la Motte, to the Richwood mines, the one on the St. Francis, and the other near the Maramek, is about sixty miles; and from Fourche Courtois, west of the Mine à Burton (which I have considered as the centre) to the mines nearest the Mississippi, is about twenty-five miles. There is no doubt but that mines equally good as any that are wrought may be found out of this tract in every direction; even within a few miles of the Mississippi. Not more than four miles from that river, between col. Hammond's farm and Herculaneum, I picked up in the road, a large lump of ore, which had been washed out by rain a short time before.

MINE A BURTON,

Is situated on a handsome stream, a branch of Big river, and large enough to turn a mill the whole year. The village, which is much superior to those which are formed near the diggings, is built on either side of it. The diggings extend around it in every direction, but the principal, which are called the Citadel Diggings, are immediately west, on a high prairie. They occupy about two hundred acres. The surface of the ground has been tolerably well searched; and very great quantities of lead, from the first discovery of this place to the present time, have been made: it will now be necessary to sink into the bowels of the earth before much more can be done: this place has been nearly abandoned by the common diggers. A shaft, and the first known in this country, has been sunk by Mr. Austin, on a part which falls within his concession. It is about eighty feet in depth, and drifts, in various directions, extend a considerable distance. Twenty hands, might work here at present to advantage, and with sure prospect of profits. They are not yet incommoded by the intrusion of the water, owing to the height of their situation.

The situation of this village is pleasant, there are some handsome dwellings; the inhabitants, about twenty families, turn their attention to agriculture. The surrounding country, although broken in many parts, yet affords a great deal of fine land: the soil, as is general throughout the mine tract, is of a deep red, and supposed to be principally produced by the decomposition of pyrites, which are known to be a manure. Col. Perry shewed me a field in which wheat had been sown for twelve successive years, and no apparent diminution in the produce.

New Diggings, about two miles east of the Mine à Burton; they were opened about the year 1806: and from the fame which they acquired, drew the miners from nearly all the other mines. It is thought, that during the year, in which these were worked, more lead was made, than has been since, in any one year throughout the mines. For two or three years past, until the present season, these diggings were almost neglected. They are now wrought by several gentlemen with hired hands and slaves. They work in a few pits that had already been sunk to a considerable depth, but had been relinquished on account of the water; this difficulty has been obviated by machinery.— There are several farms around it.

Mine Arnault: north of the Mine à Burton about six miles, is situated upon a branch of the Mineral Fork, a large creek.— It has not been wrought for many years, but a new discovery made within a short distance of it, is very flattering. The adjacent country consists of rugged hills, and one might almost fancy himself in the Allegany mountains.

Elliott's Diggings, Old Mines, and the mines of Belle Fontaine, may be considered under the same head: in half a day one may easily visit them all. Elliot's diggings have been worked for several years, by the proprietors, and to advantage. The old mines, for three or four years have been entirely neglected: the land is good, and there is a little settlement of twenty or thirty industrious people who cultivate it. These mines are from six to twelve miles from the Mine à Burton. *Brown's Diggings* are the most noted of those near Belle Fontaine. In the course of the year before last, little short of one million lbs. of lead were smelted here. A considerable quantity is still made, and the appearance of the diggings are flattering, and, but for the dispersion of the miners to other places, might be worked as profitably as any others. They are situated within a short distance of Big river: and about twenty-five miles from Herculaneum.

Bryan's Diggings, a few miles east of Big river. It is about eighteen months since these were discovered; but there has been more lead made than at any other place of the district, in the course of the present year. They are situated twenty-five miles from St. Genevieve, and twenty from Herculaneum.

Richwood Mines, are situated about twenty miles N E. of the Mine à Burton; they are said to be productive.

Mine a Joe, on Big river, higher up than Bryan's Diggings, and somewhat further from St. Genevieve. Only a few hands have been employed here during the present season.

Mine a la Motte, four miles from the St. Francis, and on a small stream which falls into that river; it is one of the oldest, and has been constantly wrought for many years, and produces a considerable quantity even on the present mode of mining.— The distance is about thirty miles from St. Genevieve. There is a handsome little village; the inhabitants sober and industrious.

Perry's Diggings, *Mine Liberty*. Fourche Courtois, are new discoveries. There are also some others of less note.

The Big river, Terre Bleu, and the Mineral Fork, are considered streams which meander through the mine tract. Big river is long, but extremely crooked; in length it falls little short of two hundred miles, from its source to where it discharges itself into the Maramek: and may be ascended upwards of sixty miles in periogues. There are extensive bodies of fine land in its neighborhood, both bottom and upland. The mine tract generally, a thing somewhat unusual in mineral countries, is well adapted to agriculture. No country can be more plentifully watered, possessing in great abundance the most delightful fountains and rivulets.

c

It is not more than three or four years since the settlements through this country commenced. The Spanish government held out encouragements to American settlers, and I have been informed that about the years 1801—2, emigration was beginning to flow in rapidly: it is probable that in a few years, unless restrained by government, there would have been a considerable population. The farmers in the mine country, will have the advantage of a ready market near them for their produce, and in the winter season, when their farms do not require attention, they will find a profitable employment in transporting the lead to the towns, for the purpose of being shipped.

The following is an estimate from the best information I can procure, of the annual produce of the different mines, and of the number of persons engaged in them; without counting smelters, blacksmiths, and others.

	lbs. lead.	hands.
Mine à Burton	50.000	15
New Diggings	200.000	40
Perry's Diggings, Mine Liberty, &c.	60.000	50
Elliott's Diggings	100.000	20
Mines of Belle Fontaine . . .	300.000	50
Bryan's Diggings	600.000	70
Richwoods	75.000	30
Mine à La Motte	100 000	40
Fourche Courtois	10.000	15
Mine à Robins & Mine à Joe	30 000	20
	1.525.000	350

From this some estimate may be formed of the produce of these mines. When they come to be extensively worked, I have not a doubt but that they will be able to supply the United States, not only with a sufficient quantity for home consumption, but also with an immense surplus for commerce.

The government has manifested by some acts, an intention of reserving to itself the mineral tracts. But the policy of this

I think, may be fairly questioned.   It is just and wise, that mines of gold or silver, or of other precious minerals, whose value is conventional or imaginary, should be reserved, or at least a proportion of them: but in ores of lead or iron, whose value depends on the labor bestowed on them, and which are besides intrinsically useful, there should be no interference with individuals. In this country, where almost every tract, and for a great extent, contains mines, the reservation would be almost impracticable. I can no more approve of this reservation, than I do that of salines.   I think they are contrary to correct principles in any government, and particularly in the United States.   A just government will never enter into competition, either in trade or manufacture, with individuals.   The individual in such cases, has to contend against fearful odds.   There is a littleness in it degrading to the magnanimity of a great republic.

By an act of congress, the governor of the territory is authorised to grant leases, of three years, to persons discovering lead mines, or salines.

The manners of the workmen and of the persons engaged in the mining business, have been represented as barbarous in the extreme.   I am told, that a few years ago, there was a collection of worthless and abandoned characters, and that the different mines were scenes of broils and savage ferocity; but the state of society, has greatly altered since that time.   There has been some very atrocious acts committed lately, but it would be unfair to infer from these the general character of those engaged about the mines.   There are many worthy and reputable men engaged in this business, and many respectable families are scattered through the mine country.

CHAPTER VIII.

RESOURCES—AGRICULTURE—MANUFACTURES—TRADE.

NATURE has been more bountiful to this territory, than perhaps to any part of the western country. It possesses all the advantages of the states of Ohio, Kentucky and Tennessee, with many which they have not. Proximity to the great mart of the west, will enable the produce of this territory to be the first in arriving, and consequently to bring the highest prices.

The agriculture of this territory will be very similar to that of Kentucky, except, that south of the 35° of latitude, cotton may be grown to advantage, and nearly as high as the Missouri, for home consumption. The soil, or climate, of no part of the United States is better adapted to the growth of wheat, rye, barley, and every species of grain. Rice and indigo may be cultivated in many parts of it: and no part of the western country surpasses it for the culture of tobacco, hemp, and flax. Except the fig, orange, and a few other fruits, every species common to the United States is cultivated to advantage. There are no where finer apples, peaches, pears, cherries, plums, quinces, grapes, melons, &c.

The manufactures which might be established are various and important. The immense quantity and cheapness of lead, naturally point out this country as the proper one for the different manufactures of that mineral: sheet lead, shot, red and white lead, &c. The abundance of iron ore, on the Maramek, St. Francis, and Osage rivers, will at no distant period, encourage the establishment of furnaces and forges. The different manufactures of hemp, requisite for the lower country, may be here carried on to advantage. There is a great abundance of the finest timber for boat or ship building; in this respect, the situation of the territory has decided advantages over the rest of the western country.

The staple articles of trade, are at present, lead, peltry, cotton, tobacco, and live stock. It will not be long before there will be added to these, the manufactures of lead, hemp, and cotton, besides the raw materials themselves; also, iron, salt-petre, and coal, wheat, flour, apples, cider, whiskey, pickled pork, and beef, and a variety of other articles of less importance.

CHAPTER IX.

STATE OF LOUISIANA.

BOUNDARIES—GENERAL SURFACE, &C.

THE state of Louisiana is bounded in the following manner; " beginning at the mouth of the river Sabine, thence by a line to be drawn along the middle of said river, including all its islands, to the thirty-second degree of north latitude, thence due north, to the northernmost part of the thirty-third degree of north latitude, thence along the said parallel of latitude, to the Mississippi;" by the accession of West Florida, the state is bounded on the east side of the Mississippi, as follows; from the thirty-first degree of north latitude on the Mississippi, along the said parallel of latitude, to the eastern branch of Pearl river, and down Pearl river to its mouth, thence to the mouth of the Sabine. It is bounded on the north and east by the Mississippi territory, the south by the ragged coast of the gulph of Mexico, and on the other sides by unoccupied lands of the United States.

I refer the reader to Mr. Darby's table for an estimate of its superficial contents, &c. Its shape is exceedingly irregular, arising from the unevenness of the coast, and from the line on the eastern side commencing only at the thirty-first degree of north latitude. Were it to begin at the thirty-third, so as to correspond with the line on the western side, the state would be left in a more compact and definite shape. Something has been said of carrying this into effect, if it should meet the approbation of the people of the Mississippi territory. Much might be said in favor of it; it would tend to lessen the expense of state go-

vernment, to both, and give that right to the Mississippi territory sooner than could be well expected without. But the great
objections, and indeed they seem almost insurmountable, arise
from the difficulty of subjecting that territory to the civil law,
after having been so long accustomed to a different system; and
to introduce the common law into this state, at once, would be
highly impolitic, if practicable.

With respect to the surface of the state, it may be easily
comprehended under three general descriptions:

      I. The tract of Upland—

      II. The Alluvia and Sunken lands—

      III. The Prairies or Savannas—

I. The tract of upland constitutes three-fifths of the whole
state; all that part of Florida above Iberville, which has been
added to the state, is of this description. For fifteen or twenty
miles from the Mississippi it is covered with heavy timber, principally oak, poplar, walnut, the magnolia grandiflora, and a
great variety of other laurels. After this, we find with little variation, open pine woods, excepting on the banks of the streams,
which are numerous and pleasant. On the other side of the
Mississippi, west of the alluvia (which are generally bounded
by the Bayou Mascon, Bayou Boeuf, and the Teche) the upland
commences, covered, with but little variation, by the long leafed pine. It is divided to the S. W. by the avenue of Red
river, beyond this, it resumes its original appearance, with
little interruption, west to the Sabine: but in advancing to
the gulph of Mexico, a change is gradually perceived. Within
thirty miles of the Opelousas church, the pine woods imperceptibly give place to groves of dwarf oak and hickory, with
spots of ground covered only with grass; these groves appear
only on the water courses, and we enter the boundless prairies
of Opelousas.

II. The prairies or savannas, and alluvia, scarcely constitute
the other two-fifths of the state. Besides those on the Washita,
and a few of no great extent, west of Black river, there are
none of any consequence, except those of the Opelousas and
Attakapas. These constitute a tract of nearly eighty miles in
length, from east to west, and fifty in breadth. The prairies of

Opelousas have a waving surface, though no where rising into hills; those of the Attakapas are flat and level, covered with a more luxuriant and a coarser vegetation. The whole country is chequered by the woody margins of streams, called bayoux,* though different from the refluent waters of the river. The parts of the country in England, where the grounds are divid-ed by hedge rows, might seem miniatures of the bold designs which nature has displayed in laying off this tract. The fringes of wood on the borders of the bayoux seldom exceed a half mile in width, and consist of live oak, magnolia, &c. and on the wet parts, of cypress. The rivers Teche and Vermillion, have the largest tracts of timbered land, and are consequently the best settled parts of the prairies. The prairies will be found in the aggregate, the least valuable of the public domain ; if they be surveyed and laid off, as at present contemplated, it will be im-possible to sell them for more than a trifle : who would purchase a tract of land situated perhaps at the distance of several miles from wood or water? The fact is, that the greater part is only fit for pasturage, and there is little likelihood, of any other use being made of it, for many years to come. From late observa-tions, however, it is probable, that in time trees might be culti-vated : the soil is growing richer from the manure left by the numerous herds of cattle which continually cover it.

III. The alluvion lands constitute the third division. Much erroneous calculation has been indulged on this head. It has been a prevailing opinion, that by far the greater part of the state is composed of this kind of land. From what I have said, it may be seen that it does not constitute more than the fifth of the state: but of this portion, there is not more than a fourth which can be considered irreclaimable. When I say irreclaim-able, I do not mean to convey the idea of any physical impossi-bility, but the great difficulty with which it must be effected, and the great length of time which must elapse before it can be done. I am well satisfied that there is much less of the west-

* They are natural drains of the waters accumulated by the rains in the prairie; ponds and even lakes are formed in places by the rains. This arises from the uneven surface of the ground.

ern side of the Mississippi rendered useless by the annual floods, than is usually stated. This observation has been several times repeated in different parts of these Views, and I find no reason to change my opinion. There is certainly much sunken and overflowed land, and perhaps not to be reclaimed without immense labor, and between the Washita and the Mississippi, perhaps one-third is of this kind. But there is nothing more incorrect than the general and vague accounts of writers on this subject, who state that the western side of the Mississippi is annually inundated to the distance of *thirty or forty, and even sixty miles*. The settlements established within a few years between the Washita and the Mississippi, prove the error of the opinion to which so many have given currency. It is true as a general rule, that the bank of the Mississippi, is the highest part of the alluvion ground, but this is not always the case; the banks of the bayoux and of the lakes are as high, if not higher. On many of the bayoux there are extensive tracts of upland, and this rarely occurs on the bank of the river itself below the Arkansas. Wherever these are to be found, we may safely conclude that the ground is but little subject to be covered by the overflowing of the waters. The road from Concordia, (opposite the town of Natchez) to the upland on the other side of Black river, is but seldom rendered impassible for travellers on horseback. I consider the extent of the lands subject to be inundated by the Mississippi, on the eastern side, as not exceeding fifteen miles, until we come to Black river. 1. From the foregoing outline it will appear that the alluvion lands are chiefly on the western side of the Mississippi, (the bottoms on the eastern side are not remarkable) and are finest along this river from the 33°, extending back to the distance of twenty miles, but suddenly widening on the approach to Red river. 2. On the Red river, of an average width of ten miles, widening on its approach to the Mississippi. 3. Below Red river and constituting the western angle of the Delta. I think it probable, that on a better acquaintance these tracts will be found to contain by far the most valuable portions of the public domain; the proportion of sunken lands, reclaimable only with great difficulty, is less than the proportion of unproductive pine woods, or of prairie not susceptible of cultivation from the want of wood and water.

In order to give the reader a more satisfactory view of the subject, I will enter into some detail on the topography of different sections, or natural divisions.

1. *Section of the state between Red river, Mississippi, and the line of the 33° of N. Lat.*

This embraces an extensive portion of the state, and of a character in many respects different from the rest. The greater part is of an uneven surface, in places hilly, and invariably covered with the long leafed pine. The soil, we may naturally suppose from this growth, to be poor, if not barren. But I have been informed by intelligent persons, that it is preferable to the pine lands of Georgia. There are no sand hills, and every where a luxuriant herbage. I have passed over some parts which are rocky, but in general we find a light grey colored earth, mixed with a considerable portion of sand. It is supposed that wheat might be grown in this soil to advantage. There are a great many beautiful streams of clear delightful water, upon whose borders, the lands are rich and clothed with a variety of trees, the magnolia and other laurels, always forming the greater proportion. These strips of land, or bottoms, rarely exceed a mile in width. On the roads between the Washita and Red river, there are a number of scattered settlers, who live tolerably well; the adjacent pine wood enabling them to keep large herds of cattle. The country is generally healthful, and when it becomes settled, will be one of the most pleasant in the state. The Washita, Catahoula, and Little river, are the principal streams by which this tract is watered. On the Washita there is said to be upland, similar to that of the Missouri, and which is well suited to the raising of wheat. The country abounds with streams, which afford mill seats, but it is feared that the torrents which they roll along after heavy rain, would sweep away any work that might be erected. On some of the more considerable creeks, or rivulets, it often happens that the whole valley is overflown. Their channels are deep, and many of them abound

w

ing in quicksands, but their beds, are usually composed of gravel or stone.

The exception to this general description consists in the
tract between the Washita and the Mississippi, the greater part
of which is low land. Black river, which loses its name at the
junction of the Tensa, Washita and Catahoula, runs through
the lower part of this tract. The lands on the borders of this river, are too low, but not annually subject to be overflown. There
had been settlers for several years on its banks, all the way to
the mouth, previous to 1811, but the flood of that year, (one of
the most remarkable experienced in this country,) compelled
the greater part of them to abandon their plantations. The lands
between the Black river, Red river, and the Mississippi, are
amongst the lowest in the alluvion tract. There are some lakes ;
that of Concordia for instance, connected with the three rivers
before mentioned, by bayoux diverging from all sides. On some
of these bayoux the land is sufficiently high to admit of settlements. The greater part of this alluvion soil is tinged with red,
from the admixture of the sediment brought down Red river,
with that of the Mississippi. The tract enclosed by the Red river, Mississippi, Tensa, and a long narrow lake connected with the
Tensa lake, called Anderson, forms the county of Concordia,
which is almost an island, the east end of this lake approaching
within a few miles of the Mississippi. Opposite this tract, on
the western side of Black river, there is another of nearly equal
size, but which is a complete island, formed by the river just
mentioned, with the bayou Saline, and the Catahoula lake and
river. In this tract, there are no settlements ; the lands are extremely low The lake called Catafouloucta, situated on this
tract, is said to have some high land on its borders. The Catahoula lake, is about thirty miles in length, and about six miles
wide. It becomes nearly dry in autumn, and at that season,
and early in the spring, the ground is covered with fine herbage,
and is resorted to by numerous herds of cattle. Besides several
smaller streams, this lake receives the Little river, a fine stream
more than two hundred miles in length ; it is discharged into
Washita, by the Catahoula river, and into Red river by bayou
Saline,

The Tensa, which enters from the eastern side, forms, with the Washita and bayou Long, another island of an oval shape, and about fifty miles in circumference. On this there are no settlers, though it is not commonly subject to be overflown; it is a level of rich soil; in 1811, it was pretty generally covered with water to the depth of about one foot. Trifling levees would secure this tract, as indeed all those islands, if it were not for the numerous bayoux of a smaller size which every where intersect the country; entirely to close up their entrances, would be attended with great labor. Immediately above this island, there is another called Sicilly island, a greater part of which, is rich upland, and supports a considerable settlement. It is about thirty miles in circumference. At the lower end of Sicilly island the bayou Tensa spreads into a lake of fifteen or twenty miles in length, and nearly parallel with the Mississippi; at one place near the settlement of Palmyra, it approaches within two or three miles of the Mississippi, and is at length connected with that river, it is supposed somewhere near Stack island, and forming one of its out-lets. Besides the Tensa lake, this bayou forms several others, of which lake Providence is the most considerable. Their banks are high, and rarely, if ever, subject to the effects of the floods of the Mississippi. The Tensa lake receives two very considerable streams; the riviere aux Boeufs, and the bayou Masçon: both are supposed to have their sources partly in the pine woods, between the Washita and the Arkansas, and partly in some lakes, formed by out-lets from the Arkansas and Mississippi: but from the clearness of their streams it is probable that they receive the greater part of their waters from the upland springs and rivulets. The bayou Masçon, may be considered the boundary of the Mississippi swamp, and seldom recedes to a greater distance than fifteen miles from the river. The land between it and the riviere aux Boeufs is generally high prairie, the lower part rises in bluffs of fifty or sixty feet high. There are several connecting bayoux between it and the bayou Masçon. The strip of land, perhaps on an average ten or fifteen miles in width, between those two bayoux, is generally above the reach of inundation. Between the riviere aux Boeufs and the Washita, the land is low, and the overflowing of either river is sometimes ready to pour over the bank of the other. On a slight glance, this country, between the Mississippi and the Washita, nearly four hundred miles on the river, and generally supposed to be annually covered with water to the depth of several feet, is divided into long narrow slips, by the parallel courses of the Mississippi, bayou Masçon, riviere aux Boeufs, and the Washita; with numerous connecting bayoux, which in time, will be as useful as artificial canals, and insterspersed with lakes whose banks are above the reach of inundation. During the flood of 1811, two Indians who had set off from fort Adams, arrived at Sicilly island, bringing with them several horses. They declared that they had to swim but two bayoux, having followed the ridges of high land.

All those bayoux are deep, and at all seasons afford sufficient water to navigate the largest barges. Their courses are generally crooked, and narrow, in places perhaps choked with logs and rafts. The Washita as high up as the 33° of N. lat. is seldom more than forty miles from the Mississippi. Two roads have been cut, one to fort Mira, and the other to bayou Berthelemie, thirty miles above; they pass through thick cane brakes, and in high water, it is necessary to swim a great number of bayoux, and to wade through places overflown.

I am conscious how difficult it is to convey any idea of a country, particularly such as this, without a map; I do not know of any extant, which I can recommend to the reader: that of Lafon, is undoubtedly the best yet published, but from my own observation, and from what I have learned from others, it is by no means to be relied on. It was, however, the best that could be made at the time of its publication, but since then the country has become much better known. The manuscript map of Mr. Darby is greatly superior, the greater part of it being taken from actual survey.

The principal settlements are those of Concordia, Catahoula, and Washita. In the two last, the settlers cultivate cotton, but in the other, their principal dependence is in the raising of stock and the culture of Indian corn, and they generally live poor having but few of the comforts and conveniences of life.

2. *The alluvion tract of Red river—Avoyelle—Land around the mouth of Red river—Atchafalaya.*

The alluvion lands of Red river are remarkably distinguish-ed from those of the Mississippi, by their deep red color, arising, as is supposed by Dr. Hunter, from the decomposition of pyrites, or a mixture of some metallic substance. The lands on the Atchafalaya, and on numerous bayoux at present fed by the wa-ters of the Mississippi, are of this description: the sediment brought down by Red river, appears to predominate through a very extensive portion of the alluvion soil west of the Missis-sippi.

If it is difficult to give an idea of the country bordering on the Mississippi, by a mere description in words, it is still more so with respect to the valley of Red river. Its irregular and con-fused shape, " if shape it can be called," baffles every attempt to compare it to any known figure in mathematics or in nature. This irregularity is principally caused by the strange and ec-centric course which that river pursues. Instead of flowing in a regular channel, it divides its waters into a hundred streams, separating and again uniting so as to render it difficult to trace the principal river. Large tracts of primitive ground, or up-land, in the ever changing course of this river, have been cut off from the main body, stand perfectly disconnected with it, and surrounded by alluvion; the current having in time entirely worn away the primitive ground. There are a great number of bayoux, or refluent streams, which show incontestable proofs, of having been at different periods, the beds of the river. It is to be observed, that on the N. E. side, the Red river is almost in-variably bounded by the primitive land, and the irregularities just mentioned, occur chiefly on the S. western side: from this it would appear, that this river, like the Mississippi, is progress-ing in its general course eastward, and that it could never have been much further in that direction than at present. Red river, would be almost as bold a stream as the Mississippi, but for the great diminution of its waters by subdivision and the forma-tion of lakes; it has had the good effect of rendering the lands in its vicinity more free from inundation, than those of the Mis-sissippi. About lat. 32° 40, long. 96° 15, Red river separates in-

to two branches, which unite within ten miles of Natchitoches. The eastern branch retains the name of the river, is
the most considerable, but obstructed by the great raft. A bayou which makes out on the east side of this branch, spreads
out into lake Bestianeau, and afterwards joins the main stream.
The western branch does not flow in a well defined channel,
but at short intervals, spreads out into lake Pisaquie, lake Mal-
doux, and lake Long, connected on the east side by bayou Pierre
(properly a continuation of the W. branch) and immediately before the junction of the two branches, the W. branch, by a
refluent bayou, contributes with the streams from the upland
in forming the lake Espagnol.* The island, or tract, enclosed by the two branches, is of an oval form, and not less than
three hundred miles in circumference; a considerable part is
said to consist of low sunken lands, but there must doubtless be a large portion of a superior quality. Immediately
below the village of Natchitoches, the river again separates
into three branches, the middle one being the principal. The
eastern is called Fausse riviere, (False river) and is connected with several lakes to the N. E. of it. The western branch
is called the river of the Post, and has on its S. W. side
a number of lakes formed partly by its own refluent waters, and
those of the upland streams: the lake à Casé is the largest of
these. Between this and the middle branch, several islands† are
formed by the connecting bayoux. In times of high water there
is but little difference in the size of these three branches; the river of the Post has been preferred on account of the distance being shorter, but the middle branch is much the clearest, though
nothing more than a deep gut or bayou, twenty or thirty yards
in width, scarcely sufficient for a long barge to turn round. The
principal settlement of Natchitoches, is situated upon it, and
forms an almost continued village for forty or fifty miles. The
water never rises so as to render it necessary to add to the na-

* This is more or less the case with all the lakes in the vicinity of
Red river. The streams from the high, or primitive ground, are extremely well supplied with water.

† Amongst others the isle of the Natchez, where that unfortunate
people made their last stand.

tural banks. These branches re-unite fifteen or twenty miles above the Rapides. The Red river receives from the N. E. side lake Yae, which discharges itself by the rivers Rara and Marteau. From the re-union of these branches, the river pursues a tolerably well defined course to the Mississippi, losing its waters by only two or three bayoux, and not forming any considerable lakes. Bayou Boeuf, which is formed partly by a large stream from the upland, and partly from the waters of Red river, may be regarded as the boundary of the Red river alluvion in that quarter.

In casting the eye over the map, it will be seen that a triangle is formed, of which bayou Boeuf is the base, and Red river and the Mississippi the two sides. It is in this triangle that the largest body of low sunken lands, are to be found in the state, particularly in the angle of Mississippi and Red river, and round the curious island of Avoyelle. From marks on the trees, it appeared to me that the land had been overflowed to the depth of ten feet. The Avoyelle is a body of primitive ground, about thirty miles in circumference, the growth similar to that of West Florida, in the neighborhood of the Mississippi; the soil is not remarkably rich, but affords a handsome settlement. The Atchafalaya of Avoyelle, flows through the triangle, in a course parallel to the bayou Boeuf, and is without any settlement; the land low. The lands on the bayou Boeuf, particularly on the upper part of it, are amongst the best in the state, commonly of two miles in width, covered with impenetrable thickets of cane; the soil extremely rich, of a red color, similar to that on the Atchafalaya of Red river. Of late years, several settlements have been formed in this bayou, and the lands were growing into high repute previous to the depreciation in the price of cotton. The lands on the Atchafalaya of Red river, are of nearly the same quality, but do not possess the same depth.* There are still but few settlers. Its navigation is interrupted by rafts and other obstructions.

The valley of Red river is susceptible of a very wealthy and extensive population; with the exception of the triangle before

* The grant of the United States, to the Marquis de la Fayette has been chiefly located on this bayou.

described, being but little subject to overflowing : the proportion of sunken ground, is scarcely equal to the part which may be cultivated, and the proportion altogether irreclaimable, is very small.   The best cotton of the United States is produced here, and brings in market, generally, one cent more in the pound.— Tobacco and indigo are also amongst the articles of culture. The principal settlements, are those of Natchitoches, bayou Rapide, bayou Robert, bayou Boeuf, and Atchafalaya.

The greater part of the tract between the Atchafalaya, bayou Plaquemine, and the Mississippi, is low and uninhabitable land, of which no use can be made in its present state.   The settlements of Pointe Coupée, West Baton Rouge, and Plaquemine, form trifling exceptions   The route to the Attakapas and Opelousas, usually taken by boats, is through the bayou Plaquemine.

The last and the largest body of alluvion in the state, is enclosed by the bayou Plaquemine, Atchafalaya, a bayou which makes out from it, (and forms the grand lake, connected with the lac d'eau Salée,) the sea, and the Mississippi.   This tract is interspersed with a number of very large lakes, connected with the sea.   Bayou la Fourche and Atchalafaya pass through it: the latter is lost in a variety of lakes and bayoux before it enters the gulph.   This land is rapidly gaining from the sea ; the large lakes are shallow, and perceptibly filling up every year, by the sediment of the Mississippi.   There is some land around them susceptible of being cultivated, but generally, there is no habitable land on this tract, except on the bayou la Fourche, and Mississippi.   The bayou la Fourche is a beautiful natural canal, admittting of settlements on its banks for eighty miles from where it issues from the Mississippi.   When the Mississippi is high, it is about one hundred and fifty yards in width, its banks, which rarely overflow, are guarded by a slight levee of two feet high: it is free from obstructions the whole way to the gulph, and there are said to be sixteen feet of water on the bar.   For the distance of sixty miles, a single horse might draw a large boat, so clean and even are its banks. In riding along it, the idea of a magnificent artificial canal was continually occurring to my mind: art cannot surpass it.   The lands are in many places a mile and

tin half in depth on both sides. It is supposed, that on this bayou, and on others connected with it, there is twice as much habitable land, as there is from its entrance, on both sides of the
Mississippi, to New Orleans. For nearly thirty miles down,
on each side, there appears a continual village; and it is tolerably well settled for thirty miles further.

3. *Attakapas and Opelousas.*

Opelousas is separated from the Attakapas by bayou Fusil-
lier, which connects the Teche with the Vermillion, and is a
natural canal, which might with ease be rendered navigable.—
On the S. W. side of the Vermillion it is separated by the Ca-
rancro, a stream which takes its rise in the prairies, and falls into
the Vermillion. The traveller, on approaching the Teche from
the Vermillion, easily discerns where the high primitive ground
gradually descends into the lower prairies of the Attakapas.—
These, I have already observed, are covered with a coarser vegetation, and are better wooded than those of the Opelousas,
but there is a much greater portion of them waste, and subject to
be drowned by rains, and are even sometimes inundated by the
Teche: the greater part is probably alluvion, at least for a mile
or two on the S. W. side, and the whole on the other. The soil
is extremely rich, though of a texture somewhat too close, liable to bake and become hard and stiff. Cotton is at present the
principal culture; the sugar-cane has been found to succeed as
well if not better than on the Mississippi. A number of planters,
of late, are turning their attention to it. Several cotton planters
of the Mississippi territory, have sold their plantations, and
commenced establishments on the Teche. On lake Tasse there
is a sugar establishment of some years standing, but this is the
only one which has yet been completed.

The Vermillion and the Teche are the principal rivers of the
Attakapas, neither of them formed by the refluent waters of other
rivers, but rising in the high prairies of the Opelousas; the
Vermillion in the neighborhood of the Opelousas church, and
the Teche considerably north of it. Their general courses are
nearly the same to the lake Tasse, where the Teche winds somewhat east of south. Their channels are deep, the waters of a

X

dark color, and not reckoned very good for use. They are connected by streams from the lake Tasse. Schooners and light
vessels may ascend in both as far as this place, from the Vermillion bay, or Berwick's bay, into which these rivers are discharged. The Teche is a much larger and longer river than
the other, being upwards of two hundred miles in length. The
Tasse is a beautiful lake of clear water, about ten miles in circumference; there are plantations around it, on the eastern side,
the other is entirely bare of wood.

The principal settlements of the Attakapas are on each side
of the Teche (though mostly on the western,) and on the Vermillion. Besides the culture of cotton, maize, &c. they have
the advantage of those extensive natural meadows to support
their herds; from the mildness of the climate, little or no trouble is requisite to keep them. The inhabitants of the Attakapas
are generally wealthy, and live as luxuriantly as the planters of
the Mississippi. It is not considered healthy, perhaps, less so
than on the coast of the Mississippi On the whole, it is destin-
ed to become one of the richest districts of Louisiana.

The immense tract of open plains or meadows, which composes
the Opelousas, boasts of advantages superior to all the riches
of the Teche or the Mississippi, in the salubrity of its air and
the beauty of its surface. Free from stagnant waters, with the
exception of a few ponds in the prairies, the atmosphere is not
poisoned by noxious vapours, and open to the breezes from the
gulph, it enjoys a cool and refreshing temperature, while the
rest of the state is suffering from the effects of a close and sul-
try air. Without fear of contradiction, I may pronounce the
Opelousas to be by far the most healthy part of the state. Nothing can be more beautiful and cheering to the traveller, than
the prospects and views which this country affords. There is
nothing wild or savage, yet the scenery is not tame or monoto-
nous; there is a sufficient variety and succession of those scenes,
which sooth the mind, or inspire with lively and pleasing emotions. I passed through them last May, when they appeared to
great advantage. The distance of my journey was forgotten
while I gazed with delight upon the waving surface of these
meadows, now covered with deep green, and of extent, in some

places bounded only by the horizon, in others by skirts of wood, dimly appearing as in some distant isle of the sea; while a thousand brilliant and odoriferous flowers shed their perfume upon the air. The plantations scattered along the water courses on the outside of the fringe of wood, the vast herds of cattle roaming at random over the plains, complete the pleasing picture.

The settlements are entirely on the water courses, which chequer this plain; settlers turn their attention principally to grazing, cotton is however cultivated to advantage. The number of cattle composing the herds which some of the wealthier possess, would in other parts of the United States, be considered incredible; there are several who mark from one to two thousand calves every year. The cattle driven to New Orleans for sale, bring from fifteen to twenty dollars a head.

The Mentou is as large as the Teche, and falls into the gulph considerably to the S. W. of it, as also does the Carcasou; on both these rivers there are said to be considerable bodies of habitable land. The Sabine, which constitutes the boundary in that quarter, is a very considerable river, but is not at present susceptible of navigation, on account of obstructions in its course. The lands immediately in its neighborhood are good.

The route to the Opelousas and to the Attakapas, is either by Plaquemine, as before mentioned, or by the ferry of la Fourche. This is also the route in time of high water, to Rapide, or Natchitoches, for persons going by land. I rode along the lower bayou la Fourche about twenty-five miles, then crossed over to the out-let of a small bayou, 15 or 20 feet wide, called the Canal, from its having been somewhat improved by labor, and forming a convenient communication with the lakes, and the Teche: following this bayou or canal about fifteen miles, I came to the ferry kept by a German, who has the exclusive right from the state, on condition of keeping suitable accommodations. Here I embarked, in the evening, on a platform erected on two large canoes, with a railing in the middle for the purpose of confining our horses, and after passing through lake Platte, and several other lakes and bayoux, landed about three o'clock next morning, two miles up the Teche. The distance twenty-three miles. The night being pleasant, and no wind stirring, I had a pleasant

passage.   The lakes are not more than three or four miles in
width, but the narrow bayoux connecting them are so numerous,
that it requires considerable experience not to lose the way. On
my return I was less fortunate; I found at the ferry several
persons who had been waiting for three days, the wind rendering it useless to attempt to cross; their patience was by this
time totally exhausted, and it was determined to start, though the
wind had abated but little of its violence. With some difficulty
we reached Berwick's bay. The wind here became too strong,
and we were compelled to put to shore on a little point of land
overgrown with palmettoes,* where we found two or three fish-
ermen stretched before a little fire.   The tide was up, the bank
of the lake not more than two feet high,   These lakes are en-
veloped in the most gloomy forests of oak, cypress and ash, upon whose boughs the long moss,† or Spanish beard, is suspended in enormous masses, almost shutting out the light from these
dreary spots, while underneath, there is an impenetrable thicket
of underwood, and smaller trees and vines.   About 12 o'clock,
the wind having somewhat abated, we struck across the bay, but
before we could reach bayou Long, the approach of a storm,
which every moment threatened to burst upon us, compelled us
to put into one of the first bayoux which communicates with lake
Platte.   We had scarcely reached the entrance, until it began
to pour down torrents of rain, accompanied by incessant peals
of thunder.   Without the slightest shelter except our great
coats, we found our situation extremely uncomfortable. About
day light we continued our voyage, opposed by wind and current,
the rain continuing with but little intermission until we arrived
on the other side, which was not until four in the evening, al-

---

* A plant very common in the lower part of Louisiana—the leaves
so disposed as to bear a strong resemblance to a very large fern. It
grows upon the more elevated spots of ground.

† I have often puzzled myself to find out some known object to which
the appearance of this curious production might be compared. Cha-
teaubriand compares them to enormous ghosts! The best I can think
of, is to the shattered sails of a ship, after a storm, the canvass hanging
down in a thousand ragged shreds.

most exhausted, having been compelled to stand up the greater part of the time, and chilled to the very heart.   Here the attention and kindness of the good people, soon made us forget what we had endured, or remembered only to felicitate ourselves on its having passed.   These accidents do not frequently occur.

4.   Settlements of La Fourche—Coast of the Mississippi—Fausse riviere.

The settlers of La Fourche, are chiefly what the French call, *petits habitants*, small planters, and are therefore, more numerous than on the coast, for it requires many cottages to make one chateau.   There are however. some extensive establishments. Lands have risen here in price, since they have grown in demand for sugar plantations, and many of the *petits habitants* bought out.   The settlers from the Canal, up to the mouth of the Fourche, are principally of Spanish origin, and speak but little French.   They are a poor and miserable population; seem lazy and careless, and are destitute of those little comforts, and that neatness, which are found in the cottage of the poorest French creole.

The most pleasant part of Louisiana, when we take into consideration the comforts and conveniences of life, is that which is called the *Coast*, and proves to us what may be done by the art and industry of man, even in those parts which nature has left rude and unsightly.   It affords one of the strongest arguments in favor of civilization, and ought to go far in reconciling the philanthropic mind to the circumstance of the present inhabitants, having shoved off the pitiable, careless race, who first possessed it.   Would it be too much to say, that this improvement and cultivation of the face of nature, was the condition on which the Creator gave to the human race the lordship of the earth! Even the garden of Eden required the fostering care of Adam and his partner:

> " On to their morning's rural work they haste,
> Among sweet dews and flow'rs; where any row

> Of fruit-trees over-woody reach'd too far
> Their pamper'd boughs,"——&c.

The borders of the Mississippi in their natural state, are far
from being agreeable to the eye; we see only gloomy forests,
close thickets of underwood and reeds, putrescent trunks of
trees, and the ragged banks heaped up with the sweepings of
the upper country, and the sides of the river filled with sawyers and planters. In lieu of these deformities, we generally
find clean, smooth banks, a stream unobstructed by these impediments, its encroachments restrained, and delightful plantations
and dwellings every where appearing. The Coast may be said
to begin at Pointe Coupée. From this to La Fourche, two-thirds
of the banks are perfectly cleared and highly cultivated: from
thence to N. Orleans, distance of near 100 miles, the settlements
continue without interruption on both sides, and present the appearance of a continued village. I was enchanted with the magnificence of the scene, as I floated down the majestic river in Dec.
1811. The continued succession of plantations laid off with regularity and taste; the various useful and ornamental trees, the fig,
peccane, ever green oak, laurels, pine, weeping willow, &c. The
delightful groves of Orange trees, bending under the weight of
their golden fruit, to one, just from the dreary solitudes of the
Missouri, or the rude wilds of Upper Louisiana, were objects
indescribably pleasing. I could have believed that I was wit-
nessing those paradisiacal scenes of which I have sometimes
dreamed; but one or two reflections which intruded themselves,
unwelcome and unbidden guests, soon caused me to view the
" fair profusion," with other sensations. The earth which bears
these ornaments has been moistened by the tears of hundreds
who labor to support,

> " A haughty lordling's pride:"

in the midst of these rich gifts which seem to invite to enjoy-
ment and delight, there lurks poison, disease, and death! Alas,
how wretched is the poor wanderer deceived, whose thoughts
are bent on discovering on this earth, some spot, possessing in

much higher degree than any other, the streams of happiness, and of pleasure unalloyed! a nearer approach dispels what the distant prospect had promised, and he is at length taught by experience, that the gifts of heaven are equally dispensed, at least that it is not in this world we are to expect a paradise.

The dwellings on the Coast are generally frame, of one story in height, but there are many constructed with tolerable elegance. The sugar houses, on either side, at intervals considerably distant, were easily distinguished, by the vast columns of smoke which they sent up into the air. Within thirty or forty miles of the city there are but few of the *petits habitants*, the lands being engrossed by the wealthy planters: this is continually progressing downwards, and the disproportion of the whites to the blacks of course increasing. Below the place, where the insurrection commenced in 1811, to the city, the distance of thirty miles, there is scarcely one white person to twenty blacks. When the lands on the coast shall be principally occupied by the larger planters, which will be the case at no distant period, it will be found absolutely necessary to station an armed force at intervals, as far up as Pointe Coupée.

The settlements of Fausse riviere, on the old bed of the river, behind Pointe Coupée, is considered one of the wealthiest in the state. In high water, Fausse riviere, is filled from the Mississippi, and is as wide as that river; after the flood subsides, the water in this place stagnates, and the settlement is rendered unhealthy. The banks are high, and there is greater safety from inundation and the breaking of the levee than on the Mississippi.

LEVEES.

IT may be thought that I have represented this country, in some respects, in too favorable a light: that I have endeavored to represent the difficulties which oppose themselves to its improvement, as less considerable than they really are. Certainly those difficulties are many and great, and when contemplated, without reflecting on what man can effect, they appear insurmountable: but when we examine what he has done in other

parts of the world, it must be acknowledged that but few im-
possibilities present themselves in the improvement of this
country. Time, and a numerous population, are doubtless, requisite, but the advantages which offer themselves, will render
it no less certain. The soil of Louisiana is the most fertile in
the world, the climate delightful during nine months of the
year, and bad the remainder, only from being irreclaimed; its
productions are of the most valuable kind, and its geographical
position, superior, perhaps to that of any part of America.
These considerations will combine to raise the lands of Louisiana to their highest value, sooner than in other sections of the
union, where the lands being more than sufficient to support ten
times the present population, and the productions every where
much alike, it is not likely that the inhabitants will soon be compelled to resort to the thousand arts, by which every acre in the
populous parts of the old world is forced to bring something.
In Louisiana, the value of its productions, the amazing fertility
of its soil, with its other advantages, will cause these arts to be
resorted to much sooner. Still many years must pass away before we can expect to become sufficiently acquainted with this
country, or before the different means can be discovered of redu-
cing it to subjection; this must be the result of long experience
and observation. It will be reduced to a science, all the inventions
of the old world for similar purposes will be put in requisition,
and new ones adapted to the peculiarities of the country will be
fallen upon. But it is the gift of man to subdue and govern the
earth; and when we have seen him not only place it under his
subjection, but even raise for himself a dominion out of the element of storms, where shall we set bounds to his labors and ingenuity?

The most considerable work of art yet constructed for the
purpose of rendering this country habitable, is the embankment
of the river, usually called the levee. We should be much deceived if we were to form an idea of this from the dykes of Holland or the embankments of the Nile. The levees are commonly constructed in the following manner. At the distance of thirty or forty yards from the natural bank, a mound of earth is raised, varying from four to six feet high, and usually from six to

nine feet at the base, with sufficient width at the top for a foot
path. A close stiff clay, common on the lower parts of the river,
is preferred. Sods are placed on the sides and at the top, and
cypress slabs are often put in the inside for the purpose of preventing the water, where there is any current, from eating away
the earth. There is a ditch for the purpose of draining off the
water which oozes through. The road lies between the levee
and the fences, and is crossed at intervals by drains, covered
with plank, as the sewers of a city, for the purpose of carrying
off the water to the swamps. An immense quantity of water
finds its way through the embankment, mostly through holes
made by crawfish, which sometimes increase so rapidly, as to
effect a breach. Several years are necessary for the levee to become perfectly solid and firm, previous to this, it is liable to be
injured by rains. The levee pursues a zig-zag course, to suit
the different curves and indentations of the river, as well as the
sinuosities, for it being too slight a work to compel the river to
hold its course, it must yield to its caprice. As the river en-
croaches upon it, or recedes, another levee is constructed nearer the river, or behind the first; from which circumstances,
there are in many places double levees. A person standing inside of the levee in a very high flood, appears to stand below the
surface of the water; but there are in few places more than
two or three feet against the levee, the ground between it and
the river being much higher than on the inside; this may be accounted for, from the quantity of sediment deposited, and the
wearing down of the road. There are besides, other modes of
constructing the levee, and the expense and size depends upon
the resistance necessary, which in some places, generally in
bends, is much greater than in others. What is considered a
good levee, may almost any where be made for four hundred
dolls. per mile. Every individual is obliged to keep up the levee
in front of his own land, and before the time of high waters it is
inspected by commissioners appointed for the purpose in each
parish, and if found insufficient, it is made at his expense. But
this is by no means adequate to the purpose, for during the season of great floods, the levees require constant attention, they
must be continually watched, and all hands are sometimes drawn

from the fields to attend them for whole days and nights. Where the levee happens not to be sufficiently high, earth must be added; where it appears to crumble in, slabs must be placed to protect it; where rains have rendered it spongy and loose, every appearance of a hole made by crawfish must be watched and filled up. Hence, it often occurs, that from the weakness or negligence of some individual, both he and his neighbors are ruined.

It has often been a matter of surprise to me that works upon which so much depend, should be constructed in a manner so rude and trifling. A few moments are sufficient to destroy the labor and industry of twenty years. It was remarked, that the steam boat in high water, under way, might with ease pass over the levee; I was never more struck with the infant state of improvements in this country, and the want of public spirit, than in viewing the work upon which the Louisianian depends for the security of his all: a prodigious volume of water rolling over his head, prevented only by a slight mound of earth from overwhelming him and all he possesses. But he does not sleep soundly. In 1811,* in the season of high water, for six weeks the coast presented a scene of continual anxiety and apprehension; the hands withdrawn from the fields, and kept watching day and night, and adding to their breastwork as the river rose. If the expense, labor, loss of time, and the destruction of property, were estimated and formed into a general fund, it would have been sufficient to have erected a work capable of withstanding the highest flood, and rendered them perfectly secure for the future. If in the season of high water, the least storm of wind were to arise, there are scarcely any of the present levees which would not give way and the whole country be laid under water. But until the season comes the danger is not feared, and nothing is done until it is too late; those who escape resolve to be prepared for the next year, but this is soon forgotten. Last year (1812) the water rose much less than in ordinary years, and scarcely passed over the banks, yet at this time, a storm of wind

---

* This was still more the case in the present year 1813, the water rose higher than in 1811, by six or eight inches, and had they not been somewhat prepared by the former season, they must have been totally destroyed.

which continued more than a day, made several breaches in
the levee, doing much injury to the plantations. Had that
storm occurred at the same season the year before, the whole
country would have been under water. A gentleman informed me that he witnessed a storm that season, but which lasted
only fifteen minutes; yet the effects which it threatened seemed to produce an universal panic; man, woman, and child, in-
voluntarily ran to the levee as it were to support it with their
hands.

The Mississippi in its natural state, at least for one hundred
and fifty miles above New Orleans, overflows its banks, *com-
munibus annis*, from two to three feet, and the descent to the
swamps is very rapid, perhaps not less than four feet a mile.
Even in this state, it must flow over its banks with great velocity; but the artificial embankments, by enclosing its waters,
cause them to rise from two to three feet higher. The natural
fall of the river itself, scarcely exceeds one foot per mile: we
may now easily conceive the velocity of a sheet of water whose
current is thus suddenly increased to five or six feet per mile.
It rushes from the river with indescribable impetuosity, with a
noise like the roaring of a cataract, boiling and foaming, and
tearing every thing before it. To one who has not seen this
country it is almost impossible to convey any idea of the terrors
excited by a *crevasse* or breaking of the levee. Like the breaking out of fire in a town, where no one knows when his own
dwelling may be assailed, it excites universal consternation;
every employment is abandoned for miles above and below, and
all hasten to the spot, where every exertion is made day and
night to stop the breach, which is sometimes successful, but
more frequently, the hostile element is suffered to take its
course.* The consequences are, the destruction of the crop, the

* There are various modes of stopping a crevasse, the most common
is the following; they begin on each side of the *crevasse*, to drive double rows of piles gradually falling with the current so as to meet less resistance, until they unite, and thus form a semicircle like a fish basket;
in the next place the piles are interwoven with small branches, or slabs
placed lengthwise between them; branches of trees are then placed
behind the piles, and some heavier materials, logs, &c. against them : if

buildings, and sometimes the land itself is much injured where
the current rushed over, carrying away the soil, or leaving numerous logs and trees drawn into the vortex as they floated down
the river; these must be destroyed before the land can again be
cultivated.   The effects of a breach of the levee are even more
desolating than those of fire.

   Though not ambitious of the reputation of a projector, I cannot refrain from expressing the following notions on the mode
which ought to be pursued.   It strikes me that this, as is the
case with every great public work in the United States, should
be resigned to a company organized for the purpose, who might
draw a benefit from the undertaking, and at the same time be res-
ponsible to the individual for the injury which he sustains. When
we see the enormous expense in constructing turnpikes for the
purpose of facilitating the transportation of goods and for travelling, it would be no great exertion of public spirit, for people to
go to the same expense in securing not only those objects, but
their all.   One hundred thousand dollars would make the levee
twenty feet wide at the base, and ten feet at the top from New
Orleans, on the east side, to Baton Rouge; the expenses then
would not be greater than in keeping a turnpike road in repair.
The travelling up and down the coast is as great as on any of
our turnpikes, and the tolls would yield as much.   There is no
planter on the coast who would not pay two dollars per acre
front per annum, to be exempt from the labor of keeping up
his levee, and for the security he would gain from one made
on such a scale.   It is a fact, there is not a planter on the Mississippi, whose plantation might not be ruined in half an hour,
and perhaps less time by some villain, wicked enough to do it :
he would only have to make a breach in the levee, which the current would soon widen sufficiently for his purpose.   Centinels
during the highest stage of water, are continually walking on
the levees, as well to prevent such attempts, as to watch any in-
roads of the water.

they can succeed this far, earth is then thrown upon the whole, and thus
a new levee formed.   As a preventative where the levee appears to be
about giving away, coffer dams are erected.

It would be adviseable to leave at intervals, openings in the levee, properly secured on each side, like the sluices of the saw
mills, in order to let off the water of the river. An immense
quantity escapes through the present levees. In proportion as
the levees extend upwards, and those below become properly
secured, so as to prevent much of the water from escaping, they
must be raised. A vast body of water at the present time passes off in those places, where there are no embankments; if this
were kept in, the levees would every where require to be several feet higher. Artificial drains at proper distances might in a
great measure obviate this difficulty. But not having leisure
for these speculations, I leave them to others, who are otherwise
interested, than as general well-wishers for the prosperity of the
country.

CHAPTER X.

ANTIQUITIES IN THE VALLEY OF THE MISSISSIPPI.

SI QUID NOVISTI RECTIUS ISTIS, CANDIDUS IMPERTI, SI NON, HIS
UTERE MECUM.

CONSIDERABLE curiosity has been excited by appearances on the Mississippi and its tributary waters, supposed to
prove a more ancient and advanced population, than the state of
the country, or the character of the tribes inhabiting it, when
first visited by Europeans, would seem to indicate. I need
make no apology for devoting a chapter to a subject, which has
been dignified by the pens of Mr. Jefferson, Dr. Barton, and
a Bishop Madison. Yet, with all possible deference to these
respectable names, I cannot but think their theories founded
on a very imperfect acquaintance with these remains: having
never themselves, visited any but the least considerable, and but
few having been described by others with accuracy. The subject is still new, and I know of none which opens a wider field for
interesting and amusing speculation.

Many, without considering the astonishing number and variety of these remains, have attributed them to a colony of Welsh, or Danes, who are supposed to have found their way by some accident to this country, about the ninth century. Without recurring to the reasoning of doctor Robertson against the probability of such a colony, I will observe, that it is absolutely impossible that they could have gained such a footing as these vestiges indicate, without at the same time, leaving others less equivocal. Excepting a wall said to be discovered in North Carolina, but which, on examination, proved to be a volcanic production, I have not heard of a single work of brick or stone north of Mexico. The fortifications in the western country are devoid of those marks which have characterised the European mode of fortifying almost time immemorial; they are mere enclosures, without angles or bastions, and seldom surrounded by a ditch. The place is usually such as convenience would dictate, or as is best adapted to the ground: two miles below Pittsburgh, on a kind of promontory called M'Kee's Rocks, nearly inaccessible on three sides, there is a fortification formed by a single line on the land side. They are sometimes, it is true, laid off with regularity, in the form of a parallelogram, semicircle, or square, but most commonly they are irregular.

We are often tempted by a fondness for the marvellous, to seek out remote and improbable causes, for that which may be explained by the most obvious. In the eagerness to prove the existence of the Welsh colony, by attributing to them these remains, we forget that the natives of the country when first discovered by Europeans, were universally in the habit of fortifying In the early wars of the New England colonists with the Indians, we are informed, that Philip, chief of the Niphet tribe, defended himself in a fort which he had constructed, and sufficiently large to contain two thousand men. Charlevoix, du Pratz, and others, relate the particulars of several sieges. A fortification is one of the first things that would naturally suggest itself in a war: they have been known to all people; the same mind which would invent means of protection for the person of a single individual, would also devise the means of security to large bodies of men. It is no difficult matter to account for the disuse of fortifications amongst the Indians, when we consider the incredible diminution of their numbers, and the little use of their forts against the whites; yet in the two last sieges of mons. Perier, in the war of the Natchez (1729), that unfortunate people, were able to withstand the approaches and cannon of the enemy for nearly two months. Imlay, in his fanciful description of Kentucky, asserts, that the Indians were not acquainted with the use of fortifications. Carver is the first who notices these fortifications, and considers them as beyond the ingenuity of the Indians. The French writers, who most probably observed them, do not speak of them, a proof that they had no doubt as to their origin, nor thought of attributing them to any others than the natives of the country. On my voyage up the Missouri, I observed the ruins of several villages which had been abandoned twenty or thirty years, and which, in every respect resembled the vestiges on the Ohio and Mississippi. On my arrival at the Arikara and Mandan villages, I found them surrounded by palisades. I have supposed these vestiges to be nothing more than the sites of pallisadoed towns or villages, and not mere fortifications. This custom of pallisadoing, appears to have been general among the northern tribes; it is mentioned by the earliest travellers. In the library of New Orleans, I found two works at present out of print, which contributed in removing all doubt from my mind; the one is by Lapiteau, a learned Jesuit, and which is sometimes quoted by Dr. Robertson, the other is a singular mixture of fable and fact, by one La Houton, published 1678, before the discovery of the Mississippi in its full extent. This writer pretends to have travelled on the part which is above the Missouri. Both these works contain a number of curious engravings, in which, amongst other things, the fortified towns are represented.

That no Welsh nation exists at present on this continent, is beyond a doubt. Dr. Barton has taken great pains to ascertain the languages spoken by those tribes, east of the Mississippi, and the Welsh finds no place amongst them; since the cession of Louisiana, the tribes west of the Mississippi have been sufficiently known; we have had intercourse with them all, but no Welsh are yet found. In the year 1798, a young Welshman of the name of Evans, ascended the Missouri, in company with Makey, and remained two years in that country; he spoke both the ancient and modern Welsh, and addressed himself to every nation between that river and New Spain, but found no Welshmen. When we reflect upon the difficulties that such a colony would have to encounter amidst ferocious savages, is it probable, that isolated and unassisted, they could have been able to exist? The history of all the European establishments, inform us, that they were opposed by the natives with great ferocity. The Welsh would certainly either form considerable establishments, or be totally annihilated; to exist in a distinct and separate tribe, without preserving any of their arts, and without gaining a superiority over the Indians, but on the contrary adopting their manners, is absolutely impossible.

Besides the fortifications, there are other remains scattered throughout the western country, much more difficult to account for, and to which the Welsh can lay no claim. It is worthy of observation, that all these vestiges invariably occupy the most eligible situations for towns or settlements; and on the Ohio and Mississippi, they are most numerous and considerable.— There is not a rising town or a farm of an eligible situation, in whose vicinity some of them may not be found. I have heard a surveyor of the public lands observe, that wherever any of these remains were met with, he was sure to find an extensive body of fertile land. An immense population has once been supported in this country. These vestiges may be classed under three different heads—1, the walled towns or fortifications, of which I have already spoken; 2, barrows, or places of interment; 3, mounds or pyramids.

2. Barrows, such as described by Mr. Jefferson, are extremely numerous in every part of the western country. The traces of a village may be always found near them, and they have been used exclusively, as places of interment, at least of deposit for the dead. The height is usually eight or ten feet above the surrounding ground, the shape manifesting little or no design.— These accumulations may be attributed to the custom prevalent amongst the American tribes, of collecting the bones of such as expired at a distance from their homes, in battle, or otherwise,

and at stated periods placing them in some common tomb. The barrows were not the only receptacles; caverns were also used, and places, which, from being extraordinary, were considered the residence of Manatoos or spirits.

3. The mounds or pyramids appear to me to belong to a period different from the others. They are much more ancient, and are easily distinguished from the barrows, by their size and the design which they manifest. Remains of palisadoed towns are found in their vicinity, which may be accounted for from the circumstance of the mounds occupying the most eligible situations for villages, or from the veneration of the Indians, for whatever appears extraordinary. From the growth of trees on some of them, they show an antiquity of at least several hundred years. The Indians have no tradition as to the founders of them, though there is no doubt but that when we first became acquainted with those people, they were used as places of defence. The old chief of the Kaskaskia Indians, told Mr. Rice Jones, that in the wars of his nation with the Iroquois, the mounds in the American bottom were used as forts. In one of the plates of Lapiteau's work, there is a representation of an attack on an Indian fort, which is evidently constructed upon one of the mounds: its form is circular, the enclosure of large pickets, and heavy beams on the outside, extending to the ground on which the mound stands. Those inside defend themselves with stones, arrows, &c. while the assailants are either aiming their arrows at such as appear above the wall, or endeavoring to set fire to the fort. Until I saw this engraving, I had frequently doubted whether these elevations of earth were intended for any other purpose than places of interment for their great chiefs, or as sites for temples. These were probably the first objects, but experience, at the same time, taught them that they might also answer as forts; perhaps the veneration for these sacred places might induce the Indians, when invaded, to make their final stand in their temples, which therefore became strong holds.— This is conformable to the history of most nations of the world.

The mounds at Grave creek and Marietta have been minutely described, but in point of magnitude they fall far short of others which I have seen.

To form a more correct idea of these, it will be necessary to give the reader some view of the tract of country in which they are situated. The *American bottom*, is a tract of rich alluvion land, extending on the Mississippi, from the Kaskaskia to the Cahokia river, about eighty miles in length, and five in breadth; several handsome streams meander through it; the soil of the richest kind, and but little subject to the effects of the Mississippi floods. A number of lakes are interspersed through it, with high and fine banks; these abound in fish, and in the autumn are visited by millions of wild fowl. There is, perhaps, no spot in the western country, capable of being more highly cultivated, or of giving support to a more numerous population than this valley. If any vestige of ancient population were to be found, this would be the place to search for it—accordingly, this tract, as also the bank of the river on the western side,* exhibits proofs of an immense population. If the city of Philadelphia and its environs, were deserted, there would not be more numerous traces of human existence. The great number of mounds, and the astonishing quantity of human bones, every where dug up, or found on the surface of the ground, with a thousand other appearances, announce that this valley was at one period, filled with habitations and villages. The whole face of the bluff, or hill which bounds it to the east, appears to have been a continued burial ground.

But the most remarkable appearances, are two groupes of mounds or pyramids, the one about ten miles above Cahokia, the other nearly the same distance below it, which in all, exceed one hundred and fifty, of various sizes. The western side, also, contains a considerable number.

A more minute description of those above Cahokia, which I visited in the fall of 1811, will give a tolerable idea of them all.

* The Saline, below St. Genevieve, cleared out some time ago, and deepened, was found to contain wagon loads of earthen ware, some fragments bespeaking vessels as large as a barrel, and proving that the salines had been worked before they were known to the whites.

I crossed the Mississippi at St. Louis, and after passing through the wood which borders the river, about half a mile in width, entered an extensive open plain. In 15 minutes, I found myself in the midst of a group of mounds, mostly of a circular shape, and at a distance, resembling enormous haystacks scattered through a meadow. One of the largest which I ascended, was about two hundred paces in circumference at the bottom, the form nearly square, though it had evidently undergone considerable alteration from the washing of the rains. The top was level, with an area sufficient to contain several hundred men.

The prospect from this mound is very beautiful; looking towards the bluffs, which are dimly seen at the distance of six or eight miles, the bottom at this place being very wide, I had a level plain before me, varied by *islets* of wood, and a few solitary trees; to the right, the prairie is bounded by the horizon, to the left, the course of the Cahokia may be distinguished by the margin of wood upon its banks, and crossing the valley diagonally, S. S. W. Around me, I counted forty-five mounds, or pyramids, besides a great number of small artificial elevations; these mounds form something more than a semicircle, about a mile in extent, the open space on the river.

Pursuing my walk along the bank of the Cahokia, I passed eight others in the distance of three miles, before I arrived at the largest assemblage. When I reached the foot of the principal mound, I was struck with a degree of astonishment, not unlike that which is experienced in contemplating the Egyptian pyramids. What a stupendous pile of earth! To heap up such a mass must have required years, and the labors of thousands.— It stands immediately on the bank of the Cahokia, and on the side next it, is covered with lofty trees. Were it not for the regularity and design which it manifests, the circumstances of its being on alluvial ground, and the other mounds scattered around it, we could scarcely believe it the work of human hands — The shape is that of a parallelogram, standing from north to south; on the south side there is a broad apron or step, about half way down, and from this, another projection into the plain

about fifteen feet wide, which was probably intended as an ascent
to the mound. By stepping round the base I computed the circumference to be at least eight hundred yards, and the height of
the mound about ninety feet. The step, or apron, has been used
as a kitchen garden, by the monks of La Trappe, settled near
this, and the top is sowed with wheat. Nearly west there is another of a smaller size, and forty others scattered through the
plain. Two are also seen on the bluff, at the distance of three
miles. Several of these mounds are almost conical. As the
sward had been burnt, the earth was perfectly naked, and I could
trace with ease, any unevenness of surface, so as to discover
whether it was artificial or accidental. I every where observed
a great number of small elevations of earth, to the height of a
few feet, at regular distances from each other, and which appeared to observe some order; near them I also observed pieces
of flint, and fragments of earthen vessels. I concluded, that a
very populous town had once existed here, similar to those of
Mexico, described by the first conquerors. The mounds were
sites of temples, or monuments to the great men. It is evident, this could never have been the work of thinly scattered
tribes. If the human species had at any time been permitted
in this country to have increased freely, and there is every probability of the fact, it must, as in Mexico, have become astonishingly numerous. The same space of ground would have suf-
ficed to maintain fifty times the number of the present inhabitants, with ease; their agriculture having no other object than
mere sustenance. Amongst a numerous population, the power
of the chief must necessarily be more absolute, and where there
are no laws, degenerates into despotism. This was the case in
Mexico, and in the nations of South America; a great number
of individuals were at the disposal of the chief, who treated them
little better than slaves. The smaller the society, the greater
the consequence of each individual. Hence, there would not
be wanting a sufficient number of hands to erect mounds or
pyramids.

Hunter and Dunbar describe a mound at the junction of the
Catahoula, Washita and Tensa rivers, very similar in shape to

the large one on the Cahokia. I saw it last summer: it has a step
or apron, and is surrounded by a group of ten or twelve other
mounds of a smaller size. In the vicinity of New Madrid,
there are a number; one on the bank of a lake, is at least four
hundred yards in circumference, and surrounded by a ditch at
least ten feet wide, and at present, five feet deep; it is about forty feet in height, and level on the top. I have frequently examined the mounds at St. Louis: they are situated on the second bank just above the town, and disposed in a singular manner; there are nine in all, and form three sides of a parallelogram, the open side towards the country, being protected, however, by three smaller mounds, placed in a circular manner. The
space enclosed is about four hundred yards in length, and two
hundred in breadth. About six hundred yards above there is a
single mound, with a broad stage on the river side; it is thirty
feet in height, and one hundred and fifty in length; the top is a
mere ridge of five or six feet wide. Below the first mounds
there is a curious work, called the Falling Garden. Advantage
is taken of the second bank, nearly fifty feet in height at this
place, and three regular stages or steps, are formed by earth
brought from a distance. This work is much admired—it sug-
gests the idea of a place of assembly for the purpose of counselling, on public occasions. The following diagram may convey a more precise idea.

A—The three sides of a
    parallelogram.

B—The single mound.

C—The Falling-garden.

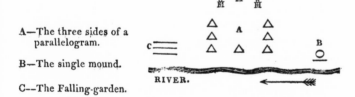

In tracing the origin of institutions or inventions amongst
men, we are apt to forget, that nations, however diversified by
manners and languages, are yet of the same species, and that the
same institutions may originate amongst twenty different people.
Adair takes great pains to prove a similarity of customs between

the American tribes and the Jews; Lapiteau shews the existence
of a still greater number common to the Greeks and Romans; the
result to the philosophic mind is no more than this, that the A-
merican tribes belong to the human race, and that men, without
any intercourse with each other, will, in innumerable instances,
fall upon the same mode of acting. The wonder would be, that
they should not shew a resemblance. Man is every where found
in societies, under governments, addicted to war, hunting, or agriculture, and fond of dances, shows, and distinction. Perhaps
the first employment of a numerous population when not engaged in war, would be in heaping up piles of earth, the rudest
and most common species of human labor. We find these
mounds in every part of the globe; in the north of Europe, and
in Great Britain, they are numerous, and much resemble ours,
but less considerable. The pyramids of Egypt are perhaps the
oldest monuments of human labor in that country, so favorable
to the production of a numerous population. The pyramids of
Mexico, which are but little known, and yet scarcely less considerable, like those of Egypt have there origin hid in the night
of oblivion. Humboldt is of opinion, that " these edifices must
be classed with the pyramidal monuments of Asia, of which
traces were found even in Arcadia; for the conical mausoleum
of Callistus was a true tumulus, covered with fruit trees, and
served for a base to a small temple consecrated to Diana." The
Greeks, who were successful in the chariot races at the Olym-
pic games, to shew their gratitude to their horses, gave them
an honorable burial, and even erected pyramids over their graves.
The great altar of Jupiter, at Olympia, was nothing more than a
huge mound of earth, with stone steps to ascend. Humboldt[*] remarks with astonishment, the striking similarity of the Asiatic
and Egyptian pyramids, to those of Mexico. The similarity of
those which he describes, to the mounds or pyramids on the Mississippi, is still more striking, but not a matter of so much wonder. The only difference is, that a few of the Mexican pyramids
are larger, and some appear to have been faced with stone or

* See Appendix, No. I.

brick. Like those of Mexico, wherever there has been a considerable town, we find two large pyramids, supposed to represent
the sun and moon, and a number of smaller ones, to represent the
stars. There is very little doubt but that they originated with the
same people, for they may be considered as existing in the same
country. What is the distance between Red river and the northern part of the intendancy of Vera Cruz, in which the pyramid of
Papantla is situated? little more than ten or fifteen days journey.
Even supposing there were no mounds in the intermediate
space, the distance is not such, as to preclude the probability of
intercourse. There is no obstruction in the way; a coach and
four has been driven from Mexico to Nacogdoches.

The Mexican histories give uncertain accounts of the origin
of those works, nor are the antiquarians able to form any satisfactory hypothesis. They are attributed by some to the Toultec nation, as far back as the ninth century, who emigrated to
Mexico from the north, perhaps from the banks of the Mississippi; and by others, to the Olmec nation, still more ancient,
who came to Mexico from the east. A curious discovery, made
a few years ago in the state of Tennessee, proves beyond a
doubt, that at some remote period the valley of the Mississippi
had been inhabited by a much more civilized people, than when
first known to us. Two human bodies were found in a coppe-
ras cave, in a surprising state of preservation. They were first
wraped up in a kind of blanket, supposed to have been manufactured of the lint of nettles, afterwards with dressed skins, and
then a mat of nearly sixty yards in length. They were clad in
a beautiful cloth, interwoven with feathers, such as was manufactured by the Mexicans. The flesh had become hard, but the
features were well preserved. They had been here, perhaps,
for centuries, and certainly were of a different race from the
modern Indians. They might have belonged to the Olmec, who
overran Mexico about the seventh century, to the Toultec, who
came centuries afterwards, or to the Aztecs, who founded the
great city of Mexico, in the thirteenth century.

These subjects can only bewilder; every nation, in tracing
back its history, must finally lose itself in fable. The Aztec
(Mexican) mode of preserving their chronicles, must necessa-

rily have been defective; the Egyptians could lay but little better claim to authenticity. The simple fact of the emigration to the country of the Oimecs, or Toultecs, may be relied on, but as to the time and circumstances, we must look for very slender accounts. It is only since the invention of letters that we can form a well grounded hope of the permanency of human institutions, of the certainty of history, and of the uninterrupted progress of improvements. Had this noble invention been unknown, how many of our most useful arts would have been lost during that night of barbarism, called the dark ages!

A French writer has fancifully observed, that civilization arises, *de la fermentation dune nombreuse peuplade*, and that it would be as idle to expect this result without a numerous population, as to think of making wine by the fermentation of a single grape. Experience shews, that a numerous population will always be attended with some degree of improvement, because, as Mr. Jefferson observes, the chances of improvement are multiplied. It is not without reason, that the Creator gave his command to increase and multiply, since many of the intellectual faculties would not otherwise be completely unfolded. It is not every country, however, which can of itself attain the full extent of the population of which it may be rendered susceptible. In unfriendly soils and climates, nature must be forced by the arts and labors of agriculture, to afford sustenance for a numerous population. The inhabitants of such have therefore been usually found in wandering tribes, engaged in constant wars, and probably unable ever to *originate* their own civilization. A mighty warrior, at the head of his own tribe, might subdue the tribes around him, and form a little empire, and peace being secured to a great proportion of his subjects, their numbers would increase, but it would fall into fragments, long before the useful arts could be invented. It has ever been in the mildest climates, gifted by nature with plenty, that civilization has had its origin. Egypt and fruitful Asia, first became possessed of a numerous population, and first cultivated the arts and sciences. In America civilization first appeared, in similar climates, where nature, with little help from man, produces abundance of food. In both the old and the new world, the

celestial spark kindled in those happy climes, would be carried
to less favored regions. But the human race has every where
experienced terrible revolutions. Pestilence, war, and the con-
vulsions of the globe, have annihilated the proudest works, and
rendered vain the noblest efforts. Ask not the sage, by whom,
and when, were erected those lingering ruins, the " frail me-
morials" of ages which have long since been swallowed up in
the ocean of time; ask not the wild Arab, where may be found
the owner of the superb palace, within whose broken walls he
casts his tent; ask not the poor fisherman, as he spreads his nets,
or the ploughman, who whistles over the ground, where is Car-
thage, where is Troy, of whose splendor, historians and poets
have so much boasted! Alas! " they have vanished from the things
that be," and have left but the melancholy lesson, of the insta-
bility of the most stupendous labors, and the vanity of immor-
tality on earth!

In the wanderings of fancy, I have sometimes conceived this
hemisphere, like the other, to have experienced the genial ray
of civilization, and to have been inhabited by a numerous, polite,
and enlightened people.* Why may not great revolutions have
been experienced in America? Is it certain, that Mexico, Peru,

* Even this idea, strange and novel as it may seem, might, by an ingenious theorist, have an air of importance given to it, by bringing into view, some vague passages of ancient authors. Plato, in one of his
dialogues, speaks of a people, who had come from the Atlantic in great
numbers, and overran the greater part of Europe and Asia. Many circumstances related of the island of the Atlantic, correspond with America. This occurrence, to which Plato alludes, was considered of great
antiquity, and preserved by obscure tradition. The island was said to
have been sunk by an earthquake. The fact is certain, that amongst
the Greeks, there prevailed a belief of the existence of another continent, in the Atlantic ocean, and inhabited by a powerful people, who,
in remote antiquity, had invaded the old world Amongst the Romans,
who borrowed the greater part of their learning from the Greeks, the
same belief prevailed. Seneca has this remarkable passage : " In ages to
come, the seas will be traversed, and in spite of the wind and waves, ava-
rice and pride will discover a New World, and Thule shall be no longer
considered the extreme part of the globe." Mons. Peyroux has in a
very ingenious essay, rendered it even probable, that the ancients had

and Chili, when first visited by Europeans, exhibited only the dawn of civilization? Perhaps it was the fiftieth approach doomed to suffer a relapse, before the sacred flame could be extended to other portions of the continent: perhaps, at some distant period the flame had been widely spread, and again extinguished by the common enemies of the human race. But I am asked, if this had been the case, should we not see indubitable proofs, in the remains of antiquity, edifices of stone, mines, and laborious works of human hands. I answer, that nature is ever laboring to restore herself, she is ever engaged in replacing in its primitive state, whatever changes the hand of man may effect in her appearance. Excavations of the earth would be filled up by the hand of time, and piles of stone when separated from the living rock, would crumble into dust. America may have been less fortunate than Europe in those happy inventions which serve in some measure to perpetuate improvements, and yet, in some of the arts she may have attained a greater excellence. The character of her civilization may have been different from any of which we have a knowledge, and her relapse produced by causes of which we can form no conjecture.

Who will assign, as the age of America, a period of years different from that allowed to, what has been denominated, the old world? A multiplicity of proofs contradict the recency of her origin; deeply imbedded stores of carbonated wood, the traces of ancient volcanoes! I could appeal on this subject to her time-worn cataracts, and channels of mighty rivers, and to her venerable mountains, which rose when the Creator laid the foundations of the earth! When the eye of Europe first beheld her, did she appear but lately to have sprung from the deep? No, she contained innumerable and peculiar plants and animals, she was inhabited by thousands of Indians, possessing different languages, manners, and appearances. Grant then, that America may have existed a few thousand years; the same causes prevailing, like effects will be produced; the same revolutions

been acquainted with America in very remote antiquity. Plato places the destruction of the Atlantides, at nine thousand years before his time.

as have been known in the old world may have taken place here.

Before the invention of letters, there would be a constant succession of advances to civilization, and of relapses to barbarism. The Chaldeans, through the glimmer of ancient history, are represented to us as the first inventors of the arts; but may not those people have been preceded by the same revolutions as have succeeded them. In long and arduous advances, they might attain to a great height in civilization, and wars, pestilence, or other calamities, precipitate them to the state of the barbarian or the savage. It is true, the traces of art would long remain undefaced; but they would not remain *forever:* Time would obliterate them.

> " He grasp'd a hero's antique bust,
> The marble crumbled into dust,
> And sunk beneath the shade."—SELLECK OSBORNE.

TO THE READER.

THE reader will easily discover that this Journal contains little more than hasty notes, taken with the intention of being extended and enlarged at leisure; but not regarding my voyage of as much importance as I had imagined it would be, when I undertook it, this idea has been abandoned I might have related many anecdotes and amusing incidents, *quorum magna pars fui*, confided to memory, and have added many remarks on Indian manners. I took some pains in making vocabularies of six or seven different Indian languages, but being informed, that Lewis and Clark had formed much greater collections than my opportunities would admit, I have not thought proper to make use of them. With respect to the natural history of the country, I have hopes that Mr. Bradbury will favor the world with the result of his observations. I have confined myself chiefly to such observations on the face of the country, as would give an idea of its capacity for the reception of population.

For the table which accompanies, I am indebted to general Clark. I take this opportunity of acknowledging my obligations to that gentleman, who politely favored me with every means of information in his power.

JOURNAL

OF

A VOYAGE, &c.

———

CHAPTER I.

M<small>R</small>. MANUEL LISA, of whom I have spoken in the " Views," was chosen by the company, to take the management of its affairs on the Missouri, and endeavor to retrieve them if possible. The profits expected, owing to a variety of unforeseen misfortunes, had not been realized; indeed, it appeared to be a prevailing opinion, that the situation of the company was desperate. Besides the loss by fire, at the Sioux establishment, and the hostility of the Blackfoot Indians, the remnant of the company's men, under Mr. Henry, had crossed the Rocky mountains, and it was not known what had become of them. To ascertain this, was therefore another object of the expedition, and if possible, to carry them assistance. Mr. Lisa, also, privately entertained the hope of being able to make peace with the Blackfoot Indians, and to be permitted to remain quietly in the country, which offered the greatest advantages to the company.

A person better qualified for this arduous undertaking, could not have been chosen. Mr. Lisa is not surpassed by any one, in the requisite experience in Indian trade and manners, and has few equals in perseverance and indefatigable industry. Ardent, bold and enterprising, when any undertaking is begun, no dangers, or sufferings are sufficient to overcome his mind. I be-

lieve there are few men so completely master of that secret of
doing much in a short space of time, which arises, from turning
every moment to advantage, as will appear in the course of the
Journal. This panegyric is due to Mr. Lisa, and it would be
unjust in me to withhold it, after the many marks of attention
I received from him. Unfortunately, however, from what cause,
I know not, the majority of the members of the company have
not the confidence in Mr. Lisa, which he so highly merits; but
on this occasion, he was intrusted with the sole direction of their
affairs, in some degree, from necessity, as the most proper person to conduct an expedition, which appeared little short of desperate. The funds of the company were at so low an ebb, that
it was with some difficulty a barge of twenty tons could be fitted
out, with merchandise to the amount of a few thousand dollars,
and to procure twenty hands and a patron. The members were
unwilling to stake their private credit, where prospects were so
little flattering. This was also the last year appointed for the
continuance of the association, and there was no certainty of its
being renewed.

With respect to myself, I must own to the reader, that I had
no other motive for undertaking a tour of several thousand
miles, through regions but selsom marked, even by the wandering footsteps of the savage, than the mere gratification, of what
he will term an idle curiosity: and I must confess that I might
have employed my time more beneficially to myself, and more
usefully to the community. Would that I were able to make
some amends, by describing the many interesting objects which
I witnessed, in such a manner as to enable the reader to parti-
cipate in the agreeable parts of my peregrinations.

We set off from the village of St. Charles, on Tuesday the
2d of April, 1811, with delightful weather. The flood of March,
which immediately succeeds the breaking up of the ice, had begun to subside, yet the water was still high. Our barge was the
best that ever ascended this river, and manned with twenty stout
oars-men. As Mr. Lisa had been a sea captain, he took much
pains in rigging his boat with a good mast, and main and top-
sail; these being great helps in the navigation of this river. Our
equipage, chiefly composed of young men, though several have

already made a voyage to the upper Missouri, of which they
are exceedingly proud, and on that account claim a kind of pre-
cedence over the rest of the crew.   We are in all, twenty-five
men, well armed, and completely prepared for defence.   There
is, besides, a swivel on the bow of the boat, which, in case of attack, would make a formidable appearance: we have also two
brass blunderbusses in the cabin, one over my birth, and the
other over that of Mr. Lisa.   These precautions were absolutely
necessary from the hostility of the Sioux bands, who, of late had
committed several murders and robberies on the whites, and
manifested such a disposition that it was believed impossible for
us to pass through their country.   The greater part of the merchandise, which consisted of strouding, blankets, lead, tobacco,
knives, guns, beads, &c. was concealed in a false cabin, ingeniously contrived for the purpose; in this way presenting as little
as possible to tempt the savages.   But we hoped, that as this
was not the season for the coming on the river of the wandering
tribes, the fall being the usual time, we might pass by unnoticed.
Mr. Wilson P. Hunt had set off with a large party, about twenty-three days before us, on his way to the Columbia; we anx-
iously hoped to overtake him before he entered the territory of
the Sioux nation; for this purpose it was resolved to strain every nerve, as upon it, in a great measure depended the safety of
our voyage.

Having proceeded a few miles above St. Charles, we put to
shore, some of our men still remaining at the village.   It is exceedingly difficult to make a start on these voyages, from the reluctance of the men to terminate the frolic with their friends,
which usually precedes their departure.   They set in to drink-
ing and carousing, and it is impossible to collect them on board.
Sometimes they make their carousals at the expense of the
Bourgeois; they are credited by the tavern keeper, who knows
that their employer will be compelled to pay, to prevent the delay of the voyage.   Many vexatious abuses are practised in these
cases.   It was found impossible to proceed any further this evening; the men in high glee from the liquor they had drank before
starting; they were therefore permitted to take their swing.

We had on board a Frenchman named Charbonet, with his wife, an Indian woman of the Snake nation, both of whom had accompanied Lewis and Clark to the Pacific, and were of great service. The woman, a good creature, of a mild and gentle disposition, greatly attached to the whites, whose manners and dress she tries to imitate, but she had become sickly, and longed to revisit her native country; her husband, also, who had spent many years amongst the Indians, was become weary of a civilized life. So true, it is, that the attachment to the savage state, or the state of nature, (with which appellation it has commonly been dignified,) is much stronger than to that of civilization, with all its comforts, its refinements, and its security.

Wednesday April 3d. About two o'clock in the afternoon, having at length succeeded in getting all hands on board, we proceeded on our voyage. Found an excessive current, augmented by the state of the waters. Having come about six miles, encamped. In the course of this evening, had as much reason to admire the dexterity of our Canadians and creoles, as I had before to condemn their frivolity. I believe an American could not be brought to support with patience the fatiguing labors, and submission, which these men endure. At this season, when the water is exceedingly cold, they leap in without a moment's hesitation. Their food consists of lied corn homony for breakfast, a slice of fat pork and biscuit for dinner, and a pot of mush for supper, with a pound of tallow in it. Yet this is better than the common fare; but we were about to make an extraordinary voyage, the additional expense was not regarded.

Thursday 4th. Last night we were completely drenched by the rain; the whole party, the bark itself, in a bad condition this morning. Weather somewhat cloudy—clearing up.— A short distance from our encampment, the hills approach the river N. E. side; they are not high, but rocky, and do not continue more than a mile, when the alluvion again commences.— About 8 a fine breeze S. E.—sailed until 12—passed several plantations S. W. side. The bottoms very extensive on the lower part of this river, the banks high, far above the reach of inundation. Timber, principally cotton wood; a few of the trees intermixed with it, are beginning to vegetate. The red-bud, the tree which blooms earliest in our woods, and so much admired by those who descend the Ohio early in the spring, appears in a few places. Passed an island where the river widens considerably; the current rapid, obliged to abandon oars and poles, and take the towing line. Above the island the high land again approaches the river; there is a brownish colored rock, with a few dwarf cedars growing on the top and in the clefts. In going too near shore, we had the misfortune to have our top mast broken by the projecting limb of a tree. Encamped some distance. This evening serene and beautiful; the sand-bars begin to appear; several deer seen. I observed on the sand bars, a kind of scaffolds, ten or fifteen feet in height, which I was informed were erected by the neighboring settlers for the purpose of shooting the deer by moon light, which usually come out of the thickets at this time, to avoid the musketoes and to sport on the smooth beach: the hunter ascends the scaffold, and remains until the deer approaches. Came this day about twenty miles; navigation comparatively easy.

Friday 5th. Wind S. E. this morning, enabling us to set off under sail—continued until ten, when it forsook us. Passed several plantations, and two islands. The bluffs disappear on the N. E. side, and are seen on the S. W. for the first time since our leaving St. Charles. They rise about two hundred feet, and are faced with rock, in masses separated by soil and vegetation. These are called the *Tavern rocks*, from the circumstance of a cave in one of them affording a stopping place for voyagers ascending, or on returning to their homes after a long absence. The Indians seem to have had some veneration for the spot, as it is tolerably well scratched over with their rude attempts at representing birds and beasts. From this place, through a *long reach*, or straight part of the river, we have a distant view of the terminating bluffs N. E. side. A violent storm of rain, wind, and thunder, compelled us to put to shore, having passed a very dangerous and difficult place. The number of trees which had lately fallen into the river, and the danger to be apprehended from others, which seemed to have but a slender hold, rendered our situation extremely disagreeable. Towards evening, a canoe with six or seven men passed on the other side, but we were unable to distinguish them. At this place I measured a cotton-wood tree, which was thirty-six feet in circumference; they grow larger on the lower parts of this river, than perhaps any where else in America. The bluffs, in the course of this day appeared higher, but not so abrupt or rocky.

Saturday 6th. Having passed a small willow island, we got beyond the hills on the S. W. side. At 11 o'clock, the wind became so high, that we were compelled to stop, as it blew directly down the river. This is near Boon's settlement—About sixty miles from St. Charles. A number of plantations at the edge of the bottom. The wind having abated in the evening, we proceeded a few miles further, and encamped.

Sunday 7th. Water rising. Crossed to the S W. side, and encountered a very swift current, at the head of the willow island. The difficulty of this navigation is not easily described. Made Point Labadie, so called from a French trader, who formerly wintered here. Forty years ago this was thought a distant point on the Missouri, at present there are tolerable plantations every where through the bottom. The carcases of several drowned buffaloes passed by us; it is said that an unusual number of them has been drowned this year—Some have been seen floating on the river at St. Louis. A gentleman lately descended, declares that he counted forty on the head of an island. Immediately below Point Labadie, the river contracts its breadth, and is confined to a channel of three or four hundred yards wide. Passed between an island and the main shore; a very narrow channel, but the current and distance less. A channel of this sort is often taken in preference, and it is one of the means of facilitating the ascending of this uncommonly rapid river: but there is sometimes danger of the upper end being losed with logs and billets of wood matted together, as it turned out in the present instance; fortunately after the labor of an hour we were able to remove the obstacles, else we should have been compelled to return. Opposite the head of the island there is a tolerarable log house, and some land cleared; the tenant, a new comer, with a wife and six children, had nothing to give or sell. Here the banks fall in very much: the river more than a mile wide.

A great impediment in opening lands on this river, is the dilapidation of the banks, which immediately ensue when the trees are cut away, from the rapid current acting upon a light soil of a texture extremely loose. It will be found absolutely necessary to leave the trees to stand on the borders of the river. The river exceedingly crooked in the course of this day. A number of plantations on both sides. Having made about fourteen miles, we put to shore, after passing a very difficult *embarras*. This word needs some explanation. Independent of the current of that vast volume of water rolling with great impetuosity, the navigation is obstructed by various other impediments. At the distance of every mile or two, and frequently at less distant intervals, there are *embarras*, or rafts, formed by the collection of trees closely matted, and extending from twenty to thirty yards. The current vexed by these interruptions, rushes round them with great violence and force. We may now judge what a boat encounters in grapling round these rafts. When the oars and grapling hooks were found insufficient, the towing line was usually resorted to with success. There is not only difficulty here, but considerable danger, in case the boat should swing round. In bends where the banks fall in, as in the Mississippi, trees lie for some distance out in the river. In doubling points, in passing sawyers, difficulties are encountered. The water is generally too deep to admit of poling; it would be absolutely impossible to stem the current further out than a few yards ; the boat usually passes about this distance from the bank. Where the bank has not been washed steep, which is most usually the case, and the ground newly formed, the young trees, of the willow, cotton-wood &c. which overhang the stream, afford much assistance in pulling the boat along with the hands.

Monday 8*th.* The water fell last night as much as it had risen. About ten came in sight of a little village N. E. side called Charette. There are about thirty families here, who hunt, and raise a little corn. A very long island lies in the bend in which this village is situated. Above this island, passed under a gentle breeze some very handsome bluffs, S. W. side to the *isle aux Boeufs;* they are about one hundred feet high, and excepting in a few places where rocks appear, covered with oak

and other timber. At this place, the river makes a considerable
bend. Instead of taking the main channel, we entered a smaller
one between the island and the shore, which will shorten the
distance; the current not so strong. The channel is about fifty
yards wide, and very handsome, having clean even banks, and resembling a small river.—It is about four miles in length.

Through all these islands, and on the Missouri bottoms,
there are great quantities of rushes, commonly called scrub
grass * They grow four or five feet high, and so close, as to
render it very disagreeable, as well as difficult, to pass through
the woods. The cattle feed upon them in the winter, answer-
ing the same purpose as the cane on the Mississippi.

At the upper end of the *isle aux Boeufs*, we were compelled, about five o'clock in the evening, to put to shore, on account
of a violent storm, which continued until after dark. In the badly constructed cabin of our boat, we were wet to the skin:
the men were better off in their tents, made by a blanket stretched over twigs.

We have been accompanied for these two days past, by a
man and two lads, ascending in a canoe. This evening they encamped close by us, placing the canoe under shelter of our boat.
Unsheltered, except by the trees on the bank, and a ragged
quilt drawn over a couple of forks, they abode " the pelting of
the pitiless storm," with apparent indifference. These people
are well dressed in handsome home made cotton cloth. The
man seemed to possess no small share of pride and self importance, which, as I afterwards discovered, arose from his being a
captain of militia. He borrowed a kettle from us, and gave it
to one of his boys. When we were about to sit down to supper,
he retired, but returned when it was over; when asked, why he
had not staid to do us the honor of supping with us; " I thank
you, gentlemen," said he, licking his lips with satisfaction, " I
have just been eating an excellent supper."—He had scarcely
spoken, when the *patron*† came to inform Mr. Lisa, they were

* This is the case for several hundred miles up the Missouri.

† The Patron is the fresh water sailing-master.

begging him for a biscuit, as they had eaten nothing for two days! our visitant was somewhat disconcerted, but passed it off with, " Poh! I'm sure they can't be suffering!"

He resides on the Gasconade; was the second family which settled in that quarter, about three years ago. He has at present about 250 men on his muster-roll. We were entertained by him with a long story of his having pursued some Pottawatomies, who had committed robberies on the settlements some time last summer; he made a narrow escape, the Indians having attacked his party in the night time, and killed four of his men after a desperate resistance. The captain had on board a barrel of whiskey to set up tavern with, a bag of cotton for his wife to spin, and a couple of kittens, for the purpose of augmenting his family: these kept up such *doleful serenades*, during the night, that I was scarcely able to close my eyes.

CHAPTER II.

Tuesday 9th. Set off this morning with a light breeze, which continued to augment until ten, when from a change in the course of the river, it was unfavorable for two or three miles. Passed a number of plantations on both sides, and *isle a la Loutr*, which is about twelve miles long, and two wide, near the N. E. side; it has a compact settlement. In the course of the day we lost sight of our captain of the Gasconade, who was not able to keep up with us in his canoe.

Passed at four o'clock, the Gasconade, a considerable river, S. W. side, which rises with the Maramek, and has been ascended upwards of one hundred miles, in canoes; but its channel is rocky and rough. It is ninety miles from the mouth of the Missouri. The lands on its borders are broken and hilly, and badly wooded. Before reaching the Gasconade, we passed a

long range of bluffs, or rather hills, well covered with wood, but
terminating at the entrance of the river in rocky precipices;
this range appears again on the other side of the Gasconade.—
There is a very long reach here, of fifteen or twenty miles; the
Gasconade hills, on the S. W. side, are washed by the Missouri
the whole of this distance.   This day was sufficient to prove the
efficacy of our sails, in navigating this river; we passed with
ease, places much worse than any we had encountered since
leaving St. Charles. Encamped six miles above the Gasconade;
heavy rains last night.

   Wednesday 10*th*. Cloudy—crossed to the bluffs, N. E. side,
which are high and rocky. Passed Montbrun's tavern and river;
another stopping place for voyagers Passed an *embarras*, N. E.
side, the most difficult since we started. There are wide bottoms
above these bluffs, on both sides of the river. The wind against
us throughout the whole of this day. The verdure is observed
to be rapidly increasing; the smaller trees and shrubs are already in gay green. From the color of the water on the S. W side,
it appears that the Osage river is paying the annual tribute.

   Thursday 11*th*. A fine morning. Current so strong S. W.
side, from the waters of the Osage, that we were compelled to
cross to an island.   Hills on the N. E. side, not high or rocky:
continued on this side to ascend throughout the day, though
with difficulty, on account of numerous *embarras*, and falling in
of the banks. This is a fine country: the lands extremely rich,
and covered with a great variety of trees.   Stopped a few moments at the cabin of a Frenchman, who is beginning to open a
plantation.   In company with the interpreter, I proceeded by
land, across a point, about two miles to the village of *Cote sans
Dessein*, where we arrived nearly three hours before the barge.
We inquired with eagerness after the party of Mr. Hunt; we
were informed that he had passed this place twenty-one days
ago. Thus far, it appears that we have gained but two days upon him.

   Friday 12*th*.   Weather fine—a gentle breeze on the river
from S. E.   Remained here until eleven, engaged in repairing
our cabin.   Mr. Lisa here employed a famous hunter, named

Castor, a Kansas Indian, who had been brought up from infancy amongst the whites.

The *Cote sans Dessein*, is a beautiful place, situated on the N. E side of the river, and in sight of the Osage. It will in time become a considerable village. The beauty and fertility of the surrounding country cannot be surpassed. It is here that we met with the first appearance of prairie, on the Missouri, but it is handsomely mixed with wood land. The wooded country on the N. E. extends at least thirty miles, as far up as this place, and not less than fifteen on the other side. The name is given to this place, from the circumstance of a single detached hill filled with limestone, standing on the bank of the river, about six hundred yards long, and very narrow.—The village has been established about three years; there are thirteen French families, and two or three of Indians. They have handsome fields in the prairie, but the greater part of their time is spent in hunting. From their eager inquiries after merchandise, I perceived we were already remote from the settlements.

We continued under way, with a light breeze, but scarcely sufficient to waft the barge of itself, without the aid of oars.— Handsome wooded upland, S. W. side, gently sloping to the river, and not rocky. For many reasons, I would prefer these situations to the bottom, where the soil is richer. Passed the Great Osage river, one hundred and thirty-three miles from the mouth of the Missouri, and navigable about six hundred miles. There is much fine land immediately on its borders, but the prairies stretch out on either side, and to the westward are almost boundless. The Osage villages are situated about two hundred miles up.

Passed a long island, called *L' isle a' Cedre*, Cedar island. A number of islands on the Missouri bear this name, from the growth of cedar upon them, in this particular, differing from the islands of the Mississippi. In this island the best part of the wood had been cut down, and rafted to St. Louis, to supply the settlements with this wood, of which there is a great consumption.

Throughout the course of this day, we found the navigation less arduous and painful; owing principally to the falling of the

waters, and to our having passed one of those rivers which add
to the current of the Missouri. The sand bars, begin to present
a pleasing appearance; several miles in length, clean and smooth.
Instead of ascending along either side, we pursued the middle
of the river, along the sand bars. Encamped N. E. side, just
above the Cedar island. The bars and the sides of the river are
every where marked with deer tracks.

Saturday 13*th.* A fine morning—somewhat cool—set off
with a favorable breeze. Passed hills on the S. W. side—saw
five or six deer sporting on a sand bar. Passed the Manitoo
rocks, S. W. side, a la *Bonne Femme* creek. The country hereabout, is delightful; the upland sloping gently to the river, timbered with oak, hickory, ash, &c. The lands on this stream are
said not to be surpassed by any in the territory.

After having had a favorable wind the greater part of the
day, encamped at the *Roche percee*, perforated rock; a high
craggy cliff on the N. E. side. This is the narrowest part of the
river I have yet seen; it is scarcely two hundred yards wide.—
Made in the course of this day about twenty-eight miles, for
which we were indebted to the favorable wind. Some of us considered this good fortune, a reward for the charity which was
manifested by us yesterday, in spending an hour to relieve a
poor ox, which was swamped near the bank. The poor creature
had remained here ten or twelve days, and the sand into which
he had sunk, was become hard and solid. The wolves had paid
him friendly visits from time to time, to inquire after his health,
while buzzards, crows, and eagles, tendered their salutations
from the boughs of the neighboring trees.

Sunday 14*th.* Violent wind all night—hoisted sail before
day light, in order to take advantage of the wind. Passed the
Maniton on the N. E. side, and high rocks. A delightful country. Wind slackened about ten   At twelve, came in sight of
the hills of Mine river, resembling those of the Gasconade. At
three, the wind again rose—passed the Mine river, S. W side.
This river is not navigable more than ten or twelve miles. Valuable saltworks are established here. The whole of this day
we found rich and extensive bottoms, N. E. side, and beautiful
sloping upland, S. W. on this side of the river some beau-

tiful situations for farms and plantations. The hills rise with a most delightful ascent from the water's edge, to the height of forty or fifty feet; the woods open and handsome. The lands on the Mine river, reputed excellent. The bottoms on the N. E. side the Missouri, uncommonly fine. There is a flourishing settlement here. As this is Sunday, the good people were dressed out in their best clothes, and came in groups to the bank to gaze upon us, as we passed by under sail. We put to shore, at the farm of Braxton Cooper, a worthy man, who has the management of the saltworks. The settlement is but one year old, but is already considerable, and increasing rapidly; it consists of seventy-five families, the greater part living on the bank of the river, in the space of four or five miles. They are, generally, persons in good circumstances, most of them have slaves. Mr. Cooper informed me that the upland, back, is the most beautiful ever beheld. He thinks that from the mouth of the Missouri to this place, the country for at least forty miles from the river, may bear the character of rich woodland: the prairies forming but trifling proportions. This place is two hundred miles up. We inquired for the party of which we were in chase—they had passed by *nineteen* days before us.

Monday 15*th*. Rain last night, but without lightning—from this it is prognosticated that the wind will continue favorable to day. Set off with a fair wind, but the course of the river became unfavorable. At half past seven, again fair—continued under sail until twelve. Passed handsome upland S. W. side, and the two Charreton rivers N. E. Had to oppose in the course of the day some very difficult places—the river extremely crooked. While the men were towing, they chased a she bear into a hollow tree; we set about chopping the tree, while several stood with guns presented to the hole at which she had entered, about twenty feet up. In a short time she put out her head and shoulders, but on receiving a volley, instantly withdrew. The chopping was renewed; madam Cuff again appeared, and was saluted as before, but without producing the same effect, as she leisurely crawled down the tree, and attempted to make off, amidst the shouts of fifteen or twenty barbarians, who were bent on the destruction of a mother and her little family. She was killed with a stroke of an axe, having been previously severely wounded. In the hollow sycamore, there were found three cubs At five, hoisted sail, and continued until seven, having this day made twenty-eight miles. Towards evening, passed beautiful undulating hills, gently sloping to the river. What charming situations for seats and farms!

Tuesday 16*th*. Set off without wind—the river rising. At eleven, the wind so much against us that we were obliged to lie by. At three we continued our voyage, and as it was resolved to tow, I set out with my rifle, expecting to meet the boat at the head of a long bend. This is the first excursion I have made into the country. I passed through the bottom with great difficulty, on account of the rushes, which grow as high as a man's head, and are matted with vines and briars. The beauty of the upland in some degree recompensed. Clean and open woods, growth, oak, hickory, &c; the grass beginning to appear green. Saw several deer, and abundance of turkeys. We are now in a country which abounds with game. I came late in the evening to the boat, I having been supposed lost in the woods. Our hunter had been more successful than I, having killed a she bear with four cubs. The river very crooked in the course of this day.— Passed some places of thin woods—not quite prairie, on the bank of the river.

Wednesday 17*th* Breakfasted under sail. Passed the GRAND river, N. E. side. It is two hundred yards wide at its mouth; a very long river, navigable six or eight hundred miles, and takes its waters with the river *Des Moines*. The traders who were in the habit of visiting the Mahas, six hundred miles above this on the Missouri, were formerly compelled to ascend this river in order to avoid the Kansas Indians, who were then the robbers of the Missouri There is a portage of not more than a couple of days, from the Grand river to the Mahas.

At the confluence on the lower side, there is a beautiful situation. The bottom is a handsome prairie, which is seen extending for the first time on the Missouri, to the water's edge, and about a mile in width: the upland then rises with a gentle ascent, with here and there a few clumps of trees. Immediately at the point of junction, there are about fifty acres of well tim-

bered land. Here is a delightful situation for a village: the distance about two hundred and forty miles from the mouth of the
Missouri There is some beautiful country lying on the Grand
river, but deficient in wood. In fact, this river may almost be
considered the boundary of the wooded upland on that side of
the river.

Here the wind failed us. The Missouri very wide; a large
bar in the middle. The beautiful green hills of the Little Osage
in sight. But for the single defect of the dilapidating banks of
the Missouri, the country bordering on it, thus far, would not
be surpassed by any in the world. Spring has already cast her
green mantle over the land ; and the scenery every where assumes a more enlivened appearance. After an arduous navigation, came this day about twenty miles.

Thursday 18*th.* Heavy rain last night, accompanied by unusual thunder and lightning. Set off at six, weather apparently
clearing up. About ten, compelled by heavy rain to put to shore
until three, when we again shoved off, came a few miles and encamped, N. E side.

Friday 19*th.* Continued our voyage at daylight, and came
through a long channel, between an island and the shore. The
wind S. E. but the course of the river such as to disable us from
profiting by it. A drizzling rain, and the weather disagreeable.
Wind favorable for an hour. Passed handsome upland and prairie S W. side. There was formerly a village of the Little Osages here, but from the frequent attacks of the Ayuwas, they
were compelled to go higher up the river. The situation is fine.
At a distance, the deep green herbage on this open ground had
much the appearance of a wheat field.

Encamped late, after having got through a channel with considerable difficulty. The slowness with which we have advanced for several days past, forms a contrast with those which preceded. Water rising.

Saturday 20*th.* A cold disagreeable morning. The men
drenched by the heavy rain of last night. Hoisted sail about six,
but the wind served us but a short distance.—Weather clearing
up—put to shore for an hour to dry our effects. Handsome hills
on the S. W. side. Got under way at three, along the N. E.

side. One of the finest tracts of land I have seen—a great proportion of the timber is walnut, poplar, and cotton wood, of enormous size. Entered a channel, at the upper end of which, fired
upon a flock of several hundred pelicans, standing on a shoal.—
These birds abound very much on the Missouri, but are shy.—
We daily kill wild fowl, ducks, geese, brandt, &c.—which ascend the river at this season of the year, to breed. Their eggs
are found at every moment, on the sand bars.

Sunday 21*st.* A delightful morning, though somewhat cool.
Got under way early—passed through the channel, and crossed
over to the S. W. side. Had some difficult *embarras*, but no
great current. After breakfast, took my gun, and struck into
the woods. On ascending the hills about two hundred feet in
height, I had a fine view up and down the river. On the other
side. (N E.) there is an extensive prairie bottom, apparently
four or five miles wide; and a evel plain of vast extent stretching out on either hand, of rich a uvion soil, from the appearance
of the luxuriant herbage. There is a singular contrast of the
sward which has remained unburnt, and the extensive tracts of
deep green of the grass of this spring. Beyond the plain, the
prairie rises into upland, of abrupt elevation, and in a thousand
fantastic forms, but without a shrub, and apparently covered with
but a thin coat of vegetation.

On this side, (S. W.) I found the soil of the upland of an
excellent quality—and notwithstanding the ravages committed
by fire, the woods, principally hickory, oak, walnut, ash, &c.—
were tolerably close.

Returned to the boat about four in the evening. We spent
an hour and an half this evening, in grappling around some rocks
of free stone, the distance of a few hundred yards. The swiftness of the current on the other side rendered it impossible to
attempt it there—Encamped some distance above an encampment of Mr. Hunt, which appeared not more than ten or twelve
days old.

Monday 22*d.* Continued until eleven, with *cordelle*, or towing line—the banks being favorable. The hills, or bluffs, are
here, about one hundred feet high, and rise abruptly from the
river. Wind from S. S. W. becoming too strong, were com-

pelled to lie by until three. Crossed to the N. E. side, and endeavored to ascend between the shore and an island, but found a
sand bar running across, at the upper end, so that we were obliged to back, and encamp nearly opposite the place of starting.

Tuesday 23*d.* Very high wind this morning. Doubled the
island which had been the scene of so much vexation. Endeavored to proceed on the outside, but met with so many difficulties, that we were compelled to cross to the S. W. side. Towed to Ibar's channel and island—then re-crossed to the N. E.
side, and found ourselves about two miles above our last night's
encampment. Remained here until three, when the wind somewhat abated its violence. Having arrived opposite the Wizzard's
island, (L'isle du Sorcier) crossed over and encamped. The
superstitious boatmen believe that a wizzard inhabits this
island; they declare that a man has been frequently seen on the
sand beach, at the point, but that he suddenly disappears, on the
approach of any one. These few days have been in a manner lost,
from contrary winds, and bad weather. Heavy rain this evening—Musketoes begin to be troublesome, for the first time during our voyage.

Wednesday 24*th.* Attempted a ripple this morning, and
were driven back five times—we had once got within half
the boat's length of being through; the oars and poles were
insufficient; ten of our men leaped into the water with the cordelle, while the rest of us exerted ourselves with the pole : and
thus by perseverance became conquerors. This ripple, like all
others of the Missouri, is formed by high sand bars, over which
the water is precipitated, with considerable noise This bar has
been formed within two or three years. The bend formerly almost impassible from the swiftness of the current, is now tolerable. There is seldom any great current on both sides : the falling in of the banks indicates the current to be there. Wherever
the river has a wider channel than ordinary, there is usually a
sand bar in the middle. This extraordinary river sometimes
pursues a straight course for ten or fifteen miles, then suddenly
turns to every point of the compass: In other places, the whole
volume of its waters is compressed into a channel of two or three
hundred yards: again suddenly opening to the width of one, or

even two miles, with islands and sand bars scattered through
the space.

Passed a canoe with four men, who had wintered up the Kansas, about five hundred miles: they had beaver, and other furs.
They could give no information respecting Hunt's party :—we
conclude he must have passed that river before they came out
of it.

From the violence of the wind, made but a few miles. While
Castor was out, he saw a *white turkey*. but was not so fortunate
as to kill it. I am told that they have sometimes been seen of
this color; but I suspect it is

Rara avis in terris, nigroque simillima cygno.

Thursday 25*th*. Contrary winds, but not such as to prevent
us from continuing our voyage tolerably well. About eleven,
came in sight of Fort Osage, situate on a bluff, three miles off,
on a commanding eminence. We stopped sometime at the
clearing of Mr. Audrain, who is about opening a farm below the
fort. A number of Indians of the Osage nation, of all ages. and
sexes, were scattered along the bank, attracted by curiosity—
some with old buffaloe robes thrown over their shoulders, others
dressed out in the gayest manner.   They gathered round us in
crowds, and manifested an idle curiosity, very different from
the Indians who live east of the Mississippi, one of whose cha-
teristics, is a studied indifference, as to every thing strange
which transpires around them.

On landing at the fort, on a very rocky shore, a soldier under arms, who waited for us at the water's side, escorted Mr.
Lisa and myself to the fort, where we were politely received by
the commanding officer.

While Mr. Lisa was transacting some business, accompanied by Mr. Sibly, the factor, and an interpreter, I went to deliver a pipe to *Sans Oreille*, (a warrior, and head man of this tribe)
sent to him by gen. Clark. He received us, seated on a mat,
and after smoking in the usual manner, requested the interpreter to inform me "that he was the friend of the Americans, and

that he was flattered with this proof of gen. Clark's good will towards him." He was surrounded by a number of young warriors, who appeared to look upon him with great respect. This man, though not a chief, is evidently intriguing to be the head of his tribe, and has great influence with them: the chief, Young White Hairs, having but little to entitle him to respect from his own character, being extremely young, and of a gentle disposition. *Sans Oreille*, as is usual with the ambitious amongst these people, is the poorest man in the nation: to set the heart upon goods and chattels, being reckoned indicative of a mean and narrow soul: he gives away every thing he can obtain, in order to procure popularity. Such is ambition! Little know they of this state of society, who believe that it is free from jealousies, envy, detraction, or guilty ambition. No demagogue—no Cataline, ever used greater art and finesse, or displayed more policy than this cunning savage. The arts of seducing the multitude are nearly the same every where, and the passion for power and distinction, seems inherent in human nature. He is a tall fine looking man, possesses very superior abilities, and is esteemed the best warrior of the village.

The fort is handsomely situated, about one hundred feet above the level of the river, which makes an elbow at this place, giving an extensive view up and down the river. Its form is triangular; this fort is small, not calculated for more than a company of men. A group of buildings is formed by the factory, suttler's house; &c. The lodges of the Little Osage, are sixty in number, and within gun shot of the fort; but they are about to remove their village to a prairie, three miles off. Their lodges are of a circular form; not more than ten or fifteen feet in diameter, constructed by placing mats, made of coarse rushes, over forks and poles.

All three of the Osage bands, together with some Kansas, were lately encamped here for the purpose of trading; to the number of fifteen hundred warriors. The officer informed me, that about ten days ago, serious apprehensions had been entertained from them. A war party, of about two hundred, having scalped a few women and children, of the Ayuwas, their enemies, had returned so elated with this exploit, that they insulted the

people of the fort. One of these warriors defied a centinel on
his post; the centinel was commanded to fire over his head, this
producing no effect, he was seized by a file of men. This he at
first treated with indifference, declaring, that if he was confined,
he would get some of the whitemen's *bread;* his tune was changed, however, by a liberal application of the cat o' nine tails to
his back. Great commotions amongst the Indians were excited; they rushed forward with their arms; but the soldiers no
sooner paraded and made ready a few pieces of cannon, than
they thought proper to retreat. They maintained a threatening
attitude for some days, and to give vent to their spite, killed a
pair of fine oxen, belonging to Mr. Audrain. The officer sent
for the chiefs, and told them, that unless two others were given
for the oxen, he would instantly fire upon their village. This
spirited deportment had the desired effect, the chief complied,
and after some counselling, the pipe was smoked, and all matters
adjusted.

These Indians are not to be compared to the nations east of
the Mississippi; although at war with most of their neighbors,
they are a cowardly race. One good trait, however, deserves to
be mentioned; they have rarely, if ever, been known to spill the
blood of a white man:—When a white hunter is found on their
lands, they take away his furs and his arms, he is then beaten
with ramrods, and driven off.

Mr. Sibly informed me, that he was just setting out on a
tour towards the Arkansas, to visit the salines,* on that river,
and also to the Kansas and Platte, to see the Pani nation.

Thus far we have gained about one hundred miles upon the
party of Hunt—we are in good spirits, and will renew the pursuit with augmented vigor.

This place is something better than three hundred miles up
the Missouri, in lat. 38° 40′.

---

* In the Appendix, there will be found, an extract from the Journal
of Mr. Sibly's tour.

CHAPTER III.

Friday, 26*th April.* Heavy rains last night, our situation extremely uncomfortable. This morning we were awakened about daylight, by the most hideous howlings I ever heard.— They proceeded from the Osages, among whom this is a custom. On inquiry. I found that they were unable to give any satisfactory reason for it; I could only learn, that it was partly religious, and if it be true, as is supposed by many, that they offer their worship only to the Evil Spirit, the orison was certainly not unworthy of him. I was told, also, that it arises from another cause; when any one, on awaking in the morning, happens to think of a departed friend, even of some valued dog or horse, which has been lost, he instantly begins this doleful cry, and all the others hark in, as soon as it is heard.

About eleven o'clock, clearing up, but wind very strong from the S. W. we set off with it, blowing directly in our faces.— About twelve we put to shore and remained for more than two hours. Crossed to the N. E. side, and continued our voyage.— Towards evening the weather moderated. Passed a small encampment of hunters. The Missouri is now what the Ohio was once, the *Paradise of hunters.* Made nine miles to day. The water is at a good stage for ascending; the navigation becomes more agreeable. Weather somewhat cool.

We have now passed the last settlement of whites, and probably will not re-visit them for several months. This reflection caused us all to think seriously of our situation. I almost repented of having undertaken this voyage, without an object in view, of suitable importance. Our men were kept from thinking too deeply, by the cheering songs, which were encouraged by Mr. Lisa, and the splashing of the oars, which kept time with them. So far removed, I seemed to look back, as from an eminence; thus abstracted, I fancied that I contemplated my country with more accuracy than I could while protected in its bosom. I heaved a sigh, when I reflected that I might never see it, or my friends again; that my bones might be deposited on some dreary spot, far from my home, and the haunts of civilized man; but this last, suggested a consolation, there is no spot however distant, where I may be buried, but will in time, be surrounded by the habitations of Americans, the place will be marked, and approached with respect, as containing the remains of one of the first who ventured into these distant and solitary regions!

Saturday 27th. We are once more to be somewhat favored. This is a delightful morning, though cool. Set off at daylight, and at six, had a light breeze from east. Passed Vincent's island, above which the river is extremely narrow, and hills S. W. side. About eleven, met a party of traders in two canoes lashed together, which form a kind of raft, heavily laden with furs, and skins. They came from the Sioux, who, they say, are peaceably disposed. They met Hunt's party, five days ago, at the Little Nimeha; it proceeds slowly, and had two days of contrary winds.— The traders think we shall be able to overtake them at the river Platte.—Hunt informed them that they would meet us below the Grand river. Wind fell shortly after leaving this party. The good news we have heard, animates our men very much.

Towards evening, passed Benito's island and sand bar, S. W. side, so called, from a trader of that name having been robbed by the Ayuwas of his peltry, and he, with his men, forced to carry enormous burdens of it on their backs, to the river des Moines. Instances of such insults were formerly very usual: several spots have been shewn to me where like acts have been committed, and even accompanied with murder. Having come within two leagues of the Kansas river, we encamped. Large sand bars begin every where to appear.

Sunday 28th. A cool morning, and somewhat foggy on the river—A light breeze from the east, but not sufficient to enable us to carry sails. Passed high land N. E side, with some rocks on the shore; we are constantly delighted with the gentle hills, or rather elevated upland of the Missouri. On a large sand bar, saw nearly thirty deer. They are very numerous on this part of the river.

Passed the Kansas, a very large river which enters on the S. W. side. It heads between the Platte and the Arkansas.— The country on its borders, is entirely open. The river can be ascended with little difficulty, more than twelve hundred miles. The Kansas nation of Indians reside upon it.

In the evening we passed the litttle river Platte, navigable with canoes fifty or sixty miles, and said to abound with beaver. We encamped near a mile above it, having made about fifteen miles.

In the course of this day, we find the river, in most places, extremely narrow, and the sand bars very extensive.

Monday 29*th.* Somewhat cloudy this morning—A light breeze from the S. E. At seven, breakfasted under sail. At nine, reached a beautiful island, called Diamond island, fifteen miles above the Kansas. From this, there is a long reach of six or eight miles. The weather is fine—the breeze still continuing.

At three o'clock we had made twenty-four miles. The wind, from the change of the course of the river, could not serve us. We lost two hours in passing one of the most difficult places I have seen on the river: after which, we had a fair wind again, until night.

Passed in the course of this day, some beautiful country on both sides: the upland chiefly S. W and a greater proportion of prairie than we have yet seen. The river generally narrow, and the sand bars of great extent.

Having made about thirty miles, we encamped a short distance below Buffaloe island, opposite a range of hills, and at the upper end of a long view. During the whole of the day, we saw astonishing quantities of game on the shore; particularly deer and turkeys. The buffaloe or elk are not yet seen.

Tuesday 30*th.* Last night there was much thunder and lightning, but little rain. At day light embarked with a favorable wind, which continued until seven, when, from the course of the river, the wind failed us for an hour. The river extremely crooked. Mr. Lisa and myself went on shore, and each killed a deer. There were great numbers of them sporting on the sand bars. There are great quantities of snipes, of a beautiful plumage, being a curious mixture of dove color, and white. I saw one of a different kind, which was scarlet underneath the wings

At two o'clock we hoisted sail at the beginning of a long
reach, to the great joy of the whole company. High prairies S.
W. side—continued under sail through another long reach, and
had a view of the old Kansas village, at the upper end of it. It
is a high prairie ; smooth waving hills, perfectly green, with a
few clumps of trees in the hollows. But for the scarcity of timber this would be a delightful situation for a town. At this
place, the bend of the river rendered the wind unfavorable.—
Continued under oars about 3 miles further, having in the course
of this day made thirty three miles.

Wednesday, 1st *May*. Very high wind all last night. Embarked this morning about daylight, and continued under sail
until six o'clock. Upland N. E. side, thinly timbered. It may
be remarked, that the hills of the Missouri are not so high as
those of the Ohio, seldom rocky, and rise more pleasantly from
the water's edge. Continued under sail until eleven, when we
were brought off by a considerable bend in the river. Passed St.
Michael's prairie, a handsome plain in front, with variegated hills
in the back ground, and but little wood. At two o'clock we
came to a very great bend in the river, but did not get through
until evening. The river from being narrow, changes to an unusual width, and very shallow. We were detained about an
hour, having been so unlucky as to run aground.

Saw but one or two deer to day, as we approach the open
country their numbers will be found to diminish, there being no
thickets to shelter them. They are said to lessen perceptibly
from Nodawa river upwards.

In the evening, the weather, which has been for some days
cloudy, cleared up, and the wind abated entirely : the Missouri
and its scenery appeared in their natural state. The wind also
became calm, and seemed to harmonize with nature. The river
is falling fast, approaching to a low stage of water—came to day
twenty-seven miles.

Thursday 2d. Embarked at daylight, the river unruffled by
a breeze ; the birds, as if rejoicing that the strife of the elements
had ceased, tuned their sweetest notes.

At seven o'clock, breakfasted opposite some bluffs N. E.
side. A very large mass appeared at no distant period, to have

slipped into the river, leaving a clay precipice fifty or sixty feet
high. A little above, there are rocks of freestone at the edge
of the water. Below this place, there is an extensive prairie,
partly river bottom, and partly upland, with a considerable rivulet passing through it. What a delightful situation for a farm,
or even a town! Description of such a country as this, can give
no idea of its peculiar character. The hills, or bluffs, begin to
appear, thinly wooded with dwarf trees, principally oak or ash.

In the evening arrived at Nodawa channel, on the N. E.
side, and about five miles in length.

Friday 3d. A beautiful morning; set off at daylight as usual, and passed the wintering ground of Crooks and M'Clelland,
some distance above Nodawa.

High hills on the S. W. side, with some bold places, and
fine land on the N. E. side. In the afternoon passed Wolf river, fourteen miles from Nodawa. Shortly after this, a breeze
from N. E. enabled us, from the course of the river, to sail four
or five miles. Passed a large prairie S W. side, and encamped
at the commencement of another. In these places there is not
even a shrub to the water's edge, the bottom of considerable
width the grass very luxuriant.

Saturday 4th. Heavy rain last night, and drizzling this morning. Passed an extensive lowland prairie, above our encampment. At half past eight, passed an encampment of Hunt. In
the evening passed the Nimeha and Tarkio creeks, and encamped a short distance above.

I overheard this evening, with considerable chagrin, while
warming myself at the fire, some bitter complaints on the part
of the men: they declared that it was impossible for them to
stand it long, that they had never so severe a voyage. This dis-
content was of course excited by some Thersites of the party.—
Great exertions have certainly been made and no moments lost,
in advancing our voyage, but much of the time we were carried along by the wind, when there was no need for any labor on
the part of the men. The weather is now fine, and their labor
diversified, when there is no wind, by the pole, the oars, or cordelle, which is little more than a promenade along the sand bars.

I represented these things to them as well as I could, and endeavored to quiet their minds.

Sunday 5th Passed an encampment of Hunt this morning. The sun shone out, but the air was cool—wind from N. E. but not so hard as to form any great obstacle. In the evening hailed two men descending in a bark canoe; they had been of Hunt's party, and had left him on the 2d of May, two days above the Platte, at Boyer's river. They had fair wind it seems all the way up. Thus, it seems we have gained upon them as much as we expected.

The weather very fine throughout the day, encamped in the evening at the upper end of a handsome prairie, opposite a large sand bar.

Monday 6th. About ten this morning, passed a river called Nis-na-botona, after which there are some long reaches very favorable for sailing. At four o'clock arrived at the little Naneha, the course of the river here is for a considerable distance nearly N. E.—Wind being N. W. were enabled to hoist sail, but having proceeded about a mile, a squall suddenly sprung up from the N. we were compelled with all despatch to take in sail, and gain the shore S. W. side. Here a dreadful storm raged during the remainder of the evening, and the greater part of the night.

Our encampment is at the edge of a large prairie, but with a fringe of wood along the bank of the river. The greater part of the country, particularly on the S. W. side, is now entirely open. The grass is at this time about six inches high.

Tuesday 7th. Continued our voyage at daylight, the weather fine, though somewhat cool. Wind still continues N. W.— Passed an island and sand bar, and towed along a prairie S. side for nearly a mile. This prairie is narrow, bounded by hills somewhat broken and stony.

At ten o'clock arrived at *L'isle a` beau soleil*; the wind here became so high that we proceeded with great difficulty. In the evening, arriving at the head of the island, were compelled to put to shore. Mr. Lisa seized this opportunity of replacing his mast, by a young oak which he found in the wood along the shore. All hands were set to work on it, in order that it might be ready the next day. This was rendered necessary on account of the old one having given way.

I took this opportunity of making an excursion into the country—ascended the hills or bluffs, which, though steep, are not much more than two hundred feet above the level of the river, and command prospects of great extent. I could see the meandering course of the river, between the two ranges of hills, or more properly of high land, for thirty or forty miles. Some of these hills are cut into precipices forty or fifty feet high, without any appearance of stone. It is a light yellow colored earth, with a considerable mixture of sand. There is an immense extent of prairie on both sides of the river. The hills are not always abrupt, but in many places rise gently, and are extremely beautiful. The river hereabout is very crooked: in following the hills, along which there is an Indian path, I could go to a point up the river, which will most probably be our place of encampment to morrow night.

On my return to the boat, killed some pigeons and wild ducks, and saw a flock of turkeys.

Wednesday 8*th.* Last night having finished our mast, we had it put up this morning before day, and at daylight set off on our voyage. Weather cool, but no wind, and the sun apparently regaining his empire.

Passed through a country in the course of this day, chiefly open, with very little wood. The river very wide: in one place it appeared to me nearly two miles. Encamped at the falling in banks, or *grand eboulment.* Wind has entirely abated.

Thursday 9*th.* Set off at daylight—continued a short distance under sail with a light breeze.

Several of the men are sick; one has a pleurisy, and others slight fevers and coughs, from frequent exposure in the water.

There appears to be no hills or bluffs on the north-east side, the whole distance to the Platte.

Encamped some distance above a hill, called *L'oeil èffroi,* from an Indian chief who was scaffolded here some years ago.

Friday 10*th.* A dreadful storm raged during the whole of last night. Set off this morning under sail, in expectation of

reaching the Platte before twelve, but in the course of an hour
it failed us, and changed to N. W.   At ten, it became so violent
that we were compelled to put to shore, where we remained
until towards evening, and again attempted to proceed, but finding the wind too strong, again landed and encamped, having
passed the mouth of the Platte.   At the mouth of this river
there is so great a number of bars and small islands, that its
entrance is scarcely perceptible.   The river enters by a number
of channels or mouths: the color of its water is the same with
that of the Missouri.   The country hereabouts is entirely open,
excepting in some spots along the river, where there are
groves of cotton wood, and on the hills a few scattered dwarf
oaks.

Saturday 11*th.*   The wind continues too high to proceed.
This morning we advance about three miles, and encamp until
near noon—very cold.

Set off with my gun to take a walk into the country. Traversed the prairie which had been burnt, and reached the high
land about three miles distant; the high land rises gradually
to the height of about two hundred feet, the country then becomes waving.   The other side of the Missouri appears extremely bare.   I wandered towards the Platte, or rather to the
point of the upland between this river and the Missouri,
which commands a very extensive prospect.   I discovered a
great extent of open country, gently rising grounds, with a
soil every where extremely rich.   The Platte is full of islands
and sand bars, and appears as wide as the Missouri.   On my return, I saw several Indian mounds.

On reaching camp I found that the wind had abated, and
that the river was rising fast.

The river Platte is regarded by the navigators of the Missouri as a point of as much importance, as the equinoctial line
amongst mariners.   All those who had not passed it before,
were required to be shaved, unless they could compromise the
matter by a treat.   Much merriment was indulged on the occasion.   From this we enter what is called the Upper Missouri.
Indeed the change is perceptible and great.

CHAPTER IV.

Sunday 12*th*. Weather pleasant—the river rising rapidly; the drift wood descends in great quantities, and the current seems to augment every moment. This may possibly be the annual flood. We were enabled to ascend the greater part of this morning with the towing line.

In the afternoon, some distance above the old Otto village, S. W. side, I went on shore, and wandered several miles through shrubby hills, and saw several elk and deer, without being able to approach them. Towards evening I entered a charming prairie, and of the richest soil. Followed a rivulet until it formed a lake in the river bottom, its banks for six or eight feet a rich black earth. In pursuing the upland I might have fallen upon the Missouri, six miles above, in the distance of a mile, the river forming here a considerable bend. The prairies or meadows to the water's edge, enabled us to continue the greater part of this day with the line.

Monday 13*th*. Water falling—continued with the towing line. At ten, a fine breeze springing up, hoisted sail. Passed the river a' *Boyer*, and the houses of M'Clelland, who wintered here. Some woody country hereabouts; but that on the upland is very inferior, chiefly shrubby oak. A short distance above this place we encountered a very difficult and rapid current, but being luckily a little aided by the sail, we passed tolerably well—We have now reached the highest point to which settlements will probably extend on the western side for many years.

In the evening passed high clean meadows, called the Council Bluffs, from the circumstance of Lewis and Clark having held a council with the Otto and Missouri Indians, when ascending this river. It is a beautiful place—Encamped four miles above this place on a large sand bar. In the course of this day found the river crooked and narrow: it appeared in one place almost closed up by drift wood and sawyers.

Tuesday 14*th.* Set off with a slight breeze—compelled by heavy rain to put to shore for some hours, after which, continued under a fine wind that lasted throughout the day; but from the winding course of the river, we were not much benefitted by it.

In some of the bends of the river, the timber, principally cotton wood, is heavy, but the prairies and upland are entirely bare of trees. The prairies compose more than two-thirds of the margin of the stream—the soil extremely rich: for the three first feet, generally a light mould, another stratum is a deep black, almost approaching the color of coal, but not hard or stiff; the lower stratum is marle. I have no doubt that these natural meadows would yield surprisingly—Encamped at the beginning of a great bend of the river, twelve miles round, and not more than three hundred paces across.

Wednesday 15*th* Although the wind is favorable, it was of no use to us, from the sudden turns of the river. At twelve hoisted sail, and passed the Soldier's river, a small stream. After doubling some points we came into a reach of some extent; wind here became very violent, and blew almost a tempest; with our sail reduced to half its size we easily encountered the strongest current. The storm became at length so serious that it was deemed imprudent to continue under way. The air was darkened by clouds of sand, and we found ourselves at the upper end of the reach, in the midst of sawyers and planters, our situation dangerous in the extreme. We fortunately escaped safely to the shore, where we remained until evening, the wind abating we proceeded a few miles further.

Thursday 16*th.* A tremendous storm of thunder and lightning last night—being fortunately in a good harbor we suffered but little. Were not able to get under weigh this morning until late. A fine serene morning, strangely contrasted with the turbulence of last night. Came in sight of the hills S. W. every one bitterly regretting that the wind of yesterday could not serve us here, where there is a view of twelve miles up the river. There appears to reign an unusual calm, the sky cloudless, the river as smooth as a mirror. Words cannot convey what I feel, and it is only the lover of nature who could understand me.

The points are tolerably woooed—At the upper end of the long reach we saw an encampment of Hunt, where there were appearances of his having remained one or two days. The bones of buffaloe which they had killed were strewed about. If it be their encampment at the time we were at the river Platte, it is not more than six days since they were here. The reaches before described are now rarely seen—the woods more free from undergrowth. Encamped before sunset on a sand bar below *la coupe à L'Oiselle.*

Friday 17th. A charming morning—slight indication of wind from the S. E. Passed *la coupe à L'Oiselle.* This name originated, in the circumstance of a trader having made a narrow escape, being in the river at the very moment that this cutoff was forming. It was a bend of fifteen miles round, and perhaps not more than a few hundred yards across, the neck, which was suddenly cut through by the river, became the main channel. This was effected in a few hours.

While remaining a short time at a sand bar in the river, a curious phenomenon occurred; the sand began to dissolve, and every instant to diminish like the melting of snow, it was thought prudent to embark immediately. This I am informed is not unfrequent. Bars are sometimes formed during the continuance of a single flood, but being principally of loose sand, without any thing to unite, as soon as the waters begin to rise again, is entirely carried off.

At ten passed a similar cut-off called *la coupe à Jacque.* At twelve continued under sail, made several long reaches—passed the Yellow banks, and encamped within a few miles of the Black-bird hill. Throughout this day the river border is chiefly wood.

Saturday 18th. A fine breeze S. W.—At seven arrived at the Black-bird hill. As this is one of the curiosities of the Missouri, a description may be amusing. It rises on the common range to the height of four or five hundred feet. The Missouri at its base, begins a strange winding course, several times returning upon its steps, and at length coming within nine hundred yards of where it is first approached; so that in a course of thirty miles the Black-bird hill is still near us. It takes its name

from a celebrated chief of the Mahas, who caused himself to be
interred on the top: a mound has been erected on the pinnacle,
with a branch stuck in it, a flag was formerly attached to it.—
He was buried, sitting erect on horse back; the reason why he
chose this spot, was to enable him to see the traders as they ascended.   This chief was as famous in his lifetime amongst all
the nations in this part of the world, as Tamerlane or Bajazet
were in the plains of Asia; a superstitious awe is still paid to his
grave. Yet, the secret of his greatness was nothing more nor
less than a quantity of arsenic, which he procured from some
trader.   He denounced death against any one who displeased
him, or opposed his wishes : it is therefore not surprising, that
he, who held at his disposal the lives of others, should possess
unlimited power, and excite universal terror.   The proud savage, whenever this terrible being appeared, rendered the ho-
mage of a slave.   The gods and heroes of antiquity, were, perhaps, little better.   We may learn this lesson, that ignorant and
savage man, can only be ruled through the means of fear.

At four o'clock, got through the last bend, and hoisted sail,
with a fine wind—sailed along some hills, S. W. side, and encamped amongst some cotton wood, in a low bottom.

Sunday 19th.   Continued our voyage this morning at daylight, with sanguine expectations of overtaking the party of Hunt,
at the Maha village.   Passed the bluffs; some of them very curious, faced with a sand rock, of variegated and fantastic hues; at
the first glance, it resembles the decorations of a theatre.   Continued with little interruption, under sail, and arrived about
twelve at some trading houses, near which, the Maha village is
situated, about two miles from the river.   We saw a few Indians on the bank, and several traders with them, men who were
on the point of setting off with their peltries.   Hunt set out from
this on the 15th, under sail.

Remaining here as short a time as possible, we continued our
voyage, having sent our interpreter and an Indian, by land, to
the Poncas, to request Hunt to wait for us.   The wind continued until towards evening, when it gradually died away.   Encamped near Floyd's bluff, and river, fourteen miles above the

Mahas. Sergeant Floyd, one of the party of Lewis and Clark, was buried here: the place is marked by a cross.

The appearance of the river is much changed—it continues a handsome width, with a diminished current. The banks low, and the trees much smaller in size; we now rarely see a large tree. The bluffs and upland on the N. E. side, are not high, and without any appearance of trees and shrubs.

Monday 20th. Passed at daylight, the Great Sioux river, which takes its rise in the plains, between the Missouri, and the waters of lake Winipec; it is five or six hundred miles in length. I ascended the bluffs, high clay banks of sixty, or an hundred feet. The current is here very strong. Hailed a trader, descending in a large canoe, made of skins of the buffaloe, upwards of twenty feet in length, who wintered at the river a' Jaque. He met Hunt eight leagues below that river, proceeding with a fair wind, and is by this time, at the *Qui Courre.*— These skin canoes are stretched over the red willow, and require to be frequently exposed to the sun, and dried, as they would otherwise become too heavy, from the quantity of water absorbed. We are now nearly half way to the place of our destination.

Perceive a sudden rise of the water. Sand bars are nearly all covered, and banks, in places, overflown.

Tuesday 21st. This morning fine, though somewhat cool. Wind increasing from the N. E. Current rapid, but for the eddies in the bends, it would be almost impossible to ascend.— There are but few embarras, or collections of trees, &c. The sand bars are fringed with a thick growth of willows, immediately behind which, there are young cotton wood trees, forming a handsome natural avenue, twenty or thirty feet wide. The banks are very low, and must be inundated every season.

Passed in the evening, a rapid, of frightful appearance, the water foaming and rolling in waves, as if agitated by violent wind in the middle of the river, while on either side it was calm. We were compelled to pass along the sand bar, and through the willows. It was with difficulty that we could obtain dry land this evening, the water, in most places, flows into the woods.— In the night, the water had risen so much, that the men were

compelled to abandon their encampment, and sleep on board.—
V..ry little prairie in the course of this day, but the timber of a
small size.

Wednesday 22d. A delightful day—the water has risen to
its utmost height, and presents a vast expanse—the current
uniformly rapid, in some places rolling with the most furious
and terrific violence. One of these places, below Vermillion
creek, was suffi..ient to appal the stoutest heart : the river forms
an elbow at the termination of some bluffs, the water, compressed between them and the sand bar, dashes against the opposite
rocks. The middle of the river appeared several feet higher
than the sides. The distance to cross, before we could reach
the opposite eddy, was not more than twice the length of the
boat, but we were not able completely to effect it, being swept
down with the rapidity of flight, but fell into the current of the
opposite side, before it had gained its full force, and were able,
with great difficulty, to gain the eddy.

The high waters enable us to cut off points, which is no
small saving of the distance. The water begins to fall, though
great quantities of drift wood descend, and thirty or forty drowned buffaloes pass by every day.

I observe a much greater variety of trees and shrubs, than
below, and some altogether new to me. There is a shrub which
the French call *graisse de boeuf*, bearing a red berry, of a pun-
gent taste; its leaves, though smaller and more delicate, bear a
resemblance to those of a pear tree. In the hollows, clumps of
trees are usually found, but what surprises me, they are very
low, though some of the oaks and ash are eighteen or twenty
inches in diameter, they look like orchard trees, and have much
greater resemblance to regular plantations than wild woods.

Thursday 23d. Water falling rapidly—a fine breeze S. E.
sailed until eleven—passed the Hot, or Burning Bluffs, on the
S. W. side. Here I observed enormous masses of pumice, and
other matter, which appeared to have undergone the action of
heat, of a very high degree. I saw what was the fragment of a
hill, the greater part at present composed of pumice. From not
being able to discover other volcanic appearances, I conclud-

ed these appearances to have been produced by the burning of coal.

About noon, espied a number of persons on a sand bar, which we at first supposed to be Indians, but on a nearer approach, recognized to be whites, amongst them, a Mons. Benit, factor of the Missouri company, at the Mandan village. These men were descending in a small boat, with some peltries. He tells us that the Indians are ill disposed to the whites, every where on the Missouri. Mr. Henry is in a distressed situation over the Rocky mountains. The Crow Indians are supposed to be inimical—and the Sioux have broken out into open hostilities, and have killed several of the whites. Mr. Benit and crew were fired upon last night, by what they supposed to be Sioux, and returned it. They did not see the boats of Hunt.

Proceeded on our voyage at three o'clock, not a little disheartened at this intelligence. Mr. Benit and one other of the company return with us. Passed some beautiful upland N. E. side, but without wood, an immense level plain stretches out, I am informed, for about an hundred miles. We observed a Sioux lodge or tent, of a conical shape, made of skins—it appears to be the custom of these people, to leave their dead in lodges of this kind, until it be convenient for them to gather up their remains.

Friday 24*th.* Set off early—weather warm. The water is falling very fast—there is still a very strong current. Passed bluffs of a chalky appearance, perhaps limestone. A piece of ice floated by us this morning, probably from the breaking up of some of the northern rivers, which have contributed to the present rise. In putting off from a bluff on the S. W. side, to cross over, my attention was called to an object which attracted the notice of the company. A huge buffaloe bull made his appearance on the top of the bluff, standing almost at the edge of the precipice, and looking down upon us. It was the first we had seen. Long and matted wool hung over his head, and covered his huge shoulders, while his body was smooth, as also the tail, except a tuft at the end. It was a striking and terrific object: he eyed us with the ferocity of the lion, seemed at length to " snuff the tainted gale," threw his head into the air, wheeled round, and trotted off.

Had a fine breeze towards evening—which enabled us to make five or six miles more than we expected.

Saturday 25th. This morning ran a ground, and were detained several hours. Passed the river *a' Jaque*; the principal rendezvous of the traders with the Yankton Sioux. It is a large handsome stream, tolerably well suited for a small settlement.

It is becoming very warm. Went out on a delightful prairie, the grass short, of a deep blue, and intermixed with a great variety of beautiful flowers. I am forbidden to wander far, on account of the Indians, who it is thought may be near. We discovered this morning, a great deal of smoke up the river— we supposed this to be a notification of the Indian spies, of our approach. We are now in the open country—no woods are to be seen, except some slender cotton wood trees in the points, and some clumps in the hollows of the upland. The beauty of the scenery, this evening, exceeds any thing I ever beheld.— The sky as clear as in a Chinese painting, the country delightful. Convert the most beautiful parts of England, or France, into one meadow, leaving a trifling proportion of wood, and some idea may be formed of this. But there appears to be a painful void—something wanting—it can be nothing else than a population of animated beings. It were vain to describe the melancholy silence which reigns over these vast plains. Yet they seem to give a spring to the intellectual faculties. One never feels his understanding so vigorous, or thinks so clearly. Were it safe, with what delight would I roam over these lovely meads!

The water has fallen, and the current is much lessened.

Sunday 26th. At daylight, discovered a canoe descending with two men, who prove to be those sent by us, to Hunt. They bring information that he has agreed to wait for us at the Poncas village, where he intends to remain some days.

Saw some buffaloe to day, and with Mr. Lisa, went several miles in pursuit of them, but without success.

Passed a beautiful island *L'isle a' bon homme*, upon which there is the remains of an ancient fortification. In the evening our hunter killed a buffaloe, upon which we all feasted.

Monday 27th. Had to oppose a contrary wind, until eleven. At one, arrived at the Poncas village, where we remained until five. On our approach, we found the whole village crowded on the bank, and several had waded up to the waist in the water.— The greater part of the men were naked; the women and children filthy and disgusting. According to custom, had a talk with the chiefs, to whom we made some trifling presents. Hunt had not waited for us, according to promise. Saw two men, who had probably deserted from him, they informed us, that as soon as he heard of our approach, which was quite unexpected, he had determined to exert himself to the utmost, to get out of our reach. The fact is, there does not exist the greatest confidence between the two commanders. Ours seems to think, that it is the intention of Hunt, to pass the Sioux, who may wish to detain him, by telling them that their trader is coming on with goods for them. While on the other hand, Hunt may believe that Lisa intends to pass him, and tell the same story. It is therefore determined to push our voyage, if possible, still more than before.

Encamped above the Qui Courre river—a most beautiful country, but very little wood. The country is much more hilly.

Tuesday 28*th.* Weather smoky, and extremely warm. High land on both sides of the river, with some dwarf trees in the hollows, principally cedar. At ten, a fine breeze springing up, we continued under sail the rest of the day, and the greater part of the night, determining to strain every nerve, in order to overtake Hunt. There is scarcely any bottoms from the Qui Courre.

Wednesday 29*th.* After lying by a few hours, at one o'clock, again continued under sail—but the moon disappearing, and it becoming dark, it was thought advisable to lie by until daylight. The hills hereabout, high and broken, and little or no river bottom on either side. At two o'clock, arrived at a beautiful island, called Little Cedar island, on which grows fine cedar, the trees uncommonly large. This is a delightful spot, the soil of the island is rich, and it may contain about three thousand acres—the middle of the island is a beautiful prairie—the adjacent country is bleak and barren. At the point of the island, discovered an encampment of Hunt, and on examination, we discovered, to the great joy of the company, that the fire was not yet extinguished; it is therefore but a few days since they were here. Continued under sail until 11 at night, having in little better than twenty-four hours, made seventy-five miles.

Thursday 30th. This morning, favored with a continuance of fair wind. The country is exceedingly rough and bro-ken—the greater part without the least vegetation. The hills have a very singular appearance. Near the top they look black, and seem to have been burnt. About noon, saw some tracks, which we supposed to be of yesterday.

In the evening, passed a very fine river, called White river, about three hundred yards at the mouth. Here there is some bottom land, and wood points; the hills covered with grass.— Heard several gun shots, which we supposed to have been from the party of Hunt. This evening the wind abated.

Friday 31st. This morning, a contrary wind, and some rain. Proceeded with the cordelle. In the course of the day, saw a large flock of antelopes—they appear to be numerous in this part of the country. Observed in the sand, a number of Indian tracks, and a place, where it appeared that the boats of Mr. Hunt had stopped with the Indians some time. One of our men discovered a curious place, contrived by the Indians, for taking fish; it was something like a fish basket—we found two fine catfish in it.

When about to put into the river, to cross to a point, we dis-covered three buffaloe, swimming towards us, and contrary to the precautions we had agreed to observe, in making no noise, least we should be discovered by the Indians, who were probably in the neighborhood, a firing was commenced upon the poor animals, which continued half an hour. The report of the guns, as might have been foreseen, brought an Indian to the top of the hill, but we were too far in the river, to return to him, or to be heard.

Towards evening, the boat having received some injury, was compelled to stop—went in pursuit of a buffaloe calf—on my return found the party somewhat uneasy on account of the length of my stay, having been drawn by the eagerness of pur-suit to a considerable distance.

Saturday, June 1st. At daylight heard a number of guns fired on the hills below us on the other side of the river We now concluded that all our precaution and labor had been vain. That we should be robbed and killed, or at least compelled to return. They soon arrived opposite to us, with an American flag, and fired one or two guns. There was but one thing to be done, which was to cross over to them at once, and meet the worst, every man preparing himself for defence. Each rower had his gun by his side—Mr. Lisa and myself, besides our knives and rifles, had each one a pair of pistols in our belts. On reaching the shore we discovered twelve or thirteen Indians on a log. Mr. Lisa and I, leaped on shore and shook hands with them.— We supposed that the principal body was concealed behind in the woods, so as to be at hand if necessary. Having no interpreter at this critical juncture, we were fearful of not being understood : however, with the aid of signs, a language with which Mr Lisa was well acquainted, he was enabled to communicate tolerably well. He told them that he was their trader, but that he had been very unfortunate, all the peltries which he had collected amongst them having been burnt, and his young men, who had passed 2 years before to go to the head of the Missouri, were attacked and distressed by the Indians of those parts, who are bad people. That he was now poor, and much to be pitied; that he was going to bring back his young men, having resolved to confine himself to the lower country. He concluded, by telling them that he intended to return in three months to establish a trading house at the Cedar island, and requested the chief to send word of it to all the Sioux bands. This story, together with a handsome present, produced the desired effect, though not without some reluctance. We remained here as short a time as possible, and re-crossed the river. The chief is a fine looking Indian, the others were very young men, nearly naked, with long braids of hair hanging down their foreheads; they are the best looking people I have seen. It is two days since Hunt passed here. We did not cease to use every exertion, considering it still possible that we might be stopped.

About twelve reached the great bend, twenty-one miles around, and only one and an half across. Two men were sent to

notify the boats of our near approach.   In the evening a strong
wind from the N E. which would hardly have been favorable
in any other part of the river, enabled us to hoist sail, and what
is singular, continued changing to suit the running of the river.
We by this means made fifteen miles—some part of the time
it blew with violence, accompanied by rain.

Sunday 2d Set out with my gun early this morning, on the
S. W. side of the river—walked about four miles along the river hills, and with much satisfaction perceived at a distance the
boats of Mr. Hunt I returned immediately to give the joyful
intelligence to our people. On coming opposite the place
where I had seen the boats, we discovered a great number of
Indians, who beckoned to us to cross; but supposing them to be
Sioux, we determined to continue on until we should overtake
the party before us. We suffered them to shout, to gallop their
horses, and to wave their robes unnoticed. Some distance above,
our men came to us, they had been with Hunt, the Indians we
had just past, were a party of three hundred Arikaras, who,
on hearing of our approach, had come for the purpose of enabling us to ascend. It appears also, that we have passed all the
Sioux bands, who had been seen by Hunt, but probably finding
his party too strong, they had resolved to stop and plunder ours,
that we must have past them in the night or under sail, as they
did not expect to hear from us so soon.

At eleven o'clock we overtook Hunt's party, to the great
satisfaction of our little company. It was with real pleasure I
took my friend Bradbury by the hand; I have reason to believe
our meeting was much more cordial than that of the two commanders. Continued under sail in company the rest of the day,
forming a handsome little fleet of five sail. Encamped in the
evening opposite the larger Cedar island, twelve hundred miles
from the mouth of the Missouri.

CHAPTER V.

Monday June 3d. A strong wind from the N. E. this morning, compelled us, after proceeding a few miles, to encamp for the remainder of the day. Took my gun, and set off to make an excursion. The country is altogether open, excepting some groves of cotton wood in the bottom. The upland rises into considerable hills, about one-third covered with a very short grass, intermixed with a great variety of plants and flowers, the rest consists of hills of clay, bare of almost every kind of vegetation. On the tops of the higher hills, at some distance from the river, there are masses of granite, of several tons weight, and great quantities of pebbles. In the course of my ramble, I happened on a village of barking squirrels, or prairie dogs, as they have been called. My approach was announced by an incessant barking, or rather chirping, similar to that of a common squirrel, though much louder. The village was situated on the slope of a hill, and appeared to be at least two miles in length; the holes were seldom at a greater distance from each other than twenty or thirty paces. Near each hole, there was a small elevation of earth, of six or eight inches, behind which, the little animal posted himself, and never abandoned it, or ceased his demonstrations of alarm, "insignificantly fierce," until I approached within a few paces. As I proceeded through the village, they disappeared, one after another, before me. There was never more than one at each hole. I had heard that the magpie, the Missouri rattle snake, and the horn frog, were observed to frequent these places; but I did not see any of them, except the magpie. The rattle snake of the prairies, is about the same length with the common rattle snake, but more slender, and the color white and black.

Mr. Bradbury has met with great success in his pursuit.— He has found nearly an hundred undescribed plants. Within a few days he has found a great number, which he calls Mexican. The country thus far, has offered nothing remarkable as to minerals. There is in company, a gentleman of the name of Nut-

tal, engaged in the same pursuits, to which he appears singular-
ly devoted; it seems to absorb every thought, so as to be troublesome to the company, which has sometimes to wait for him;
it appears to have done away every regard of personal safety.—
To the ignorant Canadian boatmen, who are unable to appreciate the science, it affords a subject of merriment; *le fou*, the
fool, is the name by which he is commonly known. No sooner
does the boat touch the shore, than he leaps out, and when his
attention is arrested by a plant or flower, every thing else is forgotten. The inquiry is sometimes made, *ou' est le fou?* where
is the fool? *il est après ramasser des racines*, he is gathering
roots. He is a young man of genius, and very considerable acquirements, but is unfortunately too much devoted to his favorite study. A characteristic anecdote of this gentleman was related to me, by Mr. Miller, who commanded one of the boats,
and shews to what an astonishing degree the pursuit of natural
history had taken possession of his mind, to the exclusion of
every thing else. The day after passing the Sioux tribes, they
met, as I have before mentioned, three hundred Arikara Indians, these were so delighted to see them, that a number rushed
into the river, to swim or wade to the boats; the party supposing them to be inimical, was on the point of firing; while every
one was in momentary expectation that this would take place,
Nuttal, who appeared to have been examining them very atten-
tively, turned to Miller, " sir," said he, " don't you think these
Indians much fatter, and more robust than those of yesterday."

   In the course of the evening, had an opportunity of seeing
the manner in which the antelope is hunted in these open plains,
where there is no possibility of approaching by insidious means.
A handkerchief is placed on the end of a ramrod, and waved
in the air, the hunter lying flat on the ground. If any of the animals be in sight, they run instantly to the place, and perform a
circuit around, approaching often within twenty or thirty yards,
which gives an opportunity of firing on them.

   The party of Mr. Hunt consists of about eighty men, chiefly
Canadians; the rest are American hunters.

   Tuesday 4th. Set off at seven—wind contrary, though not
so strong as yesterday. After doubling a point, we found that

from the course of the river, the wind would be favorable, and accordingly sailed for eight or ten miles. We saw at the mouth of a small creek, a herd of buffaloe, of several hundred. The appearance of the country has varied but little for several days past. Bleak and dreary—the bottoms narrow; in some places none at all, and clay bluffs.

Wednesday 5th. This morning, after proceeding a short distance, we were compelled, by rain, to put to shore, where we remained until the afternoon, and finding no appearance of the weather clearing up, crossed to the S. W. side, where Mr. Hunt was encamped.

I took a walk with Mr. Bradbury—in the course of which, I saw a number of antelopes, buffaloe, and villages of prairie dogs. At some distance from the river, there is not the least appearance of a tree or shrub. The country appears to rise gradually. There was something picturesque in the appearance of herds of buffaloe, slowly winding round the sides of the distant hills, disappearing in some hollow, and again emerging to view. The whole extent of the plain is covered with ordure, as in a pasture ground. Wide and beaten roads are every where to be seen.

On my return, I found that a disagreeable misunderstanding had taken place between the two chiefs of the parties. The interpreter of Mr. Hunt, had been in the employment of the company, and was indebted to it. Mr. Lisa had several times mentioned to him the impropriety of his conduct, and perhaps had made him some offers, in order to draw him from his present service. This was certainly imprudent, and placed him in the power of a worthless fellow, who, without doubt retailed the conversation to his master, with some additions. This evening, while in Hunt's camp, to which he had gone on some business, he was grossly insulted by the interpreter, who struck him several times, and seized a pair of pistols belonging to Hunt;—that gentleman did not seem to interest himself much in the affair, being actuated by feelings of resentment, at the attempt to inveigle his man. On my return to our camp, I found Mr. Lisa furious with rage, buckling on his knife, and preparing to return: finding that I could not dissuade, I resolved to accompany him. It was with

the greatest difficulty I succeeded in preventing the most serious consequences.   I had several times to stand between him
and the interpreter, who had a pistol in each hand.   I am sorry
to say, that there was but little disposition on the part of Mr.
Hunt, to prevent the mischief that might have arisen. I must, in
justice to him, declare however, that it was through him that
Mr. M'Clelland* was induced not to put his threat in execution
having pledged his honor to that effect.   I finally succeeded in
bringing Lisa off to his boat.   When it is recollected that this
was at the distance of thirteen hundred miles from all civil authority, or power, it will be seen that there was but little to restrain the effects of animosity.   Having obtained in some measure, the confidence of Mr. Hunt, and the gentlemen who were
with him, and Mr. Bradbury, that of Mr. Lisa, we mutually
agreed to use all the arts of mediation in our power, and if possible, prevent any thing serious.

Thursday 6th. Weather clearing up. The water rising very
fast—supposed the annual flood. This morning passed the ruins
of an Indian village, there were great piles of buffaloe bones, and
quantities of earthen ware. The village appears to have been
scattered round a kind of citadel, or fortification, enclosing four
or five acres, and of an oval form. The earth is thrown up about
four feet, there are a few cedar palisadoes remaining. Probably,
in cases of siege, the whole village was crowded into this space.

Friday 7th. Continued under way as usual. All kind of intercourse between the leaders has ceased. In the evening,
passed several old villages, said to be of the Arikara nation. The
bottoms, or points, become wider, and the bluffs of a less disgusting appearance; there are but few clay hills, the country
being generally covered with grass.

Saturday 8th. Contrary wind to day—though delightful
weather. This morning, passed a large and handsome river,

* A mortal enmity existed on the part of **Mr.** M'Clelland, towards
Lisa, in consequence of some conduct of the latter, in the trade—and
he had declared, that if ever he fell in with Lisa, in the Indian country,
he would shoot him. Those who know M'Clelland, would not be surprised that such a threat should be put in execution.

called the Chienne, S. W. side. It appears as large at the mouth as the Cumberland or Tennessee. Saw at this place, the ruins of an old village, and fortification. The country here-abouts is fine, and better wooded than any I have seen for the last three hundred miles. A tolerable settlement might be supported here. Game is very abundant—elk, deer, and buffaloe, without number.

Encamped a few miles above the Chienne river, in a beautiful bottom. No art can surpass the beauty of this spot; trees of different kinds, shrubs, plants, flowers, meadow, and upland, charmingly disposed. What coolness and freshness breathes around! The river is bordered with cotton wood, and a few elms, there is then an open space of 30 or 40 paces, after which begins a delightful shrubbery of small ash trees, the graisse de boeuf, the gooseberry, currant, &c. forming a most delightful avenue. We all remark, that the singing of the birds is much sweeter than in the forest of the states. This is fancifully accounted for by Mr. Bradbury, from the effects of society: from the scantiness of woods, they are compelled to crowd on the same tree, and in the same grove, and in this way, impart improvement to each other. Assuming it as a fact, that the birds of Europe sing better than those of America, he asks, can it be owing to any other reason than this?

The musketoes have been exceedingly troublesome for several days past. They disappear in the evenings, which are cool, or with the slightest wind.

Sunday 9th. Got under way this morning, with fine weather. Discovered great numbers of buffaloe; on the N. W. side, an extensive level meadow. Numbers began to swim across the river, as the party of Hunt, who were before us, got opposite; they waited, and killed as many as they wished; a number which were started from an island, swam towards us, and we killed several also.

Mr. Bradbury and I went out on the N. W. side, where the buffaloe had been first seen, and walked several miles. A very beautiful and extensive meadow, at least a mile wide, but without a tree or a shrub—the upland equally bare. Passed a Sioux encampment of last fall—from appearances there must have been three or four hundred here. Amongst other things, our curiosity was attracted, by a circular space, about twenty feet in diameter, enclosed with poles, with a post in the middle, painted red, and at some distance, a buffaloe head placed upon a little mound of earth. We are told, this is a place where an incantation for rendering the buffaloe plenty, had been performed.— Amongst other ceremonies, the pipe is presented to the head.

At four o'clock hoisted sail with a favorable wind. Passed a surprising number of buffaloe in the course of this day, some herds on the sides of the hills, not less than a thousand. Towards evening we saw a great number crowded on the sand beach at the foot of an island, proceeding with caution, we approached under sail within twenty or thirty yards, and selecting the fattest, we fired upon him at once ; and notwithstanding that he had received several wounds, he endeavored to make off — We pursued him into the island, the animal had now become ferocious from his wounds, and it was dangerous to approach him. It was not until he had received the contents of ten or twelve guns, that he was brought to the ground. The island is beautiful. It is completely surrounded by cotton wood and cedar trees, but the space within is a beautiful clear meadow. On the edges of the woods in the inside, there are great quantities of currant and gooseberry bushes ; these islands are much alike in this respect. They are more beautiful than any I have seen.

Monday 10*th.* During the whole of this day had a fine wind which enabled us to make thirty five miles. Encamped opposite a handsome stream, called Ser-war-cerna, N. W.

The country wears a handsome aspect ; the hills gently swelling and some delightful prairie on the river. There is but little wood. In the course of the day we saw great numbers of buffaloe, in herds of several hundred each.

Tuesday 11*th* Continued our voyage with a slight wind. The country much the same as that of yesterday. Encamped some distance below the island on which the Arikara village was situated some years ago—they have removed some miles further up. This evening I went to the camp of Mr. Hunt to make arrangements as to the manner of arriving at the village, and of receiving the chiefs. This is the first time our chiefs have had any intercourse directly or indirectly since the quarrel.— Mr. Lisa appeared to be suspected, they supposed his intention to be, to take advantage of his influence with the Arikara nation, and do their party some injury in revenge. I pledged myself that this should not be the case.

Wednesday 12th. Heavy rains accompanied by thunder and lightning last night.

At nine o'clock two of the chiefs with the interpreter employed by the company, came on board our boat. They are both fine looking men, much above the common size, and with much fairer complexions than any Indians I have seen. At ten we put to shore opposite the village, in order to dry our baggage, which was completely wet. The leaders of the party of Hunt were still suspicious that Lisa intended to betray them.— M'Clelland declared that he would shoot him the moment he discovered any thing like it. In the mean time, the chief spoke across the river, which is here about a half a mile wide, we understood that he was giving orders to prepare the council lodge. The village appeared to occupy about three quarters of a mile along the river bank, on a level plain, the country behind it rising into hills of considerable height. There are little or no woods any where to be seen. The lodges are of a conical shape, and look like heaps of earth. A great number of horses are seen feeding in the plains around, and on the sides of the hills. I espied a number of squaws, in canoes, descending the river and landing at the village. The interpreter informed me, that they were returning home with wood. These canoes are made of a single buffaloe hide, stretched over osiers, and are of a circular form. There was but one woman in each canoe, who kneeled down, and instead of paddling sideways, places the paddle before; the load is fastened to the canoe. The water being a little rough these canoes sometimes almost disappeared between the waves, which produced a curious effect; the squaws with the help of a little fancy, might be supposed, mermaids sporting on the billows; the canoe rising and sinking with them, while the women were visible from the waist upwards.

About two o'clock fourteen of us crossed over, and accompanied the chief to his lodge. Mats were laid around for us to sit on, while he placed himself on a kind of stool or bench. The pipe was handed around, and smoked; after which, the herald, (every chief or great man, has one of them) ascended the top of the lodge and seated himself near an open place, and began to bawl out like one of our town criers; the chief every now and then addressing something to him through the aperture before mentioned. We soon discovered the object of this, by the arrival of the other chiefs, who seemed to drop in, one after the other, as their names were called.

When all were seated, the pipe was handed to the chief, who began as is usual on solemn occasions, by blowing a whiff upwards as it were to the sky, then to the earth, and after to the east and west, after which the pipe was sent round. A mark of respect in handing the pipe to another, is to hold it until the person has taken several whiffs. After this ceremony, Mr. Lisa addressed a speech to the chiefs, in which, after the common place which would be expected, he observed, that the strangers in company with him were going a long journey to the great Salt lake to the west, and ought to be treated well, that any injury done to them, he should consider as done to himself; that in this respect they were as one people. A number of speeches were as usual made on the occasion. The chief on the proposal of trading, required time to give an answer—with this the council concluded. The boats were ordered over, and encamped a little distance below the village. A guard of Indian warriors was placed to keep off the populace and prevent pilfering.

CHAPTER VI.

Thursday 13*th.* This morning, found ourselves completely drenched by heavy rains, which continued the whole night. The chief has not given his answer as to the conditions of the trade. It is for him, usually to fix the price, on a consultation with his subordinate chiefs, to this, the whole village must conform.— The Indian women and girls, were occupied all this morning, in carrying earth in baskets, to replace that which the rains had washed off their lodges. Rambled through the village, which I found excessively filthy, the ‘ villainous smells,’ which every where assailed me, compelled me at length, to seek refuge in the open plain. The lovers of Indian manners, and mode of living, should contemplate them at a distance. The rains had rendered their village little better than a hog pen; the police appeared to me, in *some particulars*, extremely negligent. Some of the ancient cities of the old world, were probably like this village, inattentive to that cleanliness so necessary to health, where a great mass of beings are collected in one place; and we need not be surprised at the frequency of desolating plagues and pestilence. The village is swarming with dogs and children. I rank these together, for they are inseparable companions. Wherever I went, the children ran away, screaming, and frightened at my outré and savage appearance. Let us not flatter ourselves with the belief, that the effect of our civilization and refinement, is to render us agreeable and lovely to the eyes of those whom we exclusively denominate savages ! The dogs, of which every family has thirty or forty, pretended to make a show of fierceness, but on the least threat, ran off.— They are of different sizes and colors. A number are fattened on purpose to eat, others are used to draw their baggage.— It is nothing more than the domesticated wolf. In wandering through the prairies, I have often mistaken wolves for Indian dogs. The larger kind has long curly hair, and resembles the shepherd dog. There is the same diversity amongst the wolves

of this country. They may be more properly said to howl than
bark.

The lodges are constructed in the following manner: Four
large forks of about fifteen feet in height, are placed in the
ground, usually about twenty feet from each other, with hewn
logs, or beams across; from these beams, other pieces of wood
are placed slanting; smaller pieces are placed above, leaving an
aperture at the top, to admit the light, and to give vent to the
smoke. These upright pieces are interwoven with osiers, after
which, the whole is covered with earth, though not sodded. An
opening is left at one side, for a door, which is secured by a
kind of projection of ten or twelve feet, enclosed on all sides,
and forming a narrow entrance, which might be easily defended.
A buffaloe robe suspended at the entrance, answers as a door.
The fire is made in a hole in the ground, directly under the
aperture at the top. Their beds elevated a few feet, are placed
around the lodge, and enclosed with curtains of dressed elk skins.
At the upper end of the lodge, there is a kind of trophy erected; two buffaloe heads, fantastically painted, are placed on a little elevation; over them are placed, a variety of consecrated
things, such as shields, skins of a rare or valuable kind, and
quivers of arrows. The lodges seem placed at random, without
any regularity or design, and are so much alike, that it was for
some time before I could learn to return to the same one. The
village is surrounded by a palisade of cedar poles. but in a very
bad state. Around the village, there are little plats enclosed
by stakes, intwined with osiers, in which they cultivate maize,
tobacco, and beans; but their principal field is at the distance of
a mile from the village, to which, such of the females whose
duty it is to attend to their culture, go and return morning and
evening. Around the village they have buffaloe robes stuck up
on high poles. I saw one so arranged as to bear a resemblance
to the human figure, the hip bone of the buffaloe represented
the head, the sockets of the thigh bones looked like eyes.

Friday 14*th*. It rained again last night, which prevented
the trade from commencing until sometime in the day. Mr.
Lisa sent a quantity of goods to the lodge of the principal chief
before mentioned, called le Gauchée, and Hunt to the one who

accompanied him to meet us, *le Gros*, the principal war chief. The price of a horse was commonly ten dollars worth of goods first cost. Hunt had resolved to purchase horses at this place and proceed by land to the Columbia, being assured by some hunters, who met him before his arrival here, that this would be his best route.

Mr. Bradbury and I, took a walk into the upper village, which is separated from the lower by a stream about twenty yards wide—Entered several lodges, the people of which received us with kindness, placed mats and skins for us to sit on, and after smoking the pipe, offered us something to eat; this consisted of fresh buffaloe meat served in a wooden dish.—They had a variety of earthen vessels, in which they prepared their food, or kept water. After the meat, they offered us homony made of corn dried in the milk, mixed with beans, which was prepared with buffaloe marrow, and tasted extremely well; also pounded and made into gruel. The prairie turnip, is a root very common in the prairies, with something of the taste of the turnip, but more dry; this they eat dried and pounded, made into gruel. Their most common food is homony and dried buffaloe meat. In one of the lodges which we visited, we found the doctor, who was preparing some medicine for a sick lad.—He was cooling with a spoon a decoction of some roots, which had a strong taste and smell, not unlike jalap. He showed us a variety of simples which he used. The most of them were common plants with some medicinal properties, but rather harmless than otherwise. The boy had a slight pleurisy. The chief remedy for their diseases, which they conceive to be owing to a disorder of the bowels, is rubbing the belly and sides of the patient, sometimes with such violence, as to cause fainting. When they become dangerous, they resort to charms and incantations, such as singing, dancing, blowing on the sick, &c. They are very successful in the treatment of wounds. When the wound becomes very obstinate, they commonly burn it, after which it heals more easily.

Saturday 15*th.* Fine weather—Took a walk with Mr. Bradbury through the country, which is entirely open, and somewhat hilly. Large masses of granite were usually found on the highest knobs. We saw a great variety of plants, and some new ones—One or two of the vallies are beautiful, and a few dwarf plum trees scattered along a rivulet.

On our return in the evening, an alarm prevailed in the village, which appeared to be all in commotion. We were informed that the Sioux, their enemies, were near. This was probably all preconcerted. I was shewn, at the distance of about two miles, four horsemen on the top of a hill, at full gallop, passing and re-passing each other; this I understand is the signal given by the scouts, some of whom are constantly on the alert, of the approach of an enemy. To give intelligence of the appearance of a herd of buffaloe, instead of crossing each other, they gallop backward and forward abreast. Presently the warriors issued from the village with great noise and tumult, some on foot, others on horse back, and pursued the direction in which the signals were made, down the river, and past an encampment. They observed no regular march, but ran helter skelter, like persons in one of our towns to extinguish a fire—and keeping up a continued hallooing to encourage each other. Some of them were dressed in their most splendid manner. The tops of the lodges were crowded with women and children, and with the old men who could give no assistance, but by their lungs, which were kept busily employed: yet there were several who sallied forth, almost half bent with the weight of years. I counted upwards of five hundred in all. They soon after returned; whether they had chased away the enemy, or the alarm had turned out false, I never learned.

Sunday 16*th.* In the course of the day several parties arrived from different directions. According to custom they were met by warriors and conducted to the council lodge, where they gave an account of what had occurred, which was afterwards announced to the village by heralds. These contribute to enliven the village; though independent, they continually present a busy and animated scene. Great numbers of men are engaged in the different games of address and agility, others judging, or looking on, and many employed in a variety of other ways. There are a great number of women constantly at work in dressing buffaloe robes, which are placed on frames before the lodges. One of the parties which arrived to day, came from the Snake nation, where they had stolen horses. This arrested their employments for a moment, the immediate friends and relations of such as returned, spent the evening in rejoicing, while several females who had lost a relation, retired to the hills behind the village, where they continued to cry the whole afternoon.

In the evening they usually collect on the tops of the lodges, where they sit and converse : every now and then the attention of all was attracted by some old men who rose up and declaimed aloud, so as to be heard over the whole village. There was something in this like a quaker meeting. Adair labors to prove the Indian tribes to be descended from the Jews, I might here adduce this as an argument in favor of these people being a colony of quakers.

Monday 17*th.* This day arrived a deputation from the Chienne nation, to announce that these people were on their march to this village, and would be here in fifteen days. I sometimes amused myself with the idea of forming a gazette of the daily occurrences. We here see an independent nation, with all the interests and anxieties of the largest: how little would its history differ from that, of one of the Grecian states ! A war, a treaty, deputations sent and received, warlike excursions, national mourning or rejoicing, and a thousand other particulars, which constitute the chronicle of the most celebrated people.

In the evening, about sundown, the women cease from their labors, and collect into little knots, and amuse themselves with a game something like jack-stones: five pebbles are tossed up in a small basket, with which they endeavor to catch them again as they fall.

Tuesday 18*th.* Confidence had been somewhat restored between the leaders of the two parties since the council in the village. Mr. Hunt having resolved to start from this village, a bargain was made with Mr. Lisa, for the sale of Hunt's boats and some merchandise ; in consequence of which, we crossed the river, in order to make the exchange, after which we returned and encamped. We are to set off to-morrow morning to the Mandan villages.

Before I bid adieu to Arikara, I must note some general matters relating to their character and manners.

The men are large and well proportioned, complexion somewhat fairer than Indians commonly are. Generally go naked; the dress they sometimes put on, seems more for ornament than any advantage it is to them; this consists of a sort of cassoc or shirt, made of the dressed skin of the antelope, and ornamented with porcupine quills, died a variety of colors; a pair of leggings, which are ornamented in the same way. A buffaloe hide dressed with the hair on, is then thrown over the right shoulder, the quiver being hung on the other, if he be armed with a bow.*— They generally permit their hair to grow long; I have, in one or two instances, seen it reach to their heels: they sometimes increase it by artificial means; commonly with horse hair. It is divided into a number of locks, matted at intervals, with a braid of white earth, a substance resembling putty. Sometimes it is rolled up in a ball, and fixed on the top of the head. They always have a quantity of feathers about them; those of the black eagle are most esteemed. They have a kind of crown made of feathers, such as we see represented in the usual paintings of Indians, which is very beautiful. The swan is in most estimation for this purpose. Some ornament the neck with necklace made of the claws of the white bear. To their heels they sometimes fasten foxes' tails, and on their leggings suspend deers' hoofs, so as to make a rattling noise as they walk. On seeing a warrior dressed out in all this finery, walking with his wife, who was comparatively plain in her dress or ornaments, I could not but think this was following the order of nature, as in the peacock, the stag, and almost all animals, the male is lavishly decorated, while the female is plain and unadorned. I intend this as a hint to some of our petit maitres. The dress of the female consists of a long robe made of the dressed skins, of the elk, the antelope, or the agolia, and ornamented with blue beads, and strips of ermine, or in its place, of some white skin. The robe is gird-

---

* A warrior is seldom seen without his arms, even in the village.— His bow, spear, or gun, is considered part of his dress, and to appear in public without them, is in some measure disgraceful.

ed round the waist with a broad zone, highly ornamented with porcupine quills, and beads. They are no better off than were the Greeks and Romans, in what we deem at present so essential, but like them, they bathe themselves regularly, twice a day. The women are much fairer than the men; some might be considered handsome any where—they are much more numerous than the men, the consequence of the wars in which the nation is constantly engaged. Polygamy is general, they have often four or five wives. Their courtship and marriage resemble that of most Indian nations: if the parties are mutually agreeable to each other, there is a consultation of the family, if this be also favorable, the father of the girl, or whoever gives her in marriage, makes a return for the present he had previously received from the lover—the match is then concluded.

They display considerable ingenuity of taste in their works of art: this observation applies to all the American nations, from the Mexicans to the most savage. Their arms, household utensils, and their dresses, are admirably made. I saw a gun which had been completely stocked by an Indian. A curious instance of native ingenuity which came under my notice, ought not to be omitted. I was told one day, of an old Indian who was making a blanket; I immediately went to see him. To my surprise, I found an old man, perfectly blind, seated on a stool before a kind of frame, over which were drawn coarse threads, or rather twists of buffaloe wool, mixed with wolf's hair; he had already made about a quarter of a yard of a very coarse rough cloth.— He told me that it was the first he had attempted, and that it was in consequence of a dream, in which he thought he had made a blanket like those of the white people. Here are the rudiments of weaving. They make beautiful jugs or baskets with osier, so close as to hold water.

I observed some very old men amongst them—the country is so extremely healthy, that they arrive to a very great age.— About twenty years ago, the small pox destroyed a great number of them. One day, in passing through the village, I saw something brought out of a lodge in a buffaloe robe, and exposed to the sun; on approaching, I discovered it to be a human being, but so shrivelled up, that it had nearly lost the human physiognomy: almost the only sign of life discernible, was a continual sucking its hands. On inquiring of the chief, he told me, that he had seen it so ever since he was a boy. He appeared to be at least forty-five. It is almost impossible to ascertain the age of an Indian when he is above sixty; I made inquiries of several, who appeared to me little short of an hundred, but could form no satisfactory conjecture. Blindness is very common, arising probably from the glare of the snow, during a great part of the year. I observed the goitre, or swelled neck, in a few instances.

Their government is oligarchical, but great respect is paid to popular opinion. It is utterly impossible to be a great man amongst them, without being a distinguished warrior, though respect is paid to birth, but this must be accompanied by other merit, to procure much influence. They are divided into different bands or classes; that of the pheasant, which is composed of the oldest men; that of the bear, the buffaloe, the elk, the dog, &c. Each of these has its leader, who generally takes the name of the class, exclusively. Initiation into these classes, on arriving to the proper age, and after having given proofs of being worthy of it, is attended with great ceremony. The band of dogs, is considered the most brave and effective in war, being composed of young men under thirty. War parties are usually proposed by some individual warrior, and according to the confidence placed in him, his followers are numerous or otherwise. In these excursions they wander to a great distance, seldom venturing to return home without a scalp, or stolen horses.— Frequently when unsuccessful, they " cast their robes," as they express it, and vow to kill the first person they meet, provided he be not of their own nation. In crossing the river, they use canoes made of the buffaloe hide, or a few pieces of wood fastened together. They usually have some token, as a stake, which is marked so as to convey some idea of their numbers, the direction which they have taken, &c. To avoid surprise, they always encamp at the edge of a wood; and when the party is small, they construct a kind of fortress, with wonderful expedition, of billets of wood, apparently piled up in a careless manner, but so arranged as to be very strong, and are able to withstand an assault from a much superior force. They are excellent horsemen—they will shoot an arrow at full speed, and again pick it up from the ground without stopping: sometimes they will lean entirely upon one leg, throwing their bodies to that side, so as to present nothing but the leg and thigh, on the other.— In pursuit of the buffaloe, they will gallop down steep hills, broken almost into precipices. Some of their horses are very fine, and run swiftly, but are soon worn out, from the difficulty of procuring food for them in winter, the smaller branches of the cotton wood tree being almost the only fodder which they give them. Their hunting is regulated by the warriors chosen for the occasion, who urge on such as are tardy, and repress often with blows, those who would rush on too soon. When a herd of buffaloe is discovered, they approach in proper order, within a half a mile, they then separate and dispose themselves, so as, in some measure, to surround them, when at the word, they rush upon them at full speed, and continue as long as their horses can stand it: a hunter usually shoots two arrows into a buffaloe, and then goes in pursuit of another; if he kills more than two in the hunt, he is considered as having acquitted himself well. The tongue is the prize of the person who has slain the animal; and he that has the greater number, is considered the best hunter of the day. Their weapons consist of guns, war clubs, spears, bows, and lances. They have two kinds of arrows, one for the purpose of the chase, and the other for war; the latter differs in this particular, that the barb or point is fastened so slightly, that when it enters the body, it remains in, and cannot be drawn out with the wood; therefore, when it is not in a vital part, the arrow is pushed entirely through. They do not poison them. Their bows are generally very small; an elk's horn, or two ribs of a buffaloe, often constitute the materials of which they are made. Those of wood are of willow, the back covered with sinews. Their daily sports, in which, when the weather is favorable, they are engaged from morning till night, are principally of two kinds. A level piece of ground appropriated for the purpose, and beaten by frequent use, is the place where they are carried on. The first is played by two persons, each armed with a long pole; one of them rolls a hoop, which, after having reached about two-thirds of the distance, is followed at half speed, and as they perceive it about to fall, they cast their poles under it; the pole on which the hoop falls, so as to be nearest to certain corresponding marks on the hoop and pole, gains for that time. This game excites great interest, and produces a gentle, but animated exercise. The other differs from it in this, that instead of poles, they have short pieces of wood, with barbs at one end, and a cross piece at the other, held in the middle with one hand; but instead of the hoop before mentioned, they throw a small ring, and endeavor to put the point of the barb through it. This is a much more violent exercise than the other.

With respect to their religion, it is extremely difficult, particularly from the slight acquaintance I had with them, to form any just idea. They have some notion of a Supreme Being, whom they call " the Master of Life," but they offer him no rational worship, and have but indistinct ideas of a future state. Their devotion manifests itself in a thousand curious tricks, of slight of hand, which they call magic, and which the vulgar amongst them believe to be something supernatural. They are very superstitious. Besides their public resident lodge, in which they have a great collection of magic, or sacred things, every one has his private magic in his lodge about his person. Any thing curious, is immediately made an amulet, or a talisman; and is considered as devoted or consecrated, so as to deprive them of the power of disposing of it. The principal war chief lately took advantage of this, ingeniously enough. He obtained a very fine horse, which he was desirous of keeping, but fearing that some one might ask him as a gift, and to refuse would be considered as evincing a narrowness of mind unbecoming a great man, who ought not to set his heart upon a matter of so little importance, he announced that he had given him to his magic.— Some parts of their religious exercises are the most barbarous that can be imagined. I observed a great number whose bodies were scarred and cut in the most shocking manner; I was informed that this was done in their devotion; that to shew their zeal, they sometimes suspend themselves by the arms or legs, or the sides, by hooks. I was shewn a boy, who had drawn two buffalo heads by cords drawn through the fleshy part of his sides, nearly a quarter of a mile. I might enumerate a variety of other particulars, in which this strange self punishment is carried to the greatest lengths. They have frequent holy days, when the greater part of the village appears to desist from labor, and dress out unusually fine. On these occasions, each one suspends his private magic on a high pole before his door; the painted shields, quivers of a variety of colors, scarlet cloth, and highly ornamented buffaloe robes, which compose those trophies, produce a very lively effect. I several times observed articles of some value, suspended in the woods. I was told they often leave their property in this manner, without being under any apprehension that any of the same tribe will touch it, provided that there be the least sign to shew that it is not lost. A kind of superstition similar to that of the Druids, which protected their offerings hung up in the woods.

Since the affair of lieut. Prior, who commanded the party despatched by the United States, to take home the Mandan chief, these people have been friendly to the whites. They speak of the occurrence with regret, and declare that it was done by bad people whom they could not restrain.

To give an account of the vices of these people would be to enumerate some of the more gross, prevalent amongst us.—The savage state, like the rude uncultivated waste, is contemplated to most advantage at a distance. They have their rich and their poor, their envious, their proud, overbearing, their mean and grovelling, and the reverse of these. In some respects they appear extremely dissolute and corrupt—whether the result of refinement, or vice, or the simplicity of nature, I am not able to say. It is part of their hospitality, to offer the guest, their wife, sister, or maid servant, according to the estimation in which the guest is held, and to refuse, is considered as treating the host with contempt. It appeared to me while we remained at the village, that their females had become mere articles of traffic: I have seen fathers bring their daughters, brothers their sisters, and husbands their wives, to be disposed of for a short time, to the highest bidder. I was unable to account for this strange difference from all other people I had ever read of, unless from the inordinate passion which seized them for our merchandise. Chastity appeared to be unknown as a virtue Yet this may not have been universal; a more minute acquaintance with these people, might have enabled me to explain this strange phenomenon. From the remnant of a singular custom which prevails amongst them, one might suppose that this had not always been the case. On a certain occasion, a great number of young girls were collected before the medicine lodge or temple, prizes were exhibited, and a cedar bough was stuck on the lodge; the old men who reside in the temple, proclaimed, that whoever was yet a virgin, should come forward and touch the bough, and take the prize; that it was in vain to think of deceiving, the *manitou* would reveal every thing; the young men were moreover required to declare against any one who should attempt it, all they knew. A young metiff, daughter of the interpreter, a beautiful girl of sixteen, came forward, but before she could ascend to touch the bough, a young fellow stepped out and bade her remember a certain place! She withdrew, confused and abashed. There was a pause for a considerable time; I began to tremble for the maidens of Arikara, when a girl of seventeen, one of the most beautiful in the village, walked forward and asked, "where is the Arikara who can boast of having received favors from me?" then touched the bough, and carried off the prize. I feel a pleasure in adding, for the honor of the ladies of Arikara, that others followed, though I did not take the trouble of noting the number.

Seeing the chief one day in a thoughtful mood, I asked him what was the matter—"I was wondering" said he "whether you white people have any women amongst you." I assured him in the affirmative. "Then" said he, "why is it that your people are so fond of our women, one might suppose they had never seen any before?"

CHAPTER VII.

Wednesday 19*th.* It was resolved this morning by Mr. Lisa, to leave one of his men to continue the trade with the Arikaras, and continue his voyage. As part of the price of the goods bought from Mr. Hunt, was to be paid in horses, a party was sent by land to the Mandan fort, for the purpose of bringing them. Mr. Bradbury being desirous of seeing the interior of the country, accompanied them.

Set off from the village about eleven o'clock, the wind favorable, but the weather rainy and disagreeable. Having made about fifteen miles, we encamped. The musketoes are more troublesome than I have known them. I am informed that this is not the case every year.

Thursday 20*th.* Weather more pleasant, but the wind for a part of the afternoon contrary. The river is rising rapidly, it is at present at a very high stage. Having made five points, encamped.

Friday 21*st.* Set off under sail, with a fine breeze, which continued the whole day. Made upwards of forty miles. The country improves—handsome green hills, and fine bottoms.

Saturday 22*d.* A continuance of favorable wind, but the river crooked. At ten, landed to kill some buffaloe—they are numerous on the sides of the hills.

Sunday 23*d.* Bad weather—contrary wind, and violent storms. In the evening it cleared up: the wind continuing so as to prevent us from proceeding, we landed and went in pursuit of some buffaloe. The whole surface of the country appeared covered with them. I continued the chase four or five miles from the river, in the middle of a very romantic country.

Monday 24*th.* Proceeded this morning with delightful weather, the sky clear, and of a most enchanting blue. Continued the greater part of the day, with the cordelle, along the prairie. The country on either side, of a very pleasant appearance, and a number of wooded points.

Tuesday 25th. Sailed this morning with a slight breeze.—
At ten, passed an old Mandan village; and at some distance
above, saw a great number of Mandan Indians on their march
along the Prairie.   They sometimes go on hunting parties by
whole villages, which is the case at present; they are about five
hundred in number, some on horseback, some on foot, their tents
and baggage drawn by dogs.   On these great hunting parties,
the women are employed in preserving the hides, drying the
meat, and making a provision to keep.   Very little of the buffaloe is lost, for after taking the marrow, they pound the bones,
boil them, and preserve the oil.   This evening the Mandan
chief, She-he-ke, who was in the United States, came to us with
his wife.   Hearing of our approach, he had set off for the purpose.   Encamped on a prairie of a very rich soil.   The country is very fine on both sides of the river.   There are some high
hills.

Wednesday 26th.   In the course of the day, passed by the
Mandan villages, with a favorable wind, and arrived late at night,
at the fort of the company, 1640 miles from the mouth of the
Missouri.

We remained here until the sixth of July.   Mr. Bradbury
had already arrived.   He describes the country at the distance
of eight or ten miles from the river, as very handsome ; a continued succession of meadows, with some wood along the water
courses : on approaching the river, it becomes more broken and
hilly.

We made several excursions to the villages below, and to
the interior of the country, but as they afford but little new, I
shall not give any detail of them.   In the neighborhood of the
fort there are a number of clay hills, washed into the most curious shapes, by the frequent rains, generally of a whitish color,
though intermixed with strata of various hues.   Some of them
resemble clouds, being circular, and detached : at the first glance
they look like buildings.   On some of them there is a beautiful
creeping vine, or evergreen, which Mr. Bradbury informs me,
is described by Michaux, as growing on the lakes.   There are
great quantities of petrified wood scattered about: I traced a

whole tree; the stump was more than three feet high, and at least four in diameter. This is a very extraordinary fact, in a country where the trees are every where small.

On the fourth of July, we had something like a celebration of the day; the two principal chiefs happened to be with us.— The borgne is one of the most extraordinary men I ever knew. The description of Abelino might give some idea of this man. He sways with unlimited control, all these villages, and is sometimes a cruel and abominable tyrant. In stature he is a giant, and his one eye seems to flash with fire. I saw him on one or two occasions, treat She-he-ke with great contempt—Mr. Lisa citing something which She-he-ke expressed, " what" says the other, " does that bag of lies pretend to have any authority here." She-he-ke is a fat man, not much distinguished as a warrior, and extremely talkative, a fault much despised amongst the Indians.

On a visit to the village. I saw a great number of small scaffolds scattered over the prairie, on which human bodies were exposed. The scaffolds are supported with four forks, and sufficiently large to receive one or two bodies. They are covered with blankets, cloth of different colors, and a variety of offerings. In this they are different from the Arikaras, who bury their dead as we do.

On the sixth of July, we set off from the fort, to return to the Arikara village, where we arrived two days after, without any remarkable occurrence. On our arrival, we found Mr. Hunt waiting the arrival of the Chiennes, to complete his supply of horses. We continued here about ten days, Mr. Manuel Lisa having concluded to send two of his boats, with peltries, Mr. Bradbury who was desirous of returning, gladly embraced the opportunity. The boats were accordingly put under my command, with six men in each.

Two mornings before our departure, a great commotion was heard in the village, before daylight. We rose to discover the cause, and found that the war party, of about three hundred men, were within a short distance of the village, on their return, after a battle with the Sioux the evening before, in which two or three were killed, and as many wounded. All the relations of

those engaged, came out of the village to meet them. I accompanied them about a mile and an half. They advanced in a kind
of procession, which moved slowly, with some regularity; each
band separate, and sung its song.   Some carried the scalps on
poles, others the sacred standards, which consisted of a large
bow and a spear, both beautifully ornamented.   The scene which
took place, would be worthy the pen of a Fenelon; the meeting
of those connected by the most tender relations, was truly affect-
ing.   The whole would baffle description; I was touched with
the tenderness of a woman, who ran to meet her son, a youth
badly wounded, but who exerted himself to keep on his horse,
and from his countenance, one would have supposed nothing
had been the matter.   The young man died almost as soon as
he arrived at the temple, for it is the custom to carry those who
have been wounded on these occasions to this place, to be taken
care of at the public expense.   As they approached the village,
the old men who could hardly walk, whose voices were extremely shrill, came out singing their songs also, and rubbing
the warriors with their hands.   The following day was spent in
festivity by the village in general, and in grief by those who had
lost their relations.

Towards the last of July, with glad hearts, we set off, to return once more to civilized life, after more than four months absence from it.   My orders were to go day and night if possible,
and not to stop for any Indians.   The water was extremely high,
and with the assistance of six oars, we were able to make little
short of twelve miles an hour.   The first day we passed the
Chienne river, and went some time after night, but considering
this something dangerous, I landed and continued until daylight.
The next morning we reached the Great Bend, a vast number
of buffaloe were to be seen on all sides, and the most tremendous bellowing from the bulls, as this was about the time of
their mixing with the herds of cows, for they generally stay
in separate herds.   The country this far is beautiful, the
points sufficiently wooded, and the bottoms fine.   The wind
becoming high, we were compelled to lie by the whole of
the afternoon, in the Great Bend.   On the north west side,
it is bounded the whole of the way by bluffs, nearly bare,

affording but a scanty vegetation of sand cherries, gooseberries, and dwarf plum trees. The next day we passed White river, where the black bluffs begin—a barren and miserable country nearly an hundred miles; there are scarcely any bottoms, and the bluffs in most places without even grass. In some places the hills rise to the height of mountains;—it frequently afforded me amusement to see the herds of buffaloe ascending these hills by a winding path. In the evening we were compelled to land in a little recess of the bluffs, there being appearances of an approaching storm: we were not disappointed. The continued and vivid flashes of lightening, and peals of thunder, shaking the solid earth, were succeeded by a tremendous storm. The winds blew with such violence, as to threaten our boats; for an hour, we were obliged to protect the sides with wet blankets, to prevent them from filling, while it rained on us incessantly the whole night. The next day we passed the Poncas village. The Indians were absent in the plains. The islands are generally fine thus far, and excepting the tract between the White river, and the Qui Courre, there are many delightful spots, though the bottoms are mostly prairie, and the upland with little or no wood.

In the evening, near a point above isle à Bon Homme, our attention was awakened by a tremendous noise. On landing, we discovered the woods literally swarming with buffaloe, a herd of males had come amongst a number of females. The noise which they made is truly undescribable. On the hills in every direction, they appeared by thousands. Late in the evening we saw an immense herd running along the sides of the hills in full speed; their appearance had something in it, which, without incurring ridicule, I might call sublime—their footsteps resembled the roaring of distant thunder.

The next day we passed the Maha village, and had a most extraordinary run of forty-five leagues, from sun to sun. From the Qui Courre, to the Mahas, the bottoms are wider and better wooded than above, but the upland much the same. We found them almost every where overflowed; we were obliged to encamp on some driftwood—the musketoes tormenting us the whole night.

The following day we passed the Blackbird hill, and the riv
er Platte. The navigation in this part is much more dangerous
than above, from the number of trees fixed in the bottom. The
bottoms are much wider than above, and better wooded; in
some places for twenty miles and upwards, we were out of sight
of the high lands : but the low grounds were every where overflowed. The water rushed into the woods with great velocity,
and in bends it poured over the gorge into the river again; a
sheet of water sometimes for a mile, flowed over the bank.

In something better than two days afterwards, we arrived at
Fort Clark, having come a thousand miles in eight or nine days,
without meeting a living soul. Here we were treated politely
by the officers. Mr. Sibly, the factor, had returned but a few
days before, from a journey to the interior, and shewed us specimens of salt, which he had procured at the salines, on the
Arkansas.

We arrived at St. Louis early in August, having made fourteen hundred and forty miles in little better than fourteen days

A TABLE

OF DISTANCES FROM THE MOUTH OF THE MISSOURI TO THE
MANDAN VILLAGES—RIVERS—LATITUDES, &C.

Places.	Width of Rivers.	Side of Mis'ri.	Dist-ance.	Tot. Dis.	Latitude.
St. Charles . . .	"	N. E.	21	"	38° 55
Osage R. (Little) . .	30 yds.	N. E.	20	"	"
Charles' creek . .	20	S. W.	27	"	"
Shepherd's creek . .	"	S. W.	15	"	"
Gasconade R. . . .	157	S. W.	17	100	38° 45'
Muddy R. . . .	50	N. E.	15	"	"
Great Osage . . .	397	S. W.	18	133	38° 31
Marrow creek . .	20	S. W.	5	"	"
Cedar creek & island .	20	N. E.	7	"	"
Lead Mine hill . .	"	S. W.	9	"	"
Hamilton's creek . .	20	S. W.	8	"	"
Split Rock creek . .	20	N. E.	8	170	"
Saline or Salt R. . .	30	S. W.	3	"	"
Manitou R. . . .	30	N. E.	9	"	"
Good Woman's R. . .	35	N. E.	9	"	"
Mine R. . . .	70	S. W.	9	200	"
Arrow prairies . .	"	S. W.	6	"	"
The Charitons . .	30 & 70	N. E.	14	"	"
Ancient village of the Missouri Indians near which formerly stood F Orleans.	"	N. E.	16	"	"
Grand R. . . .	90	N. E.	4	240	"
Snake creek . . .	18	N. E.	6	"	"
Ancient village of the Little Osage Indians.	"	S. W.	10	256	"
Tiger creek & island .	25	N. E.	20	"	"
A creek and island .	"	S. W.	12	"	"
Fire prairie & creek .	"	S. W.	12	"	"
Fort Clark (or Osage) .	"	S. W.	6	306	"

Places.	Width.	Side.	Dis.	T. D.	Lat.
Hay Cabin creek . .	20	S. W.	6	"	"
Coal bank . . .	"	S. W.	9	"	"
Blue Water R. . .	30	S. W.	10	"	"
Kansas R. . . .	233	S. W.	9	340	39° 05
Little R. Platte . .	60	N. E.	9	"	"
1. Old Kansas village .	"	S. W.	28	"	"
Independence creek .	"	S. W.	28	"	"
2 Old Kansas village .	"	S. W.	1	"	"
St. Michael's prairie .	"	N. E.	24	"	"
Nodawa R. . .	70	N. E.	20	450	39° 40'
Loup or Wolf R. . .	60	S. W.	14	"	"
Big Nimeha . .	80	S. W.	16	"	"
Tarkio creek . .	23	N. E.	3	"	"
Nish-na-botona . .	50	N. E.	25	508	"
Little Nimeha . .	48	S. W.	8	"	"
Bald-pated prairie—the river Nish-na-botona is at this place not more than 150 yds from the bank of the Mis'r.	"	N. E.	23	"	"
Weeping-water creek .	25	S. W.	29	"	"
RIVER PLATTE	600	S. W.	32	600	41° 04'
Butterfly creek . .	18	S. W.	3	"	"
Musketoe creek . .	22	N. E.	7	"	"
Ancient village of Ottoes	"	S. W.	11	"	"
do. of Ayuwas . .	"	N. E.	6	"	"
——R. . . .	28	N. E.	11	"	"
Council Bluffs . .	"	S. W.	12	650	41° 17'
Soldier's R. . . .	40	N. E.	39	"	"
Little Sioux . . .	80	N. E.	44	"	"
Bad Spirit R. . .	"	S. W.	55	788	"
A bend in the river, 20 miles round & but 900 yds. across			21	809	"
An island 3 miles N. E. of Floyd's village.	"		27	836	"
Floyd's river & bluff .	35	N. E.	14	850	"

Places.	Width.	Side.	Dist.	T D	Lat.
Big Sioux R. . . .	110	N. E.	3	853	38° 48'
Commencement of the Co- bell, Alum and Copperas bluffs.	"	S. W.	27	880	"
Hot or Burning bluffs .	"	S. W.	30	"	♪
White Stone R. .	30	N. E.	8	"	"
An old village at the mouth of Little Bow creek	"	S. W.	20	"	"
River à Jaque, or James R.	90	N. E.	12	950	42° 53'
Calumet bluff . .	"	S. W.	13	"	"
Ancient fortification, Good Man's Isle	"	S. W.	13	976	"
Plumb creek . .	12	N. E.	10	"	"
White Paint creek .	28	S. W.	8	"	"
Qui Courre creek .	150	S. W.	6	1000	"
Poncas river & village .	30	S. W.	10	"	"
The village of dog prairies	"	S. W.	20	"	"
The island Cedar .	"		40	"	"
WHITE RIVER	300	S. W.	60	1130	"
The 3 rivers of the Sioux	36	N. E.	22	"	"
An island in the upper part of the Big Bend	"	S. W.	20	"	"
Upper part of the Big Bend the gorge 1¼ mile across	"	S. W.	30	"	"
Tyler's R. . . .	35	S. W.	6	1208	"
L'Oiselle's post, Cedar isl'd	"		18	"	44° 12
Titon R. . . .	70	S. W.	37	"	"
The upper part of five old record villages of Arikaras reduced by the Sioux	"	S. W.	42	"	"
Chienne R. . . .	400	S. W.	5	1310	44° 20'
Old Record village .	"		47	"	"
Ser-war-cerna . .	90	S. W.	40	1397	"
Waterehoo . .	120	S. W.	25	1422	45° 35'
Old village on an island .	"	S. W.	4	"	"

Places.	Width.	Side.	Dist.	T.D.	Lat.
Arikara, 3 villages	*n*	*s. w.*	4	*n*	*n*
Stone Idol creek	18	*n. e.*	18	*n*	*n*
Warecore	35	*n. e.*	40	*n*	*n*
Cannon-ball R.	140	*s. w.*	12	1500	46° 29½
Old Mandan village	*n*	*s. w.*	40	*n*	*n*
— do. —	*n*	*s. w.*	40	*n*	*n*
Mandan village	*n*	*s. w.*	20	1600	47° 13
Company's Fort	*n*		40	1640	*n*

APPENDIX.

———◆◆◆———

EXTRACT FROM HUMBOLDT'S NEW SPAIN—Vol. II,
Pages 41, 42, 43, 44, 45, & 119, '20, '21, '22, '23, & 171, '72, '73, '74.

(No. 1.)

THE only ancient monuments in the Mexican valley, which from their size or their masses can strike the eyes of a European, are the remains of the two pyramids of San Juan de Teotihuacan, situated to the north east of the lake of Tezcuco, consecrated to the sun and moon, which the Indians called Tonatiuh Yzaqual, house of the sun, and Metzli Ytzaqual, house of the moon. According to the measurements made in 1803 by a young Mexican servant, doctor Oteyza, the first pyramid, which is the most southern, has in its present state a base of 208 metres* (645 feet) in length, and 55 metres (66 Mexican vara,† or 171 feet‡) of perpendicular elevation. The second, the pyramid of the moon, is eleven metres§ (30 feet) lower, and its base is much

---

* 682 feet English. *Trans.*

† Velasquez found that the Mexican vara contained exactly 31 inches of the old pied du roi of Paris. The northern facade of the Hotel des Invalides at Paris is only 600 feet French in length.

‡ 180 feet English. *Trans.*

§ 36 feet English. *Trans.*

less. These monuments, according to the accounts of the first
travellers, and from the form which they yet exhibit, were the
models of the Aztec teocallis. The nations whom the Spaniards found settled in New Spain attributed the pyramids of
Teotihuacan to the Toultec nation;* consequently their construction goes as far back as the eighth or ninth century; for the
kingdom of Tolula lasted from 667 to 1031. The faces of these
edifices are to within 52′ exactly placed from north to south, and
from east to west. Their interior is clay, mixed with small
stones. This kernel is covered with a thick wall of porous
amygdaloid. We perceive, besides, traces of a bed of lime which
covers the stones (the tetzontli) on the outside. Several authors
of the sixteenth century pretend, according to an Indian tradition, that the interior of these pyramids is hollow. Boturini
says that Siguenza, the Mexican geometrician, in vain endeavored to pierce these edifices by a gallery. They formed four layers of which three are only now perceivable, the injuries of time,
and the vegetation of the cactus and agaves having exercised
their destructive influence on the exterior of these monuments.
A stair of large hewn stones formerly led to their tops, where,
according to the accounts of the first travellers, were statues
covered with very thin lamina of gold. Each of the four principal layers was subdivided into small gradations of a metre† in
height, of which the edges are still distinguishable, which were
covered with fragments of obsidian, that were undoubtedly the
edge of instruments with which the Toultec and Aztec priests
in their barbarous sacrifices (*Papahua Tlemacazque or Teo-*

* Siguenza, however, in his manuscript notes, believes them to be
the work of the Olmec nation, which dwelt round the Sierra de Tlasca-
la, called Matlacueje. If this hypothesis, of which we are unacquainted
with the historical foundations, be true, these monuments would be still
more ancient. For the Olmecs belong to the first nations mentioned in
the Aztec chronology as existing in New Spain. It is even pretended
that the Olmecs are the only nation of which the migration took place,
not from the north and north-west (Mongol Asia?) but from the east
(Europe?).

† 3 feet 3 inches. *Trans.*

ftixqui) opened the chest of the human victims. We know that
the obsidian (itztli) was the object of the great mining under-
takings, of which we still see the traces in an innumerable quantity of pits between the mines of Moran and the village Atoto-
nilco el Grande, in the porphyry mountains of Oyamel and the
Jacal, a region called by the Spaniards the mountain of knives,
el Cerro de las Navajas.*

It would be undoubtedly desirable to have the question resolved, whether these curious edifices, of which the one, *(the
Tonatiuh Ytzaqual,)* according to the accurate measurement
of my friend M. Oteyza, has a mass of 128.970 cubic toises,†
were entirely constructed by the hand of man, or whether the
Toultecs took advantage of some natural hill which they covered over with stone and lime. This very question has been recently agitated with respect to several pyramids of Giza and
Sacara ; and it has become doubly interesting from the fantas-
tical hypotheses which M. Witte has thrown out as to the origin of the monuments of colossal form in Egypt, Persepolis,
and Palmyra. As neither the pyramids of Teotihuacan, nor that
Cholula, of which we shall afterwards have occasion to speak,
have been diametrically pierced, it is impossible to speak with
certainty of their interior structure. The Indian traditions, from
which they are believed to be hollow, are vague and contradic-
tory. Their situation in plains where no other hill is to be found,
renders it extremely probable that no natural rock serves for a
kernel to these monuments. What is also very remarkable
(especially if we call to mind the assertions of Pococke, as to the
symmetrical position of the lesser pyramids of Egypt) is, that
around the houses of the sun and moon of Teotithuacan we find
a group, I may say a system of pyramids, of scarcely nine or ten
metres of elevation.‡ These monuments, of which there are

---

* I found the height of the summit of the Jacal 3 124 metres
(10.248 feet;) and la Rocca de las Ventanas at the foot of the Cerro de
las Navajas, 2.590 metres (8.496 feet) above the level of the sea.

† 33.743.201 cubic feet. *Trans.*

‡ 29 or 32 feet. *Trans.*

several hundreds, are disposed in very large streets which follow exactly the direction of the parallels, and of the meridians,
and which terminate in the four faces of the two great pyramids.
The lesser pyramids are more frequent towards the southern
side of the temple of the moon than towards the temple of the
sun and, according to the tradition of the country, they were
dedicated to the stars. It appears certain enough that they served as burying places for the chiefs of tribes. All the plain
which the Spaniards, from a word of the language of the island
of Cuba, call *Llano de los Cues*, bore formerly in the Aztec
and Toultec languàges the name of *Micaotl*, or road of the
dead. What analogies with the monuments of the old continent!
And this Toultec people, who, on arriving in the seventh century on the Mexican soil, constructed on a uniform plan several
of those colossal monuments, those truncated pyramids divided
by layers, like the temple of Belus at Babylon, whence did they
take the model of these edifices? Were they of Mongol race?
Did they descend from a common stock* with the Chinese,
the Hiong-nu, and the Japanese?

Another ancient monument, worthy of the traveller's attention, is the military intrenchment of Xochicalco, situated to the
S. S. W. of the town of Cuernavaca, near Tetlama, belonging
to the parish of Xochitepeque. It is an insulated hill of 117
metres of elevation, surrounded with ditches or trenches, and
divided by the hand of man into five terraces covered with ma-
sonry. The whole forms a truncated pyramid, of which the four
faces are exactly laid down according to the four cardinal points.
The porphyry stones, with basaltic bases, are of a very regular
cut, and are adorned with hieroglyphical figures, among which
are to be seen crocodiles spouting up water, and, what is very
curious, men sitting croos-legged in the Asiatic manner. The

---

* See a work of Mr. Herders: Idea of a Philosophical History of the
human species, Vol. II. page 11, (in German,) and Essay towards a Universal History, by M. Gatterer, page 489, (in German.)

platform of this extraordinary monument* contains more than
9.000 square metres,† and exhibits the ruins of a small square
edifice, which undoubtedly served for a last retreat to the
besieged.

The table-land of La Puebla exhibits remarkable vestiges of
ancient Mexican civilization. The fortifications of Tlaxcallan
are of a construction posterior to that of the great pyramid of
Cholula, a curious monument, of which I shall give a minute
description in the historical account of my travels in the interior
of the new continent. It is sufficient to state here, that this pyramid, on the top of which I made a great number of astrono-
mical observations, consists of four stages; that in its present
state the perpendicular elevation is only 54 metres,‡ and the horizontal breadth of the base 439 metres;§ that its sides are very
exactly in the direction of the meridians and parallels, and that
it is constructed (if we may judge from the perforation made a
few years ago in the north side) of alternate strata of brick and
clay. These data are sufficient for our recognising in the construction of this edifice the same model observed in the form of
the pyramids of Teotihuacan, of which we have already spok-
en. They suffice also to prove the great analogy|| between these
brick monuments erected by the most ancient inhabitants of Anahuac, the temple of Belus at Babylon, and the pyramids of
Menschich-Dashour, near Sakhara in Egypt.

---

* Description de las antiguedades de Xochicalco dedicada a los Se-
ñores de la Expedicion maritima baxo las ordenes de Don Alexandro
Malaspina, por Don Jose Antonio Alzate, Mexico, 1791, p. 13.

† 96.825 square feet. *Trans.*

‡ 177 feet. *Trans.*

§ 1.423 feet. *Trans.*

|| *Zoega de Obeliscis*, p. 380; *Voyages de Pococke, (edition de Nauf-
chatel,)* 1752, tom. i. p. 156 and 167; *Voyage de Denon*, 4to. edit. p. 86.
194. and 237; *Grobert Description des Pyramides*, p. 6. and 12.

The platform of the truncated pyramid of Cholula has a surface of 4.200 square metres.* In the midst of it there is a church
dedicated to Nuestra Senora de los Remedios, surrounded with
cypress, in which mass is celebrated every morning by an eccle-
siastic of Indian extraction, whose habitual abode is the summit of this monument. It is from this platform that we enjoy
the delicious and majestic view of the Volcan de la Puebla, the
Pic d'Orizaba, and the small cordillera of Matlacueye,† which
formerly separated the territory of the Cholulans from that of
the Tlascaltec republicans.

The pyramid, or teocalli, of Cholula, is exactly of the same
height as the Tonatiuh Itzaqual of Teotihuacan, already described; and it is three metres‡ higher than the Mycerinus, or the
third of the great Egyptian pyramids of the group of Ghize.—
As to the apparent length of its base, it exceeds that of all the
edifices of the same description hitherto found by travellers in
the old continent, and is almost the double of the great pyramid
known by the name of Cheops. Those who wish to form a clear
idea of the great mass of this Mexican monument from a comparison with objects more generally known, may imagine a
square four times the dimensions of the Place Vendome, covered with a heap of bricks of twice the elevation of the Louvre !
The whole of the interior of the pyramid of Cholula is not, perhaps, composed of brick. These bricks, as was suspected by a
celebrated antiquary at Rome, M. Zoega, probably form merely
an incrustation of a heap of stones and lime, like many of the
pyramids of Sakhara, visited by Pococke, and more recently by
M. Grobert. Yet the road from Puebla to Mecameca, carried
across a part of the first stage of the teocalli, does not agree with
this supposition.

* 45.208 square feet English. *Trans.*

† Called also the Sierra *Malinche,* or *Dona Maria.* Malinche appears to be derived from *Malintzin,* a word (I know not why) which is
now the name of the Holy Virgin.

‡ 9.8 feet. *Trans.*

We know not the ancient height of this extraordinary monument. In its present state, the length of its base* is to its perpendicular height as 8 : 1; while in the three great pyramids of Ghize, this proportion is as 1 $\frac{6}{10}$ and 1 $\frac{7}{10}$ to 1′, or nearly as 8 to 5. We have already observed that the houses of the sun and moon, or the pyramidal monuments of Teotihuacan northeast from Mexico, are surrounded with a system of small pyramids arranged symmetrically. M. Grobert has published a very curious drawing of the equally regular disposition of the

* I shall here subjoin the true dimensions of the three great pyramids of Ghize, from the interesting work of M. Grobert. I shall place in adjoining columns the dimensions of the brick pyramidal monuments of Sakhara, in Egypt, and of Teotihuacan and Cholula, in Mexico. The numbers are French feet. (A French foot = 1.066 English.)

	Stone pyramids.			Brick pyramids.		
	Cheops.	Cephren.	Mycerinus.	Of Five Stages in Egypt, near Sakhara	Of Four Stages in Mexico.	
					Teotihuacan	Cholula.
Height.	448	398	162	150	171	172
Length of Base.	728	655	280	210	645	1355

It is curious to observe. 1. That the people of Anahuac have had the intention of giving the height and the double base of the Tonatiuh Itztaqual to the pyramids of Cholula; and, 2. That the greatest of all the Egyptian pyramids, that of Asychis, of which the base is 800 feet in length, is of brick and not of stone. (*Grobert*, p. 6.) The cathedral of Strasbourg is eight feet, and the cross of St. Peter, at Rome, 4½ feet lower than the Cheops. There are in Mexico pyramids of several stages, in the forests of Papantla, at a small elevation above the level of the sea, and in the plains of Cholula and Teotihuacan, at elevations surpassing those of our passes in the Alps. We are astonished to see in regions the most remote from one another, and under climates of the greatest diversity, man following the same model in his edifices, in his ornaments, in his habits, and even in the form of his political institutions.

small pyramids which surround the Cheops and Mycerinus a
Ghize. The teocalli of Cholula, if it is allowable to compare it
with these great Egyptian monuments, appears to have been
constructed on an analogous plan. We still discover on the
western side, opposite the cerros of Tecaxete and Zapoteca, two
completely prismatical masses. One of these masses now bears
the name of Alcosac, or Istenenetl, and the other that of the
Cerro de la Cruz. The elevation of the latter, which is constructed *en pise'*, is only 15 metres.*

In the northern part of the intendancy of Vera Cruz, west
from the mouth of the Rio Tecolutla, at two leagues distance
from the great Indian village of Papantla, we met with a pyramidal edifice of great antiquity. The pyramid of Papantla remained unknown to the first conquerors. It is situated in the
midst of a thick forest, called *Tajin* in the Totonac language.—
The Indians concealed this monument, the object of an ancient
veneration. for centuries from the Spaniards; and it was only
discovered accidentally by some hunters about thirty years ago.
This pyramid of Papantla was visited by M. Dupé,† an observer
of great modesty and learning, who has long employed himself
in curious researches regarding the idols and architecture of
the Mexicans. He examined carefully the cut of the stones of
which it is constructed; and he made a drawing of the hieroglyphics with which these enormous stones are covered. It is to
be wished that he would publish the description of this interesting monument. The figure‡ published in 1788, in the Gazette
of Mexico is extremely imperfect.

The pyramid of Papantla is not constructed of bricks or clay
mixed with whin stones, and faced with a wall of amygdaloid,
like the pyramids of Cholula and Teotihuacan: the only mate-

---

* 49 feet. *Trans.*

† Captain in the service of the king of Spain. He possesses the bust
in bassaltes of a Mexican priestess, which I employed M. Massard to en-
grave, and which bears great resemblance to the *Calanthica* of the heads
of Isis.

‡ See also *Monumenti di Architettura Messicana di Pietro Marquez,*
Roma, 1804, tab. i.

rials employed are immense stones of a porphyritical shape.—
Mortar is distinguishable in the seams. The edifice, however,
is not so remarkable for its size as for its symmetry, the polish
of the stones, and the great regularity of their cut. The base
of the pyramid is an exact square, each side being 25 metres*
in length. The perpendicular height appears not to be more
than from 16 to 20 metres.† This monument, like all the Mexican teocallis, is composed of several stages. Six are still distinguishable, and a seventh appears to be concealed by the vegetation with which the sides of the pyramid are covered. A great
stair of 57 steps conducts to the truncated top of the teocalli,
where the human victims were sacrificed. On each side of the
great stair is a small stair. The facing of the stories is adorned
with hieroglyphics, in which serpents and crocodiles carved in
relievo are discernible. Each story contains a great number of
square niches symmetrically distributed. In the first story we
reckon 24 on each side, in the second 20, and in the third 16.—
The number of these niches in the body of the pyramid is 366,
and there are 12 in the stair towards the east. The Abbé Marquez supposes that this number of 378 niches has some allusion
to a calendar of the Mexicans; and he even believes that in each
of them one of the twenty figures was repeated, which, in the
hieroglyphical language of the Toultecs, served as a symbol for
marking the days of the common year, and the intercalated days
at the end of the cycles. The year being composed of 18 months,
of which each had 20 days, there would then be 360 days, to
which, agreeably to the Egyptian practice, five complementary
days were added, called *nemontemi*. The intercalation took
place every 52 years, by adding 13 days to the cycle, which gives
$360 + 5 + 13 = 378$, simple signs, or composed of the days of
the civil calendar, which was called *compohualilhuitl*, or *tonal-
pohualli*, to distinguish it from the *comilhuitlapohualliztli*, or
ritual calendar used by the priests for indicating the return of
sacrifices. I shall not attempt here to examine the hypothesis,

* 82 feet. *Trans.*

† From 52 to 65 feet. *Trans.*

of the Abbé Marquez, which has a resemblance to the astrono-
mical explanations given by a celebrated historian* of the number of apartments and steps found in the great Egyptian laby-
rinth.

THE MOUND NEAR SULTZERTOWN, M. T.

(No. 2.)

I have been favored by my friend the Rev. Mr. Schemer-
horn with an account of a mound near Sultzertown, M. T.

" A Sultzertown, M. T. six miles from Washington, is a
very remarkable Indian mound, and in every respect different
from any I have seen in Oaio, or Kentucky. It is not like those
raised on a plain, or the river alluvia, but the land around it, is
very uneven or rolling, and from the gradual descent of the
ground from its very base, we should be naturally led to conclude, that here they had taken advantage of the natural position.
Instead of raising with much labor, this huge pile of earth, they
have had little else to do than by levelling, to form the mound
agreeably to their designs.

" Its form is a parallelogram, whose sides bear the proportion to each other of two to three, and measured at the outside
of the ditch, contains more than six acres. The first elevation
is forty feet, the area of which may contain four acres. On the
west side of the parallelogram, about the middle is a circular
mount, whose diameter is fifty feet, and which measures from
the base eighty-six feet. Opposite to it on the east end, is a
similar mount, whose height is fifty feet, but appears to have
been considerably higher. The north and south sides which
are the longest, have each three or four lesser elevations, but
which are considerably washed down, the whole of the mound
having been frequently ploughed, and many a valuable crop raised on it; but were originally, I suppose, at least ten feet above
the first elevation. The whole surrounded by a deep ditch,
which, particularly at the E. and W. sides is still very perceptible. On the S. and N. sides are the passages out and in,

* M. Gatterer.

" Whether this was a place of defence against an enemy, or a place devoted to religious worship, I shall not undertake to determine. This, we may affirm with safety, that whatever of these theories we adopt, however visionary this may appear to some, many things plausible may be said on each. That it was admirably calculated as a place of defence no one can doubt, who considers its extent, its height, its ditch, particularly of palisadoed and military works erected on the highest mounds or towers. If we suppose it dedicated to purposes of devotion, and the people to be worshippers of the heavenly bodies, the first species of idolatry, the different heights of the mounds, and their situation, would lead us to conjecture, that the highest was consecrated to the sun, the next to the moon, and the lesser ones to the stars; but when we find that this has been the idolatry of some of the aborigines, is there not a foundation for the conjecture?

" Human skeletons have been found in many of those mounds. Mr. Griffin, the owner of the Sultzer mounds, informed me, that his sons some few years since, had brought some of the bones of a human skeleton, particularly the head and bones of the leg, which they discovered in this mound, on one of its sides where the earth had been washed away. The skull, he observed, was uncommonly large,* the bones of the leg and thigh much longer and larger than of common men, and that he supposed the skeleton, which unfortunately was never taken up entirely, but immediate orders given to re-deposit the bones, would have measured between six feet six inches and seven feet. It is worthy of remark, that du Pratz mentions that the Natchez (who according to their tradition came from the west,) deposited the remains of their sons or chiefs, in the part of the tem-

* It is difficult to account for the enormous size of the skeletons found in the western country. Are they only of extraordinary individuals, or do they prove a race of men of a larger size than any existing at the present day? nothing is more common than to find skeletons of this unusual size. There was for a long time preserved at fort Chartres a skull of an astonishing magnitude; and I have seen a jaw bone which I could with ease pass over my face, and leg bone which reached three inches above my knee from the ground.

ple where was kept the eternal fire. If we suppose this mound to have been a place consecrated to purposes of worship, might not the foregoing fact account for the finding skeletons in some of them, without supposing the original design mere depositories of the dead.

"That there are mounds of these different kinds is highly probable; but I see no reason why we may not suppose, some of the largest of them, to have been designed for all these purposes. The altars of religion, however absurd, may be the theology of some nations, yet superstition, if no purer principle, will render these dear to them as their lives. If so, it was necessary that in the early ages such places should be secured and defended. It is not uncommon to read in history, of nations who have made their last stand against their enemies in their temples, and around their altars

"And again, there is a principle in human nature to shew respect to great and good men, even after their spirits have returned to him who gave them. This has been instanced in almost every nation. I shall only allude to the practice amongst the British, of shewing respect to departed greatness and merit, by placing their monuments in Westminster abby. We also find that amongst christians, as a mark of respect to their departed pastors, the placing their remains beneath the pulpit.—This is not the case amongst civilized nations only, it has most probably been the custom from the earliest ages."

(No. 3.)

Communicated by the rev. Mr. Mills.

AT Sultzertown, near Washington, in the Mississippi territory, there is an ancient fortification. It is in the form of a parallelogram, including between three and four acres measured at the base. The mound was raised 46 feet above the common level of the ground; near the middle of the west line was raised a large mound of a circular form, 40 feet above the first level of the fortification, making the distance from the top of the mound 86 feet above the common level of the ground. The top of this mound had been ploughed and somewhat worn down.

It was six or eight paces across it, had it been carried up to a point, as most likely it originally was, or nearly so, it would have increased the height of the mound 30 or 40 feet, which latter number added to the 86 feet, its present height, would make it 126 feet, above the ground at the base. When the present proprietor took possession of his plantation, upon which the fortification stands, about 20 years ago, the country around was timbered and covered with lime brakes.

There was at that time no timber growing upon the fortification of more than a foot diameter, opposite the high mound on the west line was another mound, on the east, but not so high, about 50 feet above the common level of the ground.

In the middle of the north and south lines were the appearances of ways to ascend and descend the fortification; on each side of these apparent passways, was a mound, rising not more than 10 feet above the fortification, but near 50 above the level of the ground around. There was remaining part of the way round the base, a ditch, in some places, at the time I saw it, near near 20 feet deep. Human bones of a large size have been found near the mound.

—

(No. 4.)

The following interesting account of a part of the Mississippi country is extracted from a letter to the editors* dated Natchez, Mississippi Territory, Jan. 12, 1813.

MADISONVILLE

Is handsomely situated on the west bank of the river Tchefonta, which rises and runs into lake Ponchartrain in the parish of St. Tammany, in the state of Louisiana. At present this town has little more than the name, attached to an elegant, healthy, and eligible spot of ground for a seaport town. About half a dozen French built mud walled huts, and about as many log houses or cabins, and two or three small frames are all its present improvements.

* National Intelligencer—attributed to Dr. Perry of the U. S. Navy.

Correctly to appreciate the advantages of the situation of Madisonville, its terraqueous vicinity must be understood. The land east and west from this place along the borders of the lake is a sandy flat, extending from five to twenty miles from their shores, and nearly as level as the still ocean which seems to have receded from it: this flat coast is the termination of the inclined plain, with a southern exposure, extending from near the Mississippi to Pearl river, and from about lat. 31, 30, N. to the lakes: it is pleasantly diversified with pine covered plains and ridges, which alternate with rich low grounds or intervals, from half a mile to two miles in breadth, on all the numerous streams which dissect it. The largest and most westwardly of these streams is the Amite river, which interlocks its western branches with the waters of the Homochitto, Bayou Sarah, and Thompson's creek, which is the last considerable creek that feeds the Mississippi from the east. The Amite receives at Galvastown the Bayou Manchaique, an outlet in time of high water from the Mississippi, and loses its name in a round lake called Maurepas, which is about nine miles in diameter. The next stream eastward is the Tiefau, which has its source a few miles north of the old Spanish line in lat. 31; like the Amite, it inclines to the east of south in its course, and, after receiving its main branch, the Talbany, and its minor branch the Ponchartoula, both from the east, it also empties into lake Maurepas. The waters of lake Maurepas enter by a straight called the pass of Manchaique into lake Ponchartrain, which lies between the sandy coast of the continent and the river made island of Orleans. Tanchipohee creek rises several miles further north than the Tiefau, and interlocks with the eastern branch of the Amite; in its course, which is nearly south, it receives numerous small streams, and mouths into lake Ponchartrain, three miles east of Manchaique Pass: a bar at its mouth obstructs its navigation. The Tchefonta and Bouge Falia have their uttermost springs near together about twelve miles south of lat. 31; their courses are nearly parallel till they unite about three miles N. eastward from Madisonville. Bouge Falia receives from the east, little Bouge Falia, on the south bank of which is an elegant range of barracks and officers' houses, sufficient for a regiment of men, which have been built, and occupied by the United States' troops: they are now vacant. Bouge Chitto is next in size to Amite river, with the waters of which its higher branches interlock; it rises west of north from Madisonville, which place it approches in its course, but turns to the east and enters Pearl river; between which, and the river Tchefonta several small creeks and bayous rise and fall into lake Ponchartrain, but they are inconsiderable in point of size or extent.

The lakes are but the continued channel of the united waters of the Amite and the other streams from this coast; their current has been sufficiently strong to defend their shores from the annual deposits of alluvia by the Mississippi, in greater or less degrees at different points: hence the inequalities of the width of the lake: lake Maurepas is properly the lake of the Tiefau. The Mississippi has extended its delta around the mouths of these waters, and has finally bound their weakened current close to the coast, left them but a narrow straight, called the Regulee, through which as they pass they mingle with the waters of Pearl river, and flow into the gulph of Mexico, about 50 miles S. E. from Madisonville.

Lake Ponchartrain is said to be about thirty miles wide and about sixty miles long: it has an even sandy bottom, which seems to be a continuation of the inclined plain of the coast, gradually descending till it reaches the southern shore, which is characterized by a muddy bottom, and a marshy, swampy margin.

The tides of the lakes depend entirely on the winds, and are consequently irregular, ebbing and flowing as it changes, and rising occasionally from one to six feet.

The channel of the Regulees admits vessels with seven feet draft of water; and any vessel that can pass the Regulees may safely navigate the lakes. When the Mississippi is high, any vessel that can safely enter the lakes may descend Bayou Manchaique, and also the pass of that name between the lakes.

The river Amite is sufficiently large for boat navigation at the junction of its east and west branches a few miles below lat. 31. Galvastown is situated on its S. E. bank, below the mouth of bayou Manchaique.

The Tiefau, Talbana, and Ponchartoula, are capable of boat and small schooner navigation. Springfield or Bookter's landing, is situated on the W. bank of the Talbana, about ten miles from lake Maurepas.

The Tanchepehoe is accessible for boats but is unfavorable for schooner navigation.

The Tchefonta is a wide and handsome little river, affording a safe harbor and navigation for any vessel that can be sailed through the Regulees. Schooner navigation extends several miles up the eastern branch, called Bouge Falia, on the west bank of which a town is laid off by the name of St. Jack; and several buildings are erected.

Madisonville is favorably situated for the coasting and West India trade, having about two days sail in going out, and about two weeks sail in coming in, the advantage of New Orleans: it lies more convenient to the necessary supplies for repairing and building vessels; it is believed to be a more healthy situation, less infested with musketoes, and furnished with good spring water.

Madisonville is situated two miles from the mouth of the river Tchefonta; about 30 miles N. of New Orleans; about 30 miles E. from Springfield; about 70 miles E. from Baton Rouge; and about 80 miles E. by. S. from St. Francisville, at the mouth of the bayou Sarah, in the state of Louisiana. It lies about 80 miles E. S E from Woodville, the seat of justice in Wilkinson county; about 110 miles S. E from the city of Natcnez; about 60 miles S. E. from the seat of justice in Amite county; about 90 miles S. by W. from New London or Monticello, on Pearl river; about 65 miles S. W. from New Columbia, in Marion county; about 140 miles W. S. W. from fort Stoddert, and about 110 miles W. from Mobile town, in the Mississippi territory. These are the conjectured distances on rectalineal directions; for there are few or no roads leading towards Madisonville. The Old King's road, as it is called, leading in a direction from Baton Rouge to the bay of St. Lewis a few miles E. from the Regolees, crossed the river Tchefonta about half a mile above the Cockle bank, now the site of Madisonville.

The United States' troops cut a road from the vicinity of Tchefonta in a direction to fort Stoddert; but the water and the swamp obstructions on it rendered it almost useless, except in very dry weather; and the great hurricane of August last, has completely blocked it up as well as every other road approaching Madisonville; and the police laws, weak and unsettled in consequence of the many and recent changes of government, have not co-operated with public spirit to clear them out.

The country within 20 or 30 miles of the Mississippi, is generally a broken, rich land, thick wood country, with a heavy undergrowth of cane, &c. The low grounds of the many streams running towards the lakes, are extremely fertile; and above the flat woods, the low grounds of which are too moist for cultivation, it is believed by the inhabitants, that sugar cane may be cultivated to perfection and advantage; and recent experiments strengthen that opinion. Upland rice is grown in great perfection, and may be rendered a very profitable culture on these low grounds. On the second rate low grounds, and first rate piney lands, wheat grows finely and yields a heavy grain: it is harvested early in May: but wheat is an uncertain crop, on account of the rains and wind which are apt to prevail about the season of its blossoming; and it is subject to a rust. Indian corn grows as finely and yields as well as in any part of the United States, Tennessee and Kentucky excepted. This country is inferior to none for the culture of upland cotton, and is superior to any in the United States for the production of cornfield peas, sweet potatoes, and pompions. The piney plains and ridges afford excellent water, pleasant and healthy situations, and luxuriant and abundant pasturage.

Madisonville is understood to be chosen by the agents of the Navy Department for repairing, and even building of small vessels of war for the southern station; and it seems peculiarly adapted to these purposes: the vicinity abounds with oak, pine, and cypress: here also tar is made in abundance, with as great facility as in any part of the union: the spun hemp, or rope yarn of Kentucky, may be brought as cheap to this harbor as to any other, and the rigging may be laid to order at the navy yard with the greatest economy and advantage to the public service.

Provisions will also be furnished here of as good a quality and as cheap as in any other seaport: the country between the Pearl and Mississippi rivers is extremely favorable to the growth of hogs: and cattle are reared to as great perfection, and perhaps to as great an extent, on the waters of Pearl river, and particularly in the Choctaw nation of Indians, as in any part of the U. States.

Why, it may be asked, have not the singular advantages of this place sooner manifested themselves? The French were the first, and for many years the only civilized inhabitants in the vicinity of Tchefonta. Enterprise is not one of the characteristic traits of the Louisiana French. A few small fields and mud wall houses, are the most of their improvements in this neighborhood. The burning of shell lime and charcoal, making tar and raising cattle, and carrying the product of their labor to the Orleans market, were generally the extent of their pursuits. Attempts at commerce must have proved futile, as there were no country settlements to support them; the neighboring country was still within a few years past inhabited only by Choctaw Indians.

The country back of Madisonville now sustains a very considerable population; but there being no roads to accommodate an intercourse, its trade is diverted into other and unnatural channels. The capitalist will not place his stock on a coast where there are no roads to facilitate trade; and the inhabitants of the country have little inducement to make roads towards a place where they have little or no advantages of commerce.— The only measure necessary to insure an influx of capital to Madisonville, and to make it gradually assume the rank of a respectable seaport town, is the making of two or three good roads in proper directions through the flat woods, to the high and hard lands of the adjacent country. And with a capital to invite it, the natural advantages of this place would insure it the trading seaport of a country larger in extent than the state of Connecticut, and capable of sustaining an equal or greater agricultural population.

The land in the vicinity of Madisonville, with very few exceptions in favor of old Spanish and French titles, belongs to the

United States; it is therefore confidently hoped that when the peculiar properties of this port shall more fully unfold them- selves to the view of the government, it may be considered ex- pedient to cause good roads to be made at the public expense, over the public lands, in proper directions to favor and facilitate commercial intercourse between the town and country.

———

(No. 5.)

HAVING spoken of the Trappists in my account of the mounds in the American bottom, I here subjoin a description which was published in the St. Louis paper, and which, contrary to my wishes, I have understood gave great offence to the good fathers.

The buildings which the Trappists at present occupy, are merely temporary: they consist of four or five cabins, on a mound about fifty yards high, and which is perhaps one hun- dred and fifty feet square. Their other buildings, cribs, sta- bles, &c. ten or fifteen in number, are scattered about on the plain below. I was informed that they intended to build on the terrace of the large mound; this will produce a fine effect, it will be seen five or six miles across the plain, and from some points of view ten or twelve. They have about one hundred acres en- closed in three different fields, including the large mound, and several others.

On entering the yard, I found a number of persons at work, some hauling and storing away the crop of corn; others, shap- ing timber for some intended edifice. The greater number were boys from ten to fourteen years of age. The effect on my mind, was inexpressibly strange, at seeing them pass and repass each other in perfect silence. What force must it require to subdue the sportive temper of boyhood! But nothing is so strong as nature. I admired the cheerful drollery of a mulattoe lad, with one leg, who was attending the horse mill: as the other boys passed by, he generally contrived by some odd trick or gesticulation, to attract their notice, and commonly succeeded in exciting *a smile*. It was a faint watery gleam of sun-shine, which seemed to say, that their happiness was not entirely ob-

scured by the lurid gloom which the ingenuity of " distempered
imaginations" had cast around. Good God, thought I, is it possible that the gift which thou bestowedst, to distinguish us
amidst thy " vast creation" should be thus despised; for without
speech, how could we ever communicate to each other, that we
possess reasoning powers—a manation of the divine essence ?
To make the highest virtue consist in *silence*, was reserved for
the Trappists.

Fatigued and chagrined at this scene, which I contemplated
apparently unobserved, I ascended the mound which contains
the dwellings. This is nearly 25 feet in height: the ascent
rendered easy by a slanting road. I wandered about here for
some time, in expectation of being noticed by some one; it was
in vain that I nodded to the reverend fathers, or peeped into their
cabins How unaccountably the mind is sometimes affected !
I own I felt a kind of awe, for which I was unable to discover
the most distant cause. Perhaps were I to enter a Pagod for the
first time, I might experience the same feeling. At length
seating myself upon a log, I amused myself with the appearance of the different figures as they silently passed, and indulged my reflections. I had read of solitary monks, and had seen
them represented in paintings, but here they really existed.—
The recollection of the figure which this strange order of
men has made for so many centuries, in history, and in romance,
naturally awakened a variety of remembrances with their linked
associations. I admired with what rigid severity the good fathers banished from their heads, those ornamental locks bestowed by nature, leaving one wandering tuft: a symbol of the
crown of thorns!

I had the good fortune to be accosted by a young man, who
I discovered to be in their employment as a kind of steward,
though not otherwise attached to the society. I experienced relief on being able to find one who was willing to speak: I made a
variety of inquiries of him, but to very little purpose: he was
however obliging, and promised to speak in my behalf to the
Principal. In a short time Father Joseph made his appearance ;
I learned that he had the government of the monastery in the
absence of Father Urbain. He is a sprightly, and intelligent

man, and much to my surprise, talked with wonderful volubility, which excited in me almost as much surprise as Robinson Crusoe in his island, felt, when his parrot addressed him. He invited me into the watchmaker's shop, for they carry on several trades, to assist in supporting the institution. The shop was well furnished; part was occupied as a laboratory, and library; the latter but indifferent; a few medical works of no repute, and the dreams of the Fathers, with the miraculous wonders of the world of Saints. Several men were at work, and some boys busily employed. One poor fellow, ten or twelve years of age, attracted my attention and pity. He was seated by a stove, making strokes on a slate, and appeared to have just risen from the bed of sickness, or rather from the tomb. Emaciated to the last extreme, his face was pale, cold and bloodless, his lips purpled, his sunken eye marked by a livid streak, and his countenance overspread with a listless stillness. Had it not been for the feeble motion of his hand as he drew it over the slate, and the occasional raising of his heavy and languid eyelid, I could have believed that the tenant of this sad and melancholy ruin, had gone to seek a happier abode. I felt my heart swell in my breast.— Alas! poor lone creature, thou hast no mother, no sister, to watch over thee with the tenderness and solicitude which none but a mother or sister can feel! I was pleased when I saw Father Joseph advance towards him with a tenderness and benignity of countenance, which does not belong to a monk: he endeavored to cheer him by speaking pleasantly to him, but the poor fellow had lost the power of smiling; his physiognomy was locked up in rigid coldness, which nothing but returning health, or the the warmth of parental affection could soften.

Father Joseph inquired whether I had dined, and being informed in the negative, had something prepared. My fare was simple; consisting chiefly of vegetables; though not less acceptable for it was given with good will. Having returned thanks to the Father for his hospitality, I took my leave.

I learned that the family of the Trappists consists of about eighty persons, a considerable number of whom are not at home. The boys are generally American; the men principally German and French. They expect a considerable accession from

N n

Europe. It is about a year since they have been fixed in this place. Last summer proved fatal to five or six, and few escaped the prevailing fever. They deny the place to be unhealthy, and say that those who died were chiefly old men; the meager diet, and scanty nourishment, which is taken by such as have made the vow, must certainly contribute. They first settled in Kentucky, afterwards came to Florisant near St. Louis, and from thence to their present residence. They are supposed to be an industrious well meaning people; and I should be willing to see them treated with respect, and even encouragement in all but one thing; the education of children. This is foreign from the original design of their institution, which is a total exclusion from the world Such a place is for a thousand reasons not calculated for a school; a boy brought up here to the age of one and twenty, can never be fit for any thing but a Trappist. It may be said that an asylum is here offered to those in extreme distress—to those unfortunate wretches, who, aged and friendless, are in danger of perishing of want Happily for our country such instances are rare indeed. Or for those unhappy orphans, who may be exposed from their helplessness to be without support, and to whom, inhuman barbarity may have denied a home and a protection. I may safely say that these are as rare as the others. In America, it is not necessary as in Europe, to give a fee with a boy who is bound apprentice to any particular calling; on the contrary there is scarcely any mechanic who will not gladly take him and teach him his trade for the service which he may render, before the expiration of the apprenticeship

A brief history of this singular institution, may not be unentertaining. The monastery of La Trappe was situated in the province of Perche in France: in one of the most solitary spots that could be chosen. It was founded in 1140 by Rotrou Count of Perche. This monastery had fallen into decay, and its discipline much relaxed, when reformed by the Abbe Rancé 1664. Rancé had met with some misfortune, which rendered life hateful to him, some assert the sudden death of madam Montbazor, whose favorite lover he was. He had been a man of fashion, and possessed some pretensions to literature; he is said to have

translated the poems of Anacreon. Into this monastery, whith-
er he came, he carried a reform of the most savage austerity.—
The vow was perpetual silence; the miserable Trappist denied himself during his existence, every comfort of life. He
laid himself on a stone, and was frequently called in the dead
of night to his devotions. His food was bread and water, and
this but once in the twenty-four hours. Each day he was to
remove from his intended grave one spadefull of earth, in order
to keep ever present to his mind that he must soon entirely
cease to be of this world. A French writer, (who is however,
influenced by enmity) observing upon this monastery, says—
C'est la' qu'ils se retirent, ceux qui ont commis quelque crime se-
cret dont les remords les poursuivent; ceux qui sont tourmentés
de vapeurs melancholiques et religieuses; ceux qui out oublié que
Dieu est le plus miséricordieux des pères, et qui no voyent en lui,
que le plus cruel des tyrans, &c.

I think it unnecessary to give my opinion on the nature of
the institution—such institutions it must be acknowledged are
not treated with much respect in the United States; we can
hardly speak of them with candor, or think of them without prejudice. It is true, this is the land of freedom and toleration,
but it is also the land of good sense. Every one may pursue his
spiritual or temporal happiness, in what way he pleases; but his
neighbors have also the liberty of laughing at him, if in the
pursuit of that happiness, he exhibits singularities which appear to the rest of the world ridiculous.

(No. 6.)

The following articles of the treaty of '63, raise a necessary
implication that France was the lawful owner of what is called
West Florida. It will be seen that the cession was in fact made
by France to Great Britain.

ARTICLE 7.

In order to re-establish peace on solid and durable foundations, and to remove forever all subject of dispute with regard
to the British and French territories on the continent of Ame-

rica. It is agreed that for the future the confines between the dominions of his Britannic majesty and those of his Most Christian majesty in that part of the world, shall be irrevocably fixed by a line drawn along the middle of the river Mississippi, from its source to the river Iberville, and from thence by a line drawn along the middle of this and the lake Maurepas and Ponchartrain, to the sea; *and for this purpose the Most Christian king cedes in full right and guarantees to his Britannic majesty, the river and port of the Mobile, and every thing which he possesses or ought to possess on the left side of the river Mississippi, except the town of New Orleans and the island on which it is situated, &c.*

ARTICLE 20.

" His Catholic majesty cedes and guarantees in full right to his Britannic majesty, Florida, with Fort St. Augustin, and the bay of Pensacola, as well as all that Spain possesses on the continent of North America, to the E. or to the S. E of the river Mississippi, and in general, every thing that depends on the said countries and lands, with the sovereignty, property, possession, and all rights acquired by treaties, or otherwise, which *the Catholic king and crown of Spain* have had till now over the said countries, lands, places, and their inhabitants, so that the Catholic king cedes and makes over the whole to the said king, and to the crown of Great Britain, &c.

This country must necessarily, therefore, have formed part of Louisiana, and as such, appertained to France. Spain cedes to France, by the treaty of Ildefonso, Louisiana as it had been held by France, and not in the extent held by her at the time of cession.

In the 2d chapter of the first book, there are some observations which would seem to attach blame to the commissioners. But I am induced to believe from further inquiry, that I have merely taken up the popular opinion. Gov. Claiborne has promised to favor me with the *process verbal*, which I will publish should this book ever be thought worthy of second edition.

(No. 7)

Extracts from the account of a journey from Fort Clark, on the. Missouri, to the Salines, on the Arkansas, by Mr. Sibly.

AFTER giving a number of medals to the Paunee chiefs, and having various councils with them, Mr. Sibly, on the 4th of June left their villages, and proceeded to the Little Osage camp, on the Arkansas, about 75 miles south, and 16 east from the Panis, where he safely arrived on the 11th. I remained, says he, several days with the Osages, who had abundance of provisions, they having killed 200 buffaloe within a few days. Where they had their camp, the Arkansas was about two hundred yards wide, the water shallow, rapid, and of a red color.— On the 16th, the Indians raised their camp, and proceeded towards the hilly country on the other side of the Arkansas.— I continued with them about 50 miles west, and 30 miles east, when we fell in with some men of the Chaniers band, who informed us that their camp was at no great distance, and the camp of the Big Osage still nearer, in consequence, I determined to pass through both on my way to the Grand Salines. On the 21st, I rode S. 40 miles, E. 30, to the Big Osage camp; nearly all the warriors were at war, or abroad hunting. I was remarkably well treated by Young White Hair, and family, I however, remained but one night with them. On the 22d, I rode 20 miles S. 15 E. to the Chaniers camp, where we arrived about one o'clock. We were treated well by the head men, and indeed, this is one of the tribes most attached to the Americans. The chief's name is Clermont. From hence forty miles to the Grand Saline, which we reached early on the 24th. I hasten to give you a description of this celebrated curiosity. The Grand Saline is situated about 280 miles S. W. of Fort Osage, between two forks of a small branch of the Arkansas, one of which washes its southern extremity, and the other the principal one, runs nearly parallel within a mile of its opposite side. It is a hard level plain of a reddish colored sand, and of an irregular or mixed figure; its greatest length is from N. W. to S. E. and its circumference full 30 miles—from the appearance of driftwood that is scattered over, it would seem that the whole plain is at times inundated by the overflowing of the streams that pass near it. This plain is entirely covered in dry hot weather, from two to six inches deep, with a crust of beautiful clean white salt, of a quality rather superior to the imported blown salt; it bears a striking resemblance to a field of brilliant snow after a rain, with a light crust on its top. On a bright sunny morning, the appearance of this natural curiosity is highly picturesque. It possesses the quality of looming or magnifying objects, and this in a very striking degree, making the small billets of wood appear as formidable as trees. Numbers of buffaloe were on the plain. The Saline is environed by a strip of marshy prairie with a few scattering trees, mostly of cotton wood. Behind, there is a range of sand hills, some of which are perfectly naked, others thinly clothed with verdure, and dwarf plum bushes, not more than thirty inches in height, from which we procured abundance of the most delicious plums I ever tasted. The distance to a navigable branch of the Arkansas, about 80 miles, the country tolerably level, and the water courses easily passed.

About 60 miles S. W. from this, I came to the Saline, the whole of this distance lying over a country remarkably rugged and broken, affording the most romantic and picturesque views imaginable. It is a tract of about 75 miles square, in which nature has displayed a great variety of the most strange and whimsical vagaries. It is an assemblage of beautiful meadows, verdant ridges, and rude misshapen piles of red clay thrown together in the utmost apparent confusion, yet, affording the most pleasing harmonies, and presenting in every direction an endless variety of curious and interesting objects. After winding along for a few miles on the high ridges, you suddenly descend an almost perpendicular declivity of rocks and clay, into a series of level fertile meadows, watered by some beautiful rivulets, and here and there adorned with shrubby cotton trees, elms and cedars. These meadows are divided by chains formed of red clay, and huge masses of gypsum, with here and there a pyramid of gravel. One might imagine himself surrounded by the ruins of some ancient city, and that the plains had sunk by some convulsion of nature, more than 100 feet below its former level; for some of the huge columns of red clay rise to the height of 200 feet perpendicular, capped with rocks of gypsum, which the hand of time is ever crumbling off, and strewing in beautiful transparent flakes along the declivities of the hill, glittering like so many mirrors in the sun.

AMERICAN ENTERPRISE.

[*From the Missouri Gazette.*]

(No. 8.)

WE last week promised our readers an account of the journey of the gentlemen attached to the New York Fur Company, from the Pacific Ocean to this place—We now lay it before our readers, as collected from the gentlemen themselves.

On the 28th June 1812, Mr. Robert Steuart, one of the partners of the Pacific Fur Company, with two Frenchmen, Messrs. Ramsey Crooks and Robt. M'Clellan, left the Pacific Ocean with despatches for New York.

After ascending the Columbia river 90 miles, John Day, one of the hunters, became perfectly insane, and was sent back to the main establishment, under the charge of some Indians; the remaining six pursued their voyage upwards of 600 miles, when they happily met with Mr. Joseph Miller, on his way to the mouth of the Columbia; he had been considerably to the south and east, among the nations called Blackarms and Arapahays, by the latter of whom he was robbed; in consequence of which, he suffered almost every privation human nature is capable of, and was in a state of starvation and almost nudity when the party met him

They now had fifteen horses, and pursued their journey for the Atlantic world, without any uncommon accident, until within about 200 miles of the Rocky mountains, where they unfortunately met with a party of the Crow Indians, who behaved with the most unbounded insolence, and were solely prevented from cutting off the party, by observing them well armed and constantly on their guard. They however pursued on their track six days, and finally stole every horse belonging to the party.

Some idea of the situation of those men may be conceived, when we take into consideration, that they were now on foot, and had a journey of 2000 miles before them, 1500 of which was entirely unknown, as they intended and prosecuted it considerably south of Messrs. Lewis and Clark's route; the impossibility of carrying any quantity of provisions on their backs, in addition to their ammunition, and bedding, will occur at first view.

The danger to be apprehended from starvation was immi-
nent. They however put the best face upon their prospects,
and pursued their route towards the Rocky mountains at the
head waters of the Colorado, or Spanish river, and stood their
course E. S. E. until they struck the head waters of the great
river Platte, which they undeviatingly followed to its mouth.
It may here be observed, that this river for about 200 miles, is
navigable for a barge; from thence to the Otto village, within
45 miles of its entrance into the Missouri, it is a mere bed of
sand, without water sufficient to float a skin canoe.

From the Otto village to St. Louis, the party performed
their voyage in a canoe, furnished them by the natives, and arrived here in perfect health on the 30th of last month, (May).

Our travellers did not hear of the war with England until
they came to the Ottoes; these people told them that the Shaw-
noe Prophet had sent them a wampum, inviting them to join in
the war against the Americans; that they answered the mes-
senger, that they could make more by trapping beaver than
making war against the Americans.

After crossing the hills (Rocky mountains) they happily fell
in with a small party of Snake Indians, from whom they purchased a horse, who relieved them from any further carriage of
food, and this faithful four-footed companion performed that service to the Otto village. They wintered on the river Platte,
600 miles from its mouth.

By information received from these gentlemen, it appears
that a journey across the continent of N. America, might be performed with a wagon, there being no obstruction in the whole
route that any person would dare to call a mountain, in addition
to its being much the most direct and short one to go from this
place to the mouth of the Columbia river. Any future party
who may undertake this journey, and are tolerably acquainted
with the different places where it would be necessary to lay up
a small stock of provisions, would not be impeded, as in all probability they would not meet with an Indian to interrupt their
progress—although on the other route more north, there are
almost insurmountable barriers.

Messrs. Hunt, Crooks, Miller, M‘Clelland, M‘Kenzie, and
about 60 men who left St. Louis in the beginning of March,

1811, for the Pacific ocean, reached the Arikara village on the 13th day of June, where meeting with some American hunters who had been the preceding year on the waters of the Columbia with Mr. Henry, and who, giving such an account of the route by which they passed, as being far preferable in point of procuring with facility an abundant supply of food at all times, as well as avoiding even the probability of seeing their enemies the Black Feet, than by the track of captains Lewis & Clark; the gentlemen of the expedition at once abandoned their former ideas of passing by the falls of the Missouri, and made the necessary arrangements for commencing their journey over land from this place.

Eighty horses were purchased and equipped by the 17th of July, and on the day following they departed from the Arikaras, 60 persons in number, all on foot except the partners of the company. In this situation they proceeded for five days, having crossed in that time two considerable streams which joined the Missouri below the Arikaras, when finding an inland tribe of Indians calling themselves Shawhays, but known among the whites by the appellations of Chiennes, we procured from these people an accession of 40 horses, which enabled the gentlemen to furnish a horse for every two men. Steering about W. S. W. they passed the small branches of Big river, the Little Missouri above its forks, and several of the tributary streams of Powder river, one of which they followed up, they found a band of the Absaroka or Crow nation, encamped on its banks, at the foot of the Big Horn mountain.

For ammunition and some small articles, they exchanged all their lame for sound horses with these savages; but although that this band has been allowed by every one who knew them, to be by far the best behaved of their tribe, it was only by that unalterable determination of the gentlemen to avoid jeopardizing the safety of the party without at the same moment submitting to intentional insults, that they left this camp (not possessing a greater force than the whites) without coming to blows.

The distance from the Arikaras to this mountain, is about 450 miles over an extremely rugged tract, by no means furnishing a sufficient supply of water; but during the 28 days they were getting to the base of the mountain, they were only in a few instances without abundance of buffaloe meat.

Three days took them over to the plains of Mad river, (the name given the Big Horn above this mountain) which following for a number of days, they left it where it was reduced to 80 yards in width, and the same evening reached the banks of the Colorado or Spanish river. Finding flocks of buffaloe at the end of the third day's travel on this stream, the party passed a week in drying buffaloe meat for the residue of the voyage, as in all probability those were the last animals of the kind they would meet with. From this camp, in one day, they crossed the dividing mountain, and pitched their tents on Hoback's fork of Mad river, where it was near 150 feet broad, and in eight days more having passed several stupendous ridges, they encamped in the vicinity of the establishment made by Mr. Henry, in the fall of 1810, on a fork about 70 yards wide, bearing the name of that gentleman; having travelled from the main Missouri about 900 miles in 54 days.

Here abandoning their horses, the party constructed canoes and descended the Snake or Ky-eye-nem river, (made by the junction of Mad river, south of Henry's fork) 400 miles, in the course of which they were obliged by the intervention of impassable rapids to make a number of portages, till at length they found the river confined between gloomy precipices at least 200 feet perpendicular, whose banks for the most part were washed by this turbulent stream, which for 30 miles was a continual succession of falls, cascades and rapids. Mr. Cook's canoe had split and upset in the middle of a rapid, by which one man was drowned, named Antonie Clappin, and that gentleman saved himself only by extreme exertion in swimming. From the repeated losses by the upsetting of canoes, our stock of provisions were now reduced to a bare sufficiency for five days, totally ignorant of the country where they were, and unsuccessful in meeting any of the natives from whom they could hope for information.

Unable to proceed by water, Messrs. M'Kenzie, M'Clelland and Reed, set out in different directions, inclining down the river, for the purpose of finding Indians and buying horses. Mr.

1811, for the Pacific ocean, reached the Arikara village on the 13th day of June, where meeting with some American hunters who had been the preceding year on the waters of the Columbia with Mr. Henry, and who, giving such an account of the route by which they passed, as being far preferable in point of procuring with facility an abundant supply of food at all times, as well as avoiding even the probability of seeing their enemies the Black Feet, than by the track of captains Lewis & Clark; the gentlemen of the expedition at once abandoned their former ideas of passing by the falls of the Missouri, and made the necessary arrangements for commencing their journey over land from this place.

Eighty horses were purchased and equipped by the 17th of July, and on the day following they departed from the Arikaras, 60 persons in number, all on foot except the partners of the company. In this situation they proceeded for five days, having crossed in that time two considerable streams which joined the Missouri below the Arikaras, when finding an inland tribe of Indians calling themselves Shawhays, but known among the whites by the appellations of Chiennes, we procured from these people an accession of 40 horses, which enabled the gentlemen to furnish a horse for every two men. Steering about W. S. W. they passed the small branches of Big river, the Little Missouri above its forks, and several of the tributary streams of Powder river, one of which they followed up, they found a band of the Absaroka or Crow nation, encamped on its banks, at the foot of the Big Horn mountain.

For ammunition and some small articles, they exchanged all their lame for sound horses with these savages; but although that this band has been allowed by every one who knew them, to be by far the best behaved of their tribe, it was only by that unalterable determination of the gentlemen to avoid jeopardizing the safety of the party without at the same moment submitting to intentional insults, that they left this camp (not possessing a greater force than the whites) without coming to blows.

The distance from the Arikaras to this mountain, is about 450 miles over an extremely rugged tract, by no means furnishing a sufficient supply of water; but during the 28 days they were getting to the base of the mountain, they were only in a few instances without abundance of buffaloe meat.

Three days took them over to the plains of Mad river, (the name given the Big Horn above this mountain) which following for a number of days, they left it where it was reduced to 80 yards in width, and the same evening reached the banks of the Colorado or Spanish river. Finding flocks of buffaloe at the end of the third day's travel on this stream, the party passed a week in drying buffaloe meat for the residue of the voyage, as in all probability those were the last animals of the kind they would meet with. From this camp, in one day, they crossed the dividing mountain, and pitched their tents on Hoback's fork of Mad river, where it was near 150 feet broad, and in eight days more having passed several stupendous ridges, they encamped in the vicinity of the establishment made by Mr. Henry, in the fall of 1810, on a fork about 70 yards wide, bearing the name of that gentleman; having travelled from the main Missouri about 900 miles in 54 days.

Here abandoning their horses, the party constructed canoes and descended the Snake or Ky-eye-nem river, (made by the junction of Mad river, south of Henry's fork) 400 miles, in the course of which they were obliged by the intervention of impassable rapids to make a number of portages, till at length they found the river confined between gloomy precipices at least 200 feet perpendicular, whose banks for the most part were washed by this turbulent stream, which for 30 miles was a continual succession of falls, cascades and rapids. Mr. Cook's canoe had split and upset in the middle of a rapid, by which one man was drowned, named Antonie Clappin, and that gentleman saved himself only by extreme exertion in swimming. From the repeated losses by the upsetting of canoes, our stock of provisions were now reduced to a bare sufficiency for five days, totally ignorant of the country where they were, and unsuccessful in meeting any of the natives from whom they could hope for information.

Unable to proceed by water, Messrs. M'Kenzie, M'Clelland and Reed, set out in different directions, inclining down the river, for the purpose of finding Indians and buying horses. Mr.

Crooks with a few men returned to Henry's fork for those they had left, while Mr. Hunt remained with the main body of the men, in trapping beaver for their support. Mr. Crooks finding the distance much greater by land than he had contemplated, returned at the end of three days, where waiting five more, expecting relief from below—the near approach of winter made them determine on depositing all superfluous articles, and proceed on foot. Accordingly, on the 10th of Nov. Messrs. Hunt & Crooks set out, each with 18 men, one party on the S. side of the river.

Mr. Hunt was fortunate in finding Indians with abundance of salmon and some horses, but Mr. Crooks saw but few and in general too miserably poor to afford his party assistance; thirteen days travel brought the latter to a high range of mountains through which the river forced a passage, and the banks being their only guide, they still by climbing over points of rocky ridges projecting into the stream, kept as near it as possible, till in the evening of the 3d Dec. impassible precipices of immense height put an end to all hopes of following the margin of this water course, which here was no more than 40 yards wide, ran with incredible velocity and was withal so foamingly tumultuous, that even had the opposite bank been fit for their purpose, attempt at rafting would have been perfect madness, as they could only have the inducement of ending in a watery grave a series of hardships and privations, to which the most hardy and determined of the human race, must have found himself inadequate. They attempted to climb the mountains, still bent on pushing on, but after ascending for half a day, they discovered to their sorrow that they were not halfway to the summit, and the snow already too deep for men in their emaciated state to proceed further.

Regaining the river bank, they returned up, and on the third day met with Mr. Hunt and party, with one horse proceeding downwards; a canoe was soon made of a horse hide and in it transported some meat, what they could spare to Mr. Crooks's starving followers, who for the first 18 days after leaving the place of deposite, had subsisted on half a meal in 24 hours, and in the last nine days had eat only one beaver, a dog, a few wild cherries, and old moccasin soals, having travelled during these 27 days at least 550 miles. For the next four days, both parties continued on up the river, without any other support than what little rosebuds and cherries they could find, but here they luckily fell in with some Snake Indians, from whom they got five horses, giving them three guns and some other articles for the same. Starvation had bereft J. B. Provost of his senses entirely, and on seeing the horse flesh on the opposite side of the river, was so agitated in crossing in a skin canoe, that he upset it and was unfortunately drowned. From hence Mr. Hunt went on to a camp of Shoshonies about 90 miles above, where procuring a few horses and a guide, he set out for the main Columbia, across the mountains to the south west, leaving the river where it entered the range, and on it Mr. Crooks and five men unable to travel.

Mr. H. lost a Canadian named Carrier, by starvation, before he met the Shy-eye-to-ga Indians in the Columbia plains; from whom getting a supply of provisions he soon reached the main river, which he descended in canoes and arrived without any further loss at Astoria, in the month of February.

Messrs. M'Kenzie, M'Clelland and Reed, had united their parties on the Snake river mountains, through which they travelled twenty one days, to the Mulpot river, subsisting on an allowance by no means adequate to the toils they underwent daily; and to the smallness of their number (which was in all eleven) they attribute their success in getting with life to where they found some wild horses; they soon after reached the torks called by captains Lewis and Clark, Koolkooske; went down Lewis's party, and the Columbia wholly by water, without any misfortune except the upsetting in a rapid of Mr. M'Clelland's canoe, and although it happened on the first day of the year, yet by great exertion they clung to the canoe till the others came to their assistance, making their escape with the loss of some rifles, they reached Astoria early in January.

Three of the five men who remained with Mr. Crooks, afraid of perishing by want, left him in February on a small river on the road by which Mr. Hunt had passed in quest of Indians, and have not since been heard of. Mr. C. had followed Mr. H's. track in the snow for seven days, but coming to a low prairie he lost every appearance of a trace and was compelled to pass the remaining part of winter in mountains, subsisting sometimes on beaver and horse meat, and their skins, and at others, on their success in finding roots. Finally on the last of March the other only Canadian being unable to proceed was left with a lodge of Shoshonies, and Mr. C. with John Day, finding the snow sufficiently diminished, undertook from Indian information to cross the last ridge, which they happily effected and reached the banks of the Columbia in the middle of April, where, in the beginning of May they fell in with Messrs. Steuart and company, having been a few days before stripped of every thing they possessed by a band of villains near the falls. On the 10th of May, they arrived safe at Astoria, the principal establishment of the Pacific Fur Company, within 14 miles of Cape Disappointment.

THE END.